a Western
Jesus

a Western Jesus

the wayward americanization of Christ and the church

mike minter

PUBLISHING GROUP

nashville, tennessee

ISBN: 978-0-8054-4486-5

Published by B&H Publishing Group,
Nashville, Tennessee

Dewey Decimal Classification: 261
Subject Heading: JESUS CHRIST \ WESTERN CIVILIZATION \
CHRISTIANITY AND WESTERN CIVILIZATION

Unless otherwise noted, all Scripture references are taken from
the Holman Christian Standard Bible® © 1999, 2000, 2002, 2003
by Holman Bible Publishers. Also used is the NKJV, New King James
Version, copyright © 1979, 1980, 1982, Thomas Nelson, Inc., Publishers,
NIV, New International Version, copyright © 1973, 1978, 1984 by
International Bible Society, and the KJV, King James Version.

1 2 3 4 5 6 7 8   10 09 08 07

TO MY WIFE KAY

Thanks for your tireless support through love, counsel, prayer, encouragement, patience, and endurance while raising four godly children in your spare time. You have been the wind beneath my wings.

ACKNOWLEDGMENTS

I suppose that most books are written by one author, but the thoughts contained therein are the musings of many. My thinking has been shaped through the years by the wonderful saints at Reston Bible Church along with the leadership team of staff and elders who have been an extension of God's loving hand in giving me clear direction in a life that otherwise would have been shipwrecked. Thanks to the kind people at B&H who have shown much grace to this first-time author whose naivete has probably been the source of much laughter during coffee breaks.

A very special thanks to my executive assistant Jacki Herring, who through careful attention to detail coupled with a servant spirit, has made this undertaking possible.

CONTENTS

INTRODUCTION

ANYONE WHO HAS BEEN a believer for at least ten years begins to notice trends in Christianity. The trends are more noticeable in our western culture than in the underground church in places where Christianity is forbidden—where there is no margin for such discussions. Given enough leisure time, of which the West has an abundance, the church becomes a breeding ground for new theological fads and cycles of philosophy of ministry that are not transcendent in nature, and we begin to lose our way as pilgrims who are called to be salt and light in this present evil world.

This is not a book about theology or philosophy of ministry. It is a book about how our western culture, led by a western jesus, has negatively influenced how we view Scripture. In our theological debates, each side often accuses the other side of "not searching the Scriptures to see if these things are so" (Acts 17:11). In our defense we often toss out such statements as "thus saith the Scriptures" or "thus saith the Lord," when what we really mean is "thus saith the Scriptures as viewed through my traditional and culturally biased view."

If one looks through the finely polished lens of a microscope or telescope and the object in view is distorted and lacking in definition, it is not the fault of the skillfully crafted lens but due to the distortion of the eye. Similarly, when we look into the perfect law of liberty (see James 1:25) that has been layered over with culture, tradition, and human bias, distortion is sure to follow; but if we look at culture, tradition, and human bias through the perfect lens of Scripture, the Christian life will come into sharper focus. I realize that no one will ever achieve this perfectly, as we are fallen people; but we need to do all we can to see clearly what God has revealed to us.

I have approached this subject with thirty-two years of pastoral experience behind me. This doesn't make me an expert, but it does give me a measure of credibility. I have tried to be fair in my approach, and in this writing, with fear and trepidation, I have sacrificed many sacred cows on the altar of the western church. In no way do I seek to imply that all western thinking is wrong. This book is more of a reminder, if not a warning, that we are not the salt and light we have been called to be. In the following pages we will look at morality, theology, faith, materialism, what it means to "go to church," and a host of other subjects that have been influenced by our western culture. I only ask that you read with an open mind and see if you are following a western jesus or the transcendent Christ.

[CHAPTER 1]

My Story

■ ■ ■ ■ ■

IT WASN'T LONG AFTER entering the United States Naval Academy in the summer of 1964 that I began to realize I was over my head with the rigorous academic challenge set before me. I had no problem with the physical demands of plebe (freshman) summer, but there were a few simple math courses that were given prior to the academic year so that we might taste the mental challenge that would soon be upon us. What seemed elementary to everyone else was not elementary to me. I was drowning in equations, formulas, and the basic math skills needed to survive. The proverbial handwriting was on the wall, and I sensed that I would soon be an academic casualty. When the first grades were released in mid-fall, I was the proud owner of a .56 GPA out of a possible 4.0. Things were not looking good. I felt like I had shown up at the Dayton 500 with a tricycle.

Word spread quickly, and it wasn't long before an upperclassman took pity on me and decided to coach me on those subjects where I was struggling (which, in my case, happened to be all of them). We met regularly, and since he was at the top of his class, he was most qualified to be my tutor. As time went on, we developed a close relationship, and it wasn't long before I noticed a unique confidence in God that permeated his life. He acted as if he knew God personally. He would pray for wisdom before each session (and believe me, with the challenge he was facing, he needed it more than I did).

There were other midshipmen who started to show up on my doorstep who had this unusual relationship with the Lord that was so foreign to my thinking. I was very religious but had never really understood the gospel. At the end of my plebe year, I faced the academic board with two choices: I could leave or repeat my plebe year. I chose the latter. After repeating my plebe year, I eventually got through my sophomore then junior year with a GPA of 1.97. The academic board felt, and rightly so, that my senior year would be too much for me to handle, and I was thus dismissed on academic grounds. It was very hard, almost traumatic. I had invested four years of my life in one of the world's greatest schools. I had many deep friendships that would be severed. I would not toss my cap into the air at graduation. I would not put on my ensign shoulder boards. In fact, I would not be a naval officer, but life must go on.

I pursued a political science degree at another college and finished in 1970. Another classmate of the gentlemen who tutored me had just returned from Vietnam. Since he knew I was in the area, he called and invited me to his place for dinner, which I gladly accepted. We became fast friends and decided to tour Europe together in June 1970. The timing was perfect; he was transitioning out of the military to work for the Fellowship of Christian Athletes and I was transitioning from college into the business world. We had this window of opportunity and spent a wonderful month traveling and seeing parts of the world we had never seen.

Here again I was introduced to someone who seemed to know God personally. My friend would pray spontaneously throughout our travels, and I saw answers to those prayers that were so amazing that I knew he was in touch with a God I was totally unfamiliar with. He gave me a copy of the Bible and asked me to read the Gospel of John. Since we traveled by train, there were long stretches during which I could settle back and read. By the time we arrived at Copenhagen, Denmark, I had completed my assignment. Yes, I had questions, but once I discovered that salvation had nothing to do with how good or religious I was, I got on my knees and called on Christ to save me.

I'm not sure what Shakespeare meant when he said, "There's something rotten in the state of Denmark," but for me it was the birthplace of my soul. It was where my pilgrimage began. The scales had fallen from my eyes (see Acts 9:18), and I began to see life through the clear lens of Scripture and not through the clouded lens of human reason. The confusion of the world began to make sense. I could see why humanity was furiously struggling to extricate itself from a fallen world. I became fascinated with the power of God's Word and how precise it was in examining not only my own heart but the hearts of those around me. I knew I had been born again. The pilgrimage began, and what a journey it has been!

Today as I write, I have known the Lord for about thirty-six years. For thirty-two years I have pastored the same church, one the Lord graciously called me to start in the summer of 1974. I am a student of people, which I assure you, I study much better than I study math. (I might not be a 4.0, but I'm a lot higher than .56.)

Throughout my years in ministry, I have seen many inconsistencies, not only in my own life, but in the life of the western evangelical church. Statistics show that professing believers live no differently than the world. Something is clearly wrong when followers of Christ are not following. Something is clearly wrong when believers don't really believe. I once heard an old pastor say, "You believe only what you act on; all the rest is just religious talk." This is a book about a western jesus and the transcendent Christ. It is a book about how we have diluted, watered down, and compromised Jesus in our western culture to the point that he is hardly recognizable. We have made Jesus fit our culture to the point that he follows us. We call the shots, for our yoke is easy and our burden is light. We direct his steps, for we are a lamp unto his feet, and a light unto his path. We tell him to trust in us with all his heart and that he should not lean on his own understanding. This is a book about how our pilgrimage has been made shipwreck by western thought.

Our thinking has been twisted and distorted, as the evangelical mind-set has been shaped by its own bias and Jesus has been made to conform to our image.

This is a book about our pilgrimage. It is about a destination. It is a book about the temptations pilgrims feel along the way. It's about mid-course corrections. It is about a jesus that has no teeth in his bite. He is tame, anemic, and timid. He has been fashioned by our western culture to accommodate our flesh. He doesn't rule. He calls no shots. He is, in fact, not the Jesus of Scripture, not the transcendent Christ, the King and sovereign Lord who makes no suggestions and offers no opinions but speaks with great earthshaking authority. The transcendent Christ cannot be tamed nor does he bow to the western church and its compromised views. This book is about seeing life through the eyes of a pilgrim and his temptation to follow a western jesus.

I want to take you on a journey, the one Scripture describes. This is as much about my life as it is about yours, and I have come to realize that even through thirty-two years of teaching the Scripture, I believe only what I act on; all the rest is just religious talk. I have seen many areas of my life that fall well short of the biblical standard. Still, this is not a book designed to make us feel guilty at every turn, though we may feel a twinge from time to time. On the contrary, I trust that each chapter may help free us from such angst. We will see many verses that the western church does not believe. One could say we are "unbelieving believers." I hope that through a careful study of God's Word, everyone's feet will be held to the fire, including pastors, theologians, Sunday school teachers, and just plain church attenders with no special title.

I have put myself under biblical scrutiny and been found wanting. I point no fingers. I only want to put my arm around your shoulder and take you for a long walk. I want to help you think through this thing we call the Christian life. I want to push you into some areas which, perhaps, you have not wandered or have been reluctant to explore. I will ask some hard questions. I will press western evangelical thought to the wall. I hope to make you think hard about what you really believe and distinguish it from culture, tradition, and western thinking.

How I Met the Western Jesus

The entire message of a western jesus was born out of the muddy clay (see Ps. 40:2). Through my years of ministry, I have experienced what all pastors experience—praise, satisfaction, and great joy coupled with criticism, hopelessness, and great sorrow. The apostle Paul says it comes with the territory. He dedicates the entire book of 2 Corinthians to this truth.

Since I started the church that I presently pastor and knew its personality from its inception, many years down the road I began to grieve at how much it had changed over time. I didn't like what I was seeing. Change is inevitable, and I could accept that fact, but we seemed to be losing our way. Our church was becoming more of a business than a community of believers. We were conducting four services, with about 2,500 in attendance. Yet getting big wasn't what bothered me. What bothered me was that we were losing the spiritual dynamic that had characterized our body for many years, particularly in its early stages. I had always taught our people that there should be no human explanation for our lives, and certainly no human explanation for the church. But all this was changing. Transfer growth was quickly replacing conversion growth, the latter being what made up the bulk of our body in its earlier years.

After many years of a growing staff, attendance pushing capacity, and giving on the rise, the church began to encounter numerous obstacles. I found myself to be the senior leader of a large and growing church, and the demands were way beyond my capabilities. I felt I was reliving my days at the Naval Academy, only I wasn't drowning in equations but leadership decisions. All I wanted to do was teach. My spiritual gift is not leadership, but like it or not I was forced to make some hard decisions, and decisions made under pressure in a hasty fashion are rarely if ever profitable.

People I cared for and had shepherded for years began to leave. Attendance dropped dramatically and giving took a nosedive. The domino effect took over, causing close friends to depart without explanation. Our church was giving $1.7 million a year to support 260 missionaries, and I started to worry that missionaries would be forced to come off the field due to my faulty leadership. How would our staff be paid? Suddenly there were many differing opinions as to how things should be remedied—all of them seemingly backed by Scripture, yet somehow opposing one another. To make matters worse, we were in the middle of a building program. Someone once said the reason God invented time was so everything wouldn't happen all at once. Not so this time. It happened all at once and I found myself in the crossfire. The pain was excruciating.

Although it was one of the darkest times in my ministry, I can honestly say God spared me from bitterness. Still I did not understand why so many left. I spent long hours, weeks, and months grieving over the loss of such sweet fellowship. Not that I'm minimizing my shortcomings, but my failures were not moral or ethical, but rather a failure in leadership. I wondered why people couldn't forgive me and continue serving as part of our community. Hadn't I walked many of them through their pain, buried their parents, taught their children, visited them in the hospital, and taught them faithfully through the years? Of the many who left, only one actually met with me prior to leaving to thank me and tell me why he was moving on. The rest just drifted away, probably not wanting to hurt me, but fully realizing I would eventually discover their disappearance.

It was during this two-year trial that my understanding of a western jesus was birthed. I was forced to look deeply into Scripture to see what God intended his church and the Christian life to be. As people left, I began to realize they were leaving for the same reason they would leave a bank, a job, or a country club: there was a better deal somewhere else. More pay, benefits, and better hours. Reasons for departure were simply expressed in "Christianese": "The Lord is leading us to fellowship elsewhere," "The Spirit is moving us on," and so on. All these reasons were actually manifestations of a western mind-set. We think church is a place you go to. We think it is a building. This is western thinking, and I began to wonder how many other areas in the church had been impacted by it. I realized that the fault was squarely on my shoulders. Had I done a better job of teaching about what the church is, I suspect many would have remained. However, God is good and my church has bounced back with a good spirit and giving at an all-time high in spite of my faulty leadership.

I believe that every pastor should feel that God has given him the greatest people in the world to shepherd. That is how I feel about those I presently minister to and those I have shepherded in the past. These are all wonderful people whom God is using to advance his kingdom.

Theology

All of what I experienced caused me to think about many areas of the Christian life. A western view of Jesus had infected the thinking of believers in nearly every area. It wasn't just church but the Christian life. I started to take inventory of all that I had experienced as a believer as well as a pastor. I thought of all the difficult questions people had asked me through the years regarding the Christian life. I could feel a book being shaped that would confront some of the tough issues that I feel have more simplistic answers than we have given them and much of what we believe has been sanitized by western thinking. The grid in which we view the Christian life is distorted and much of what we claim to believe, we don't really believe. When a new believer enters the kingdom, he is immediately faced with a myriad of views on how the Christian life should be lived. Most believers go through many changes in their journey. It reminds me of a mouse entering a maze looking for the cheese at the other end. But which way should he go? He could choose charismatic cheese, reformed cheese, Pentecostal cheese, or dispensational cheese. Is it any wonder that the world looks over our shoulder and smells a rat? We have a smorgasbord mentality. We mix theological systems and doctrines in order to build on our theology much like we do in making a pizza with our favorite toppings. We tend to swing from legalism to extreme liberty and everything in between.

From all of this I have distilled the theme of this book into the following statement: *This is a book about our pilgrimage and how it has been shaped by a western jesus who has been shaped by a western bias.* In the chapters before you, we will cover a wide variety of subjects, all of which will be examined in light of tradition, culture, and Scripture, exposing our western thought patterns. We will compare a western jesus who has led many astray, with the transcendent Christ who will never leave us or forsake us. This journey may surprise you. I pray most of all that it will delight you and that God may have his rightful place in the western church.

A Pilgrim's View of the Journey

I have always been fascinated with nature. I love to take hikes and observe whatever nature, through the hand of God, delivers up that day. From spiders to snakes, from birds to bamboo, I love nature. I am particularly mesmerized by the migration habits of different creatures. Whales migrate for thousands of miles, as do certain species of birds, such as Canadian geese. Various fish travel long distances in order to spawn at a particular time and place. There is one particular creature that migrates up to 2,800 miles—the Monarch butterfly. This tiny insect has a most unusual pattern for migration. In the spring, a certain species leaves Mexico and heads north for Canada, but because they have such a short lifespan, they die along the way. Therefore they must reproduce so the next generation can move northward. Several generations come and go before they reach Canada, but only one generation can fly the whole way back to Mexico. They leave in late summer and are called the Methuselah generation. They are citizens of Mexico but have never been there. They are hardwired with genetic coding that stays the course until they arrive at their final destination. You could say, "They are looking for a city." They run into natural forces, such as wind and rain, that knock them off course, yet they make every necessary midcourse correction because they are in a relentless pursuit of their citizenship. They are, in fact, on a pilgrimage referred to in the world of nature as migration.

We can draw a number of comparisons and contrasts between our pilgrimage and that of the Monarch butterfly. For instance, they are born again and so are we. They are genetically predisposed to look for a city; at the moment of our new birth, we are spiritually predisposed in search of our heavenly country. "You previously walked according to this worldly age," says Paul in Ephesians 2:2. The butterfly's life is short, and so is ours—"a bit of smoke" according to James 4:14. Monarchs have certain forces that resist them on their journey and so do we.

Yet despite all the comparisons, we are faced with one major contrast—Monarch butterflies are never tempted to settle in anywhere but home. We, on the other hand, are drawn away daily by a spiritual enemy and a fleshly nature that wars against us in our journey. The apostle Peter states, "I urge you as aliens and temporary residents to abstain from fleshly desires that war against you" (1 Pet. 2:11). We meet with temptation at every turn. The Monarch always stays focused and allows nothing to distract it from its course. Sadly, the same cannot be said about us.

One of the main purposes in our pilgrimage is to invite others to join us. Our heavenly focus will impact how we live our lives and what kind of testimony we will have for impacting those we come in contact with. This is no small matter. Will others glorify God on the "day of visitation" (1 Pet. 2:12) because of our testimony? Will others see our good works and glorify our Father in heaven (see Matt. 5:16)? Will others be prompted to ask us about the hope that is in us (1 Pet. 3:15)? Will our lives be consistent with the gospel (Phil. 1:27)? These are serious issues with eternal consequences.

Much of our journey in this book will carry us over rugged terrain, and there may be a sense of conviction along the way. Now understand, there is a difference between conviction and guilt. Good biblical preaching will convict. *Conviction* is designed by God to reveal to us things about ourselves that need correction. It exposes "the sin that so easily ensnares us" (Heb. 12:1). *Guilt* is the result of not properly responding to the conviction. In our pursuit of the heavenly city, remember the Monarch.

CHAPTER 2

Home of the Western Jesus

*For he was looking forward to the city that has
foundations, whose architect and builder is God.*

Hebrews 11:10

WHEN MY BROTHER AND I were just little guys, my dad would take
us hiking in the beautiful Blue Ridge Mountains of West Virginia. We
had an old friend who owned thirty-six thousand acres of land and let
us use it whenever we were in the area. One of the things Dad taught us
about the woods was the need to be very quiet and still or we would scare
off the wildlife. We would hike for a while and then find an old log and
park there quietly for about twenty minutes. It wasn't long before different
creatures from the forest emerged from their hiding places. Deer would
wander by and snakes would make an occasional appearance along with
squirrels and other wildlife.

I was reminded of this years later while teaching a Bible class on
the subject of meditation. One of the men in the class commented that
meditation is much like sitting still on a log in the woods; things begin

to appear that you would normally miss while hiking. What a great illustration.

One of the great blessings of Scripture is the joy of meditation, which God invites all of us to participate in. What is implied in a text is often more refreshing than what is explicitly stated. Anyone can scratch around on the surface of the Bible and tell you what it says, but meditation gives life to the truth of God's Word so that what is hidden to the unregenerate mind is revealed to believers. "But the natural man does not welcome what comes from God's Spirit, because it is foolishness to him; he is not able to know it since it is evaluated spiritually" (1 Cor. 2:14).

As we read through Scripture and meditate on its message to us, we begin to see ourselves portrayed as strangers, sojourners, and pilgrims (see Heb. 11:13 KJV). Each such expression makes clear that we belong to another world. Webster's defines a *pilgrim* as "one who journeys in foreign lands." Because I have traveled much, I know what it is like to long for home. I know the feeling of being out of my element, when the languages and customs are alien and I feel out of touch. So when Scripture calls us to be pilgrims or sojourners in this world, it is no small matter.

Sadly many of us are no longer pilgrims but tourists. Rather than longing for home, our attitude has become "I'm a native of this present world and love it." An eternal perspective has been replaced by a temporal one. Our love for the good life has obscured any dream of a better place because we don't really believe that "living is Christ and dying is gain" (Phil. 1:21).

We can, however, regain our sense of the pilgrimage we are called to if we study the lives of those in Scripture who lived it out, not in theory but in practice. It wasn't just Abraham who was looking for a city. Note how many Old and New Testament saints were searching for that same city. David said in the twenty-third psalm that he would "dwell in the house of the Lord" forever. Why? Because he was looking for a city. It is said of Moses: "For he considered reproach for the sake of the Messiah to be greater wealth than the treasures of Egypt, since his attention was on the reward" (Heb. 11:26). Why? Because he was looking for a city.

Daniel's three companions told Nebuchadnezzar that God was able to deliver them from the fiery furnace, but even if he didn't, they would not bow down. Why? Because they were looking for a city. Asaph in Psalm 73 said God would lead him to glory, which was all the counsel he needed to be refreshed in his spirit and no longer wonder why the wicked seemed to prosper. Why? Because he was looking for a city. Paul said, "For me, living is Christ and dying is gain." (Phil. 1:21). Why was death gain? Because he was looking for a city.

Abraham

One of my favorite characters in Scripture is Abraham. If you follow his life closely, you will see that it represents the Christian life. He starts out in full obedience to the call of God: "By faith Abraham, when he was called, obeyed and went out to a place he was going to receive as an inheritance; he went out, not knowing where he was going" (Heb. 11:8). It was not long, however, before he lied about his wife Sarai and said that she was his sister. Note carefully that God had promised him a son; thus he was protected by the very word of Almighty God and the covenant relationship he had established. Abraham could not have been killed by Pharaoh or anyone until the promised son was born, but self-focus obscured his understanding of what God had told him. He then began to show signs of growth in faith and understanding only to relapse by raising up Ishmael through Hagar. However, in spite of such ups and downs, Abraham eventually became a great man of faith, "for he was looking forward to the city that has foundations, whose architect and builder is God" (Heb. 11:10). King David shared the same sentiments in Psalm 119:19: "I am a stranger on earth; do not hide Your commands from me."

Somehow these great men of God had lost interest in this present world and were able to see beyond their natural horizons to treasure where Christ would dwell. They truly believed what God had said. As the old hymn says, "And the things of earth will grow strangely dim in the light of His glory and grace."

Looking Beyond the Promise

A number of years ago, while studying the life of Abraham, I noticed something I had never seen before, a personal revelation I've titled "Looking Beyond the Promise." It all began as I studied Genesis 22, where Abraham was told by God to offer up his son as a sacrifice. This has always been a most troubling portion of Scripture for unbelievers and believers as well. It seems to go against the grain of all that God stands for. One can't help but see this as some form of mental torture. Why would God do such a thing? Imagine the torment of killing your child whom you have spent about fifteen years raising.

When Abraham instructed his two servants to remain with the donkey while he and Isaac went to worship, God was setting the stage for one of the greatest principles to live by in the Christian life. Faith was being tested at its highest level. The command of God went counter to the promise of God. God appeared to be putting himself in a bind. He had promised Abraham a son who would be the necessary link in carrying out the Abrahamic covenant: "your offspring will be traced through Isaac" (Gen. 21:12). Yet here God was commanding Abraham to kill the promise, which in effect would destroy the covenant. Was Abraham serving two gods? Was he faced with a god who couldn't make up his mind? Was he faced with a god who couldn't keep his promise? Or was he facing a God who never lies but says, "Trust me to reconcile the irreconcilable"?

By this stage of Abraham's life he believed that God could be trusted. He had walked with his Lord for many years and had seen that "what He had promised, He was also able to perform" (Rom. 4:21). Still, this was a situation unlike any other. This was not a promise that was seemingly delayed, as in the birth of Isaac. This was the promise of God, "your offspring will be traced through Isaac," challenging the command of God, "take your son, . . . your only son." Abraham saw the dilemma, yet he was unfazed. He told his servants that he and Isaac would return. Yet God had not promised him that they would return. He had not promised him that Isaac would be raised from the dead. But because Abraham had learned to walk by faith and not by sight (see 2 Cor. 5:7) and since he knew that

God cannot lie (see Titus 1:2), he was forced to look beyond the promise and believe that God was able to raise Isaac from the dead. Listen to what Hebrews tells us about Abraham's thoughts.

> He considered God to be able even to raise someone from the dead, from which he also got him back as an illustration. (Heb. 11:19)

In other words he believed that God would fulfill the promise in a greater way, that is, resurrection.

This is a profound lesson for all of us. God was showing the world what it looks like to believe what God says even if the circumstances tell another story. This is hard for us to do. We in the West want everything laid out and neatly explained. Mystery and seeing through a glass dimly (see 1 Cor. 13:12) are not our style. Yet through the example of Abraham, we are called to examine the principle of looking beyond the promise. Abraham knew about the promise of his son carrying on the family line, but he didn't know how this would take place if Isaac were to die. Yet his faith in God's promise forced him to believe that it would be fulfilled in a greater way than originally promised. God's promise, "your offspring will be traced through Isaac" was sacrificed on the altar of his command, "offer up your son." If Isaac had simply lived out his life, the promise would have been fulfilled, but Abraham would have missed the blessing of looking beyond the promise and believing in resurrection. God's command to offer up Isaac took Abraham's faith to new levels of trust.

Moses

We find this same truth in the life of Moses. He was told to take the children of Israel into the land of Canaan. He obeyed the Lord but soon found himself trapped, facing a wall of water (the Red Sea) with Pharaoh's troops rapidly in pursuit. God did not tell Moses in advance that he would part the Red Sea, but Moses knew this couldn't be the end of the road because of God's covenant promise to Israel and his command for them to occupy Canaan. The Red Sea challenged the promise of God. So what was Moses forced to do? He was forced to look beyond the promise and believe that God would fulfill the promise in a greater way. He turned to his people and said, "Don't be afraid. Stand firm and see the Lord's salvation He will provide for you today; for the Egyptians you see today, you will never see again" (Exod. 14:13).

Throughout Scripture impossible situations that seemingly thwarted the promises of God were met with a faith that believed God would never lie. Even if his promises seemed to be negated by his own commands, these saints believed that he would fulfill his promises in a greater way. Now this is not to be confused with those who believe that if you have enough faith, God is obligated to carry out your wishes. This faith is based on a promise that appears to be nullified, but since God must keep his promise, then it will be fulfilled in a way greater than what was originally promised.

David knew he would defeat Goliath, not because of a previous promise of God that he would kill Goliath, but because he knew he had been anointed as king, which was not yet fulfilled. Mordecai telling Esther that if she didn't go before the king, deliverance would come from another place (see Esther 4:14) is yet another example.

No doubt few of us will be called of God to carry out such heroics, but we have been given promises that often seem thwarted by circumstances or we find ourselves in seemingly impossible situations that God brings into our lives. His promise to never leave us or forsake us is often dimmed by the difficulties of the pilgrimage. Yet like the man in Mark 9:24, we can call out to God: "I do believe! Help my unbelief." Our new nature says, "I believe," while our flesh, which is married to the circumstances of life, says, "Help my unbelief."

These All Died in Faith

Hebrews 11 is rich with the great truths of our pilgrimage. "These all died in faith without having received the promises, but they saw them from a distance, greeted them, and confessed that they were foreigners and temporary residents on the earth" (Heb. 11:13). There are several things to ponder that will yield much fruit if we can grasp the great reality of this verse. First we find "these all died in faith," referring to the saints previously mentioned in the first twelve verses of Hebrews 11. They died **IN** faith. Their faith was still strong up to the very end. Then comes a most troubling statement: "without having received the promises." Why would they keep faith in a god who does not keep his promises? This subject of unfulfilled promises is again highlighted in Acts 7 when Stephen, the first martyr, says this as he addresses the Sanhedrin regarding the life of Abraham: "Then he came out of the land of the Chaldeans and settled in Haran. And from there, after his father died, God had him move to this land in which you now live. He didn't give him an inheritance in it, not even a foot of ground, but He promised to give it to him as a possession, and to his descendants after him, even though he was childless" (vv. 4–5). So far we have these words: "These all died in faith without having received the promises." The key, however, is what follows: "but they saw them from a distance." When at death's door what were they looking for that was at "a distance"? They were looking beyond the promise and seeing that God would fulfill his promise in a much greater way in the next world. Their lives were based on such promises. That was how they met their daily challenge.

The Scripture doesn't end there. "And were persuaded of them, and embraced them . . ." (KJV). In 2 Timothy, Paul said, "I know whom I have believed and am persuaded that He is able to guard what has been entrusted to me until that day" (2 Tim. 1:12). Being persuaded and embracing God's promises will shape every facet of our lives. Money, security, pleasure, and a host of other western dreams are brought under submission to such revelation. How much of our lives would change if this were really believed? Imagine the peace and joy that would escort us through life if we had an eternal perspective as portrayed here.

The truth continues to unfold as we read how they "confessed that they were foreigners and temporary residents on the earth." Foreigners and temporary residents? Is this how the western church sees itself? Would the world look at us and say, "Now there is a different breed." There was a time in the early church when the lost world was deeply impacted by the lives of Christians, as evidenced by this letter written by Piagnetus, an early historian, in the year AD 180. Describing believers, he states:

> They are not distinguished from the rest of mankind by country, by speech, nor by customs. But although they live in both Greek and foreign cities and follow the local customs both in clothing and food and the rest of life, they exhibit the wonderful and strange nature of their own citizenship—but as sojourners. They live in their own homelands. They share all things as citizens and suffer all things as aliens. Every foreign country is a homeland, and every homeland is a foreign country. They marry as all do. They bear children, but they do not discard their children as some do. They offer a common table, but not a common bed. They find themselves in the flesh, but they do not live according to the flesh. They pass their time upon the Earth, but are citizens of Heaven. They obey the established laws and supposit the laws in their own lives. They love all and are persecuted by all. They are put to death—and are made alive. They are poor—but make many rich. They lack all things, yet abound in all things. They are abused and give blessing. They are insulted and give honor. When they do good they are punished as evildoers. When they are punished, they rejoice as those receiving life.

Does the contemporary world view us this way? Peter reminds us that our lives should so reflect our faith that many will come to the truth as a result (see 1 Pet. 2:12). Jesus, as he began the Sermon on the Mount, said, "Let your light shine before men, so that they may see your good works and give glory to your Father in heaven" (Matt. 5:16).

Hebrews 11:14 in the King James gives us another great insight into the text. Here we are told that those who state that they are strangers and pilgrims declare that they seek a country. This country they are seeking is defined as a heavenly country. Therefore we can conclude that when God's promises are not fulfilled in a natural way, faith extends its sight and interprets the promise to be fulfilled in a spiritual way, which may very well be carried into the next life. According to Hebrews 13, we have no "endur-ing city" in this world (v. 14).

Another truth arises by virtue of meditating on some of God's prom-ises and declarations. For example, we are told that our citizenship is in heaven (see Phil. 3:20). We are told that we are (present tense) strangers on the earth. By definition if I am a stranger, then I am from another place. As an American, if I am a stranger in California, then I must be from another state. As an American, if I am a stranger in France, then I must be from another country. If, however, I am a stranger in this world, then I am from a place I have never been. Does that strike you as a bit bizarre? Remember that the Monarch butterfly was from a place it had never been. I am from a place I have never been. Try telling a Frenchman that you are from the United States but have actually never been there. But this is exactly what Scripture tells us. Our western thinking doesn't allow for such illogical reasoning, yet our minds must engage the text and believe what it says. Can you imagine how this would impact our daily lives if we embraced the fact and confessed the truth that we are just passing through? What value would be put on the mall and movies if we cherished such truth? How might this change our priorities regard-ing early retirement, investment portfolios, and the American dream of living happily ever after? These great saints trusted God for what he said and worshipped him for who he is. May we do the same.

Suffering and the Pilgrimage

The Scriptures relate clearly that trials and tribulation will be part of the Christian life (see James 1, 1 Peter, and John 16). It isn't that we are just assigned trials, though that is clearly part of God's sovereign plan. Trials come as we are obedient in following the Lord because it means we are going against the grain. That always results in splinters. We are going uphill, which always results in a certain amount of spiritual sweat. We are going against the current, which means we feel like we are drowning from time to time.

I might at this juncture add a little sunshine. The Christian life is not to be thought of as boring, tedious, bland, and filled with misery. The most joyful people on planet Earth should be Christians. We are the only ones with the potential of enjoying the fruit of the Spirit, and joy happens to be one of those. Nonetheless Scripture makes clear that difficulties come as we follow Christ. This is one reason I believe Christians don't share their faith. They fear being labeled. They fear ridicule. They don't share their faith in the marketplace because they fear that once it has been disclosed that they are a believer, their life will be on display. Their every word and action will be weighed on different scales, and they may actually have to live a life consistent with the gospel. No more dirty jokes, deception, or lying to make the sale. No more getting a little tipsy after work at the local bar.

Early Christians and many in foreign cultures know they will lose their lives if they share their faith, yet they gladly do so. In the West, however, we fear being laughed at or being held to a higher standard. How embarrassed would you be if you introduced a Christian friend to one of your unbelieving coworkers, and while at lunch, your friend started to witness to this coworker—someone you have worked with and traveled with for years but have never mentioned Christ to?

How is it that many have done the following but we can't even get a conversation moving in a spiritual direction?

> Quenched the raging of fire, escaped the edge of the sword, gained strength after being weak, became mighty in battle, and put foreign armies to flight. Women received their dead raised to life again. Some men were tortured, not accepting release, so that they might gain a better resurrection, and others experienced mockings and scourgings, as well as bonds and imprisonment. They were stoned, they were sawed in two, they died by the sword, they wandered about in sheepskins, in goatskins, destitute, afflicted, and mistreated. The world was not worthy of them. They wandered in deserts, mountains, caves, and holes in the ground. All these were approved through their faith, but they did not receive what was promised. (Heb. 11:34–39)

Many who lost their lives paved the way for us to have a better life, yet "go into all the world and preach the gospel to the whole creation" (Mark 16:15) is another verse the western church simply doesn't believe. The statistics on giving to missions by the rich western church is appalling. While we build bigger barns and say, "You have many goods stored up for many years. Take it easy; eat, drink, and enjoy yourself" (Luke 12:19), the world continues to live in darkness. Or is this another part of Scripture that we don't believe? I know I fall far short of the biblical mandate. I live in a very nice home in the western suburbs of Washington, D.C. I know what weights and sins have kept me from running the race with endurance (see Heb. 12:1). I keep a running inventory, not for the sake of legalism or beating myself up, but as a discipline that helps me stay spiritually fit. This is a marathon, not a sprint.

Every Pilgrim Has a Signature Verse

There are some truly magnificent golf courses in the United States, and I have had the privilege of playing a few of them. Every major championship course has what we call a signature hole. It is often the most difficult hole on the course or perhaps the most beautiful by design. It reflects the heartbeat of the course architect and showcases his style, talent, and intent. Perhaps the most famous hole in golf is the spectacular par three sixteenth hole at Cypress Point on the Monterey peninsula in California. The hole is 220 yards long from tee to green, but all of it is over the ocean. I have never played Cypress, but I have seen pictures of this famed par three.

As I have walked through the Christian life for the last thirty-six years, I have rubbed shoulders with many believers, all of whom are unique in their journey. After I know someone for a while, I begin to sense a passion and a special reflection of God's glory. There seems to be a spiritual DNA that makes them different. Some love to study and lay out doctrinal issues, while others are more contemplative and spend their time in prayer or meditation. Still others love fellowship and desperately want to see the body connected. If we were to assign a verse to every believer's life, that verse would define who they are and what their spiritual contribution is to the church. We could say that they have a signature verse. Think about the great people in Scripture. What verse comes to your mind when you think of David? I think most of us would respond that David is known as a man after God's own heart (see 1 Sam. 13:14 KJV and Acts 13:22). For Noah, I think Genesis 6:9 tells his story: "Noah walked with God." It is said of Abraham that he "believed the Lord, and He credited it to him as righteousness" (Gen. 15:6). Paul is perhaps best defined by "For me, living is Christ and dying is gain" (Phil. 1:21).

Let's take just a moment to look at each one of these verses and how they define the individual. David was known for many things. He was the greatest king of Israel. He was a mighty warrior. He was a leader of men. But on the spiritual side David seems to be best known for the psalms, which reveal his heart for God. He failed in many ways, and his dark side is on display regarding his murder of Uriah and his adulterous relationship with Bathsheba. However, as we read his journal in the psalms, we are invited behind the curtain to see how he thinks. We see great emotion, tears, depression, anxiety, fear, joy, praise, and other displays of his deep sense of God's presence.

When we read that Noah walked with God, we can understand why. He lived in a time when there were many people on the earth, but no believers. There were no Bible conferences, church services, home Bible studies, or fellowship groups. It was only he and his family. Life must have been most difficult. I have many friends to lean on for encouragement, counsel, and prayer support, and I still find it difficult. He lived at a time when God said that every imagination of man was evil continually (see Gen. 6:5). It was a dark time, yet here was a man who depended totally on God. Who else could he walk with? Scripture asks the question, "Can two walk together without agreeing to meet?" (Amos 3:3). Noah must have agreed with God. If he agreed with God, then he must have known the thoughts of God. You cannot walk with someone unless you are moving in the same direction. Nor can you walk with someone unless you walk at the same pace. People you walk with, you talk with. You are in their presence and you choose to maintain fellowship. All of this was true of Noah and his relationship with God.

Abraham is known as the father of all who believe (see Gal. 3:7). His life was a life of ups and downs, but in the end he proved himself to be a man of great faith. Thus his signature verse, Genesis 15:6, reflects this truth. We are challenged by his life of faith as he continued to see the heavenly city.

Paul was most unusual. He desired to go home and be with Christ, but he felt he was still needed here to continue the sojourn. For Paul, "living is Christ." Christ was central to his life, and so his doctrine and teaching reflected his passion. He truly believed that dying would be gain. Talk about an eternal perspective. This was a passionate man who saw the trials of life as momentary and light. His eternal focus gave birth to a theology that made Christ central.

We could also add Esther to our list. She is known for her great statement: "I will go to the king even if it is against the law. If I perish, I perish" (Esther 4:16). She made this pronouncement just before she entered the king's presence to plead for her people, knowing she could lose her life by doing so. She was known for her great bravery.

These great people of Scripture have a distinct signature verse that summarizes their story. We are no different. However, our western thinking, which likes everything in a neat little package, has little sympathy for those who don't share our signature verse. Some draw from verses on grace, while others draw from the law of holiness. Some say prayer is the key to the Christian life, while others highlight Bible study. We can't, with our western jesus, seem to get past these differences, which are not really differences but complementary reflections of God.

I've been in church work long enough to know that unity is the fruit of corporate humility. Unfortunately, as pilgrims, we tend to collect the dust of the world in our travels, which clogs our thinking. Pride enters the arena, and signature verses become scriptural weapons employed against those who differ. I'm not suggesting doctrinal or ethical compromise, but I am suggesting that we learn to see how others view the Christian life. Signature verses in our lives are not given to us to become independent thinkers but to join with those who see things differently and thus complete the picture. Paul develops this in 1 Corinthians 12 when he talks about spiritual gifts. The body will never function well until the gifts are coordinated and used in harmony. Paul is also careful to mention the infighting that was taking place in the church at Corinth because of pride as it related to giftedness.

I admit that the term *signature verse* is not found in Scripture, but my observations from Scripture and life tell me this is true. All the well-known evangelicals who preach on the radio have their own life verse. Some have a passion for God's glory, while others showcase revival and prayer. Still others stress the importance of sound doctrine. These narrow focuses frequently leave the listening audience trying to figure out who is right and which path should be followed. Would you like to know which of the big names is right? None of them are. They are all partially right, seeing through a glass dimly just as you and I do. Some of us may be attracted to a certain style reflected in a certain preacher's delivery while others may not be drawn to them. How well I remember hearing J. I. Packer speak to a small gathering in Washington, D.C., back in the late seventies. Someone asked him how God could bless a particular body of believers, since they were off on a particular doctrine. Packer wisely replied, "I'm off on my doctrine and God blesses me." We all sat there stunned that Packer would admit to being off doctrinally. He followed up with, "I just don't know where." By this, he meant that he must be off doctrinally somewhere in his theology. He couldn't be perfect in his interpretation of every fact and thus he humbly admitted that he must be off the mark somewhere. He went on to clarify his statement by telling us that God blesses us not because of our right doctrine but even in spite of our wrong doctrine.

I have a dear friend who held up his Bible one day in front of a small gathering of believers and said, "Luke 4:18 should be everyone's favorite verse" and then he proceeded to read it. I too love the verse he read, and it is certainly important; but to say that all of us should claim this as the foundational truth is a bit strong. However, knowing this man as I do, he really lives out the passage and blesses many with it. I equally rejoice with others who claim different verses as their favorite and bless others with it.

Every church has those who love sound doctrine and see it as the glue that holds the body together, mixed with those who say Jesus is the answer and not doctrine. Both sides offer Scripture to support their claim. Here again we need humble dialogue and biblical balance. More on this later.

There are a few believers who seem to prize every verse in Scripture. They are a rare breed. As believers we tend to see life through the lens of our signature verse, but we might be careful that we are open to how others see things or there will be friction. We must try and see our differences as potentially complementary rather than competitive or combative. Paul continually reminds us to maintain a wartime mentality. We are at odds with the world system and its commander-in-chief. Our western culture, which puts a premium on leisure and the good life, has found its way into the church and diluted its eternal focus.

[CHAPTER 3]

A Western Jesus and His Church

IMAGINE YOU HAVE LIVED in Siberia all your life. At the age of thirty-seven a missionary arrives with the best news you have ever heard. The glory of the transcendent Christ penetrates your darkened heart and you pass from death unto life. Something in you cries out for fellowship and a connection with other believers; it's inherent within your new divine nature. The missionary dies shortly after sharing the gospel, and you are left with no one to disciple you. All he left you was a copy of the Bible written in your own language. You devour every word and savor every verse as though it were honey dripping from the comb.

Having finished the Old Testament and arriving at the New Testament, you experience a sense of excitement that seems uncontainable. It compels you to tell your story to others. You develop a real intimacy with the Savior and have a passion to know him in an even greater way. Having read through the Gospels, you now find yourself grazing in the rich fields of early church history in the book of Acts. What do you make of the gospel explosion and church multiplication? You find yourself fascinated with all-night prayer meetings, persecution, and resistance to the overwhelming power of the gospel. Your excitement swells and you can no longer contain yourself. The epistles reveal the depth of the gospel and a glimpse of what church life is about.

You long to find a community where this real life manifests itself as told in Acts. Through a series of divinely appointed circumstances, you are able to visit the United States. You believe your dream has come true, having read about the millions of believers and the many church fellowships in the United States. You inquire about where you might gather with believers, and several church locations are brought to your attention. Enormous structures are on nearly every corner with service times listed out front. You wonder what this means? You don't recall Scripture mentioning services times or large structures, but then again, you're just a novice.

You attend the 10:00 a.m. service of a large church, and with great anticipation you wait to experience the power of the Holy Spirit and hear preaching that will bring great revelation to your soul. Surprisingly, what you find is a far cry from what you anticipated. Hundreds if not thousands pour into a large auditorium. The music is joyful and uplifting, though you see many not participating. The message is powerful, but somehow the power seems to come from personality more than divine revelation. The message is well crafted but doesn't seem to measure up to Paul's description of preaching as found in 1 Corinthians 2:1–5:

> When I came to you, brothers, announcing the testimony of God to you, I did not come with brilliance of speech or wisdom. For I determined to know nothing among you except Jesus Christ and Him crucified. And I was with you in weakness, in fear, and in much trembling. My speech and my proclamation were not with persuasive words of wisdom, but with a demonstration of the Spirit and power, so that your faith might not be based on men's wisdom but on God's power.

Conversation in the foyer after the service has more to do with the 12:30 p.m. kickoff (whatever that is) than the sermon. People are leaving just as they came in. What about the lost who should have fallen on their faces and said, "God is really among you" (1 Cor. 14:25)? Where was the powerful testifying that you read about in 1 Thessalonians 1:8–9 regarding the great faith of the believers? Why was the meeting over so quickly? Where was the participation of the body and their gifts (see 1 Cor. 14)? Where was the prayer meeting like what you read about in Acts 12? The seriousness of the gospel you had become familiar with in the New Testament was somehow lacking. There was more of a cavalier attitude and a general sense of a temporal focus. Life went on as usual. "These aren't pilgrims," you say to yourself, "they're tourists." You soon become disillusioned and begin to wonder if this Christian life you have read about isn't just some big sham. Returning to Scripture your faith is restored and you soon come to realize the transcendent Christ had been replaced by a western jesus who is tame, domesticated, and controlled by a sterile environment. Church in the West is something you go to and do while the church of Scripture is who you are. It is your total identity. The church of Scripture is salt and light that penetrate a decaying and dark world, while the western church collects itself under one roof for one hour a week. The salt has lost its savor and the light is under a basket.

A Desire for Authenticity

There has been much written today about the lack of power in the body of Christ. Terms like *authenticity, intimacy,* and *relevance* are hot-topic issues that pervade the church, demanding dialogue. Every brand and flavor of church can be found in our western culture. They all seem to be looking for the same thing. There is a spirit of competition for the market share. Endless articles and books have glutted the Christian bookstores. Not only are individuals trying to find themselves, but the church is trying to do the same thing. It is trying to reinvent itself.

We try new ways to bring people in. We give sermon series to meet needs only to find there is nothing new under the sun. Real spiritual transformation and change is simply not taking place. The statistics show that believers live no differently than unbelievers. So we try harder to figure out this conundrum. My concern is that in the attempt to get real and relate to society and postmodern thinking, we have pushed the envelope of grace way too far. We want to show the world that we are not prudes and that a great life is in store for the believer. Grace covers it all and there is freedom in Christ. Legalism is despised, as it should be, but it is often confused with holiness, which it shouldn't be. There has been a moral fall, if you will— a departure from Christ and his teaching. We, as the church, have concluded that relating to society requires joining society. We now have Christian magazines with weekly movie reviews. I have actually read statements like, "If you don't mind a little frontal nudity, I think you will find this film very powerful." (Can you imagine the apostle Paul providing movie reviews?) Crude language is even showing up in the pulpit and seminaries in order to win over the masses. These actions are justified in the name of relevance when in reality they are nothing more than a western jesus.

The True Church

Every true believer is on a journey. The ultimate destination is known, but the temporal pilgrimage is unknown. We know from Scripture certain generic elements of the journey. There will be trials and tribulations (see John 16:33). There will be feelings of abandonment (see Ps. 10:1). There will be broken relationships (see Ps. 147:3). Yet the Lord will never forsake us (see Heb. 13:5), and there will be days of great gladness of heart (see Ps. 4:7) as we experience victory and closeness to God (see Phil. 3:10).

Only in the West Do We "Go to Church"

If you had lived during the New Testament era and asked somebody where the church was located, they would have wondered where you came from. If you had inquired about service times, they would have asked for clarification. If you had asked who the senior pastor was, they would have responded, "What's that?" What time it starts, what time it's over, what is the address—are all foreign concepts in Scripture. Listen to these words by Paul: "If the whole church assembles together" (1 Cor. 14:23a). Notice that the church didn't become the church only after they gathered. They already were the church. In our western culture, even the most mature believer still thinks the sanctuary, programs, music, or stained-glass windows and pews make up the church. If you don't believe me, just try to make a change. There is much heated dialog today about plastic pulpits versus wooden pulpits, chairs replacing pews. We recently brought up a pastor from a church that was wiped out by hurricane Katrina. He said, "You will never understand church until your building is gone." The marquee in front of his church building now says, "Bring your own chair."

A while back we decided to make one of our back rooms a place for visitors to have coffee. The next thing I heard was that we had become worldly and we would soon be known as the coffeehouse church. Some mind-sets will not change easily. However, take those—who have left because of music, or chairs replacing pews—to a foreign culture, preferably a third-world country, and allow them to assemble with believers in an abandoned warehouse—they will soon be worshipping with tears streaming down their faces. No pews, no narthex, no pulpit, no organ, no hymnals—but the very presence of God will resurrect their soul. The music will be unfamiliar, a style they would never tolerate at their home church in the West. There will be tambourines, bongo drums, hand clapping, and hand raising—all foreign to much of our western culture. The message may lack deep theological content, but the revelation of Christ himself will be evident. For the very reason they left their old church, they will rejoice in another culture. They will leave a western jesus and find the transcendent Christ.

No one fights over the issues we fight over here. They get it, and I'm not sure we do. I have worshipped in a Russian prison, in the jungles of Bolivia, in big cities, in fancy auditoriums, and in the suburbs. I once spoke in a church in New Hampshire during the winter. The wood to feed the potbelly stove was stacked behind the pulpit. The sanctuary never got above 55 degrees and the kids classes were hovering around zero. I have actually worshipped in all these places without pews or wooden pulpits because the transcendent Christ can slice through western minutiae.

Having seen the church in its nonwestern attire has naturally given rise to a more discerning view of how the body of Christ should function. I have always had to keep this in the back of my mind in order to temper my thoughts and not become judgmental of those who have not had equal exposure. When I see people upset over what I would call *minutiae*, I grieve. My tendency, right or wrong, is to run the situation through the grid of a Chinese believer who is meeting in an underground church, hoping he survives long enough to pass on his faith to others. I try to imagine him being upset over the fact that his favorite songs weren't played at their clandestine meeting. Would there be an uprising over using the New International Version as opposed to the King James Version? Was the guest speaker off on his theology such that some may threaten to leave?

We had a cantata last year and left the decorations up on the back wall behind the pulpit. They were hiding some verses that had been etched in the wall some twenty years earlier. Yes, I should have known from experience that this would be a stumbling block but since there were no complaints and the staff liked the new look better, we decided to keep it as is. Later, I was informed that four families left the church because the verses were hidden and we were heading down a dangerous path. I couldn't help but think where would these folks attend church? In their search would they require their new church building to have verses on the back wall? Are all churches without verses on the back wall in danger of God's judgment? If it is the only real way to honor God, should churches in Muslim countries do the same? Are churches that meet outdoors in rebellion? Suppose you are renting a school cafeteria where it is illegal to put up verses on the back wall. Will God refuse to visit you in worship? This is an example in which the transcendent Christ was buried by tradition. I often hear the more formal crowd get upset with the new design for churches. The sanctuary is often less formal and can double for a recreation hall. Somehow this seems to show less reverence for God. If this is a biblical truth, then all churches in poor foreign cultures need to have formal sanctuaries, or this is not a transcendent truth, but a western bias.

I could give many such examples and they would all point to a western mind-set. Does God feel more respected if I wear a coat and tie, or could he tolerate nice slacks and a button-down shirt? Suppose the pastor said just before his message, "Would the ushers come forward and pass out the snacks?" After everyone has their beverage and fruit, the pastor sits down on a stool and delivers a powerful expository message on the doctrine of imputed righteousness. Question: Has there been any violation of Scripture? Did Jesus ever teach while food was present? There is clear teaching in Acts 2 and 1 Corinthians 11 that the early church gathered for food, fellowship, and instruction. If it was OK then, why wouldn't it be OK now? I'm not advocating such a departure from the norm, but I just want believers to realize that much of what they count as sacred is just tradition, and much of what they consider an abomination is actually biblically sanctioned. I'm convinced that we are so programmed to think in a western way that we miss the real Jesus.

The Dog and Pony Show

Worship services today are so varied that it appears that each church is trying to outdo the next. Some favor a choir with robes backed by an orchestra, while others prefer a worship band backed up with drama. Who's right? Does Scripture clearly address this? The more formal church will often say that bands and drama are a dog and pony show. The truth of the matter is that both styles are a dog and pony show if the hearts of those in attendance aren't right. If people leave the service talking about the magnificent choir and the great talent in the orchestra but are not drawn to genuine worship, then it is just another form of entertainment. It's all a dog and pony show if the hearts of those leading in worship and those worshipping do not have a pure heart before God. If little children put on a skit in a home church, why can't an adult drama team do the same in a formal sanctuary? Is one holier than the other or is one more western than the other?

As a pastor, when I'm in my own church's worship service, I have trouble worshipping. I am constantly thinking about the temperature, the music, my message, and so forth. I try to see the service through the eyes of a visitor or a lost person. What do they think? Are they connecting? When I visit other churches, I look through a different lens. What do they do different from what we do? Do I like it better? How could the pastor have gotten his point across more effectively? Again, I tend to miss the worship.

A number of years ago I was at a high school basketball game and happened to sit next to a referee. I had seen him at many games wearing his black-and-white striped shirt, but he was now sitting in the stands. At halftime I introduced myself and told him that I knew he was a referee. "Do you mind if I ask you a question?" I inquired. He was most obliging, and I suspect he thought I was going to ask him about a certain foul in the game or what team was playing best. That's not, however, what I asked. I asked if he could enjoy the game or was he always judging the refs on the floor. Without hesitation he told me that he couldn't sit back and just enjoy the competition, but was always looking for some infraction that was missed or some call he disagreed with. I saw this as an illustration for those who are pastors, scholars, elders, and such. Do we get so involved in doctrinal, cultural, and traditional minutiae that we miss the game?

The western jesus has taught us to judge every aspect of the local church. "That's not the way we did Sunday school at my old church." "The pastor wasn't very relevant today." "How could they possibly have a skit at the service?" "Looks like the world is creeping in." Etcetera, etcetera. But what saith the Scriptures? The truth of the matter is that Scripture has very little to say about what a service should look like. "Plastic pulpits lead to plastic theology." "Chairs lead us to Hollywood." The negative sound bytes are too numerous to mention. Yes, I do have a concern about what is happening. What we do to a sanctuary may very well be the prelude to what we do with doctrine and in many cases does. This, however, is judging a book by its cover. There are some excellent expositors who have carefully looked over the cultural landscape and felt the need to be relevant in their dress, music, and philosophy of ministry. I have no problem provided the dress is moral, the music doctrinally sound, and the philosophy within the bounds of Scripture. Ninety-nine percent of what the apostle Paul teaches in his letters deals with the church scattered, and less than 1 percent deals with the church gathered. The western church, on the other hand, spends 99 percent of its energy putting on a worship service and 1 percent of its energy carrying the message to a lost world. Note carefully my wording about "putting on a service." There is more bickering over what a service looks like than concern for gospel outreach. This is western to the core.

Let's take another look at the term *in church*. If we look at it through the lens of Scripture with no western lens to interfere, then everything changes. The world creeping "into the church" is actually what happens to the local body of believers when they are not in the building. It's what happens over the Internet, on TV, in *People Magazine*, at the movies, and through a host of other influences that affect the church. We can have all the "appropriateness" we want when we gather, but if the rest of the week makes us a slave to the world, then appropriate dress and well-crafted worship is a farce.

The greatest battle any pastor has is how to effectively help his people live a godly life for the 167 hours they are not in the building, although what takes place during a worship service may well impact how they live the other 167 hours. What are the most effective ways to do this in our present culture without violating Scripture?

The younger generation must learn why the older generation loves tradition, steeples, pews, and hymnbooks. The older generation must be willing to see the younger generation as liking change. Good healthy dialogue in a teachable atmosphere can bring much fruit. Trying to prove that drums are of the devil or that hymns are boring become senseless arguments often birthed out of pride and a refusal to hear the other side. The truth often lies in the middle. I love the hymns because many of them tell a story that reflects what the church was dealing with in bygone years. "A Mighty Fortress Is Our God" should be carefully read and understood in light of the Reformation. The lyrics are a powerful expression of the intense warfare of the day. The younger generation should be thankful for past generations that ran interference for them. These were the giants upon which our churches stand today.

But let us not forget that God has his giants in every generation, and the battles are different as satanic strategies change. The church will always have common-denominator struggles with a lust for the world, but it may show its face differently. Jonathan Edwards didn't have to raise children in a day of Internet pornography, video games, amusement parks, shopping malls, cell phones, and TVs with 350 channels. Many of our praise songs reflect a battle that is different from battles fought before us. Hymns are often *about* God while praise songs are often *to* God. "A Mighty Fortress Is Our God" if written today would be "You, Oh Lord, Are a Mighty Fortress." There seems to be more despair in our present culture, which is why we so often read about postmodernism and the emerging church, and our bookshelves are filled with titles on anorexia, bulimia, and self-image. Such topics would have been foreign to Spurgeon, Luther, and Edwards.

So what does the church do? It must reflect its culture. Every culture has a story, and each generation within that culture has a story—and the transcendent Christ must be the answer no matter what the generation. The story is told in its music, worship, philosophy of ministry, and literature. If the church doesn't know the story, then its music, preaching, and philosophy of ministry miss the mark. It starts reading Shakespeare to four-year-olds and Little Bo Peep to sixty-year-olds. The dialogue ceases and the church begins to die.

Unfortunately, cultural change within the church is often interpreted as doctrinal change—a watering down of theology. This is usually not the case, though it can be. This is why careful dialogue must take place among generations. Each generation can learn from the other and listen for the story line. What upsets one culture or one generation may not affect another.

I was preaching at a church retreat in Trinidad. The accommodations were far from what we are used to here in the United States. However, what was most interesting is that in the auditorium there was a tarantula spider that lived up in the rafters and would crawl out and hang over the pulpit when I preached. I kid you not. When I finished, he would retreat. Now try to imagine a massive spider crawling out on the ceiling next Sunday in your beautifully lit, air-conditioned, freshly vacuumed sanctuary. It is quite possible that many would be trampled in an effort to escape. That congregation in Trinidad merely chuckled and proceeded to listen to the sermon. The tarantula was eventually converted. I tell this story to show the vast difference between one culture and another regarding the meeting place but no difference in the message.

Church on the Edge

Is it wrong to show a movie clip in a church service? It all depends. If it replaces preaching, then it is wrong. If the movie is immoral, then it is wrong. If the scene from the clip is perfectly clean, but the movie is immoral and there is no disclaimer made by the pastor prior to or after the clip is shown, then this would be tantamount to putting your seal of approval on a movie unfit for viewing and would thus be wrong. If, on the other hand, the clip was clean and related to the sermon, there would be no violation. I would, however, not advocate doing this in a church that has strong formal traditions because it could be a stumbling block.

So what is the irreducible minimum of what a service should contain? Though Scripture does not go into detail regarding the subject, there are some things that all serious gatherings must incorporate. Some of these may not be weekly, though they might be, such as communion or baptism. The Scriptures are not clear as to how long a service might be or the depth of exposition, but certainly there must be some amount of time devoted to fellowship, worship, and teaching. I find myself getting a little huffy when I hear of pastors who give twenty-minute sermons when mine are usually in the forty- to forty-five-minute range. However, the Puritans would have rebuked me for giving a sermonette, because they spent a couple of hours in exposition and long periods in prayer.

I was in Guatemala speaking at a Bible school a few years back. Each morning before I spoke the students would stand and sing. There was never a set time as to when the singing would end. On about the third or fourth day, they started worshipping at 8:00 a.m. and sang nonstop until 9:00 a.m. My legs were killing me as we stood the whole time. Surely they were going to introduce me at any moment. We continued from 9:00 to 10:00 a.m. I thought I was going to drop. *This must be the end,* I thought. No way. We went on until 11:00 a.m.—three straight hours of standing in worship. I was then invited to preach at their Sunday worship service. After what I thought was a lengthy message, the pastor came up and told me to keep going, that his people were used to long messages and would feel cheated if I cut things short.

Of course, the length is not as important as the content. How well I remember the teaching of the great Oswald Sanders. Twice I heard him give a devotional to a mission board. Both times I walked away saying to myself, "He can say more in twenty minutes than I can say in a month of sermons."

Pilgrims want and need to be under good Bible exposition. This is clear in Paul's exhortation to Timothy: "Proclaim the message; persist in it whether convenient or not; rebuke, correct, and encourage with great patience and teaching" (2 Tim. 4:2). Note carefully the three elements: rebuke, correct, and encourage. The western jesus preaches only the last part of Paul's instruction. We in the West don't like correction. It's too negative and it invades our privacy. Just tickle my ears with some good practical advice that will meet my needs. Personally, I believe that every message delivered by a pastor must be prophetic and revelatory. What do I mean? To preach means to herald forth. It is a warning and must be substantive in content. *Prophetic* does not mean telling the future in the way I am using the word. It means to speak with divine authority, and it should be penetrating because the Word is penetrating (see Heb. 4:12). It should be *revelatory* in that hearers should leave with new understanding about life and eternal matters that they could not glean from another source. All pastors can have the Spirit of God, and through prayer and meditation, the Lord will reveal to them what those under their care should know (see 1 Cor. 2:1–4).

Leaving a service and remembering all the jokes, without being convicted or challenged, reflects a message that missed the mark. Though humor has its place, the West is so used to being entertained that this is now the new sermon content. I try to have a good sense of humor, and I don't believe all sermons should be gloomy and irrelevant, but they must have biblical substance. This should not be a time when the pastor puts his people on a diet. The Word invites us to a banquet. Scripture is a veritable smorgasbord of rich food: "I have treasured the words of His mouth more than my daily food" (Job 23:12). "Come, eat" is the call from Proverbs 9:5. Too often the pulpit is an empty cistern where masses walk away with no sense that they have met with God. Messages filled with rules and no Christ just frustrate God's people, while entertaining messages blind people to what will really set them free. Good preaching will always take people to where they don't want to go. Taking people to where they naturally desire to go only feeds their flesh and egos. Taking people to where they don't want to go will make them uncomfortable but in the end will bear much fruit.

Since the early church met in homes, I don't think the Lord really cares about the actual venue, but he does care about being central to what takes place. God raises up pastors and teachers to deliver the Word to the people. However, sometimes we are so immersed in a "me" culture that hard sayings are minimized and diluted in order to keep people attending church. I'm reminded of the hard words of Jesus in John 6, when many of the disciples turned and walked away. I've been told that 70 percent of what Jesus said was negative. Yet he didn't plead with them to stay. He didn't apologize for being hard. Preaching that does not have Christ at its center is just information. It may be good information, but we can get that elsewhere. A moralistic attempt to change without Christ as the real answer is basically humanistic.

Western Formulas

Another nasty little western habit is to try and impose on others our personal formula for the Christian life. Even those who despise formulas have a formula designed to teach others how to avoid formulas. Perhaps the best way to view this is to imagine that biblical Christianity is a nation with many states. Each state represents a particular biblical discipline or truth. When we become citizens of this nation (kingdom), we also become a state resident. Perhaps you are a resident of the great state of Grace or maybe the state of Prayer or Meditation.

Our tendency is to settle into a state that most fits our spiritual giftedness, personality, and intellectual makeup. If, for example, you are a highly cerebral person, you may become a resident of the state of Theology. You might even live in Doctrine, which is the state capital, or perhaps you decide to settle down in the state of Faith.

Each state is part of the whole and is not an island unto itself. The problem arises when we try to recruit other believers to become residents of our state. Sometimes we fight over boundary lines and claim that the other states just don't get it. Our state really understands the Christian life, and the others had better join us before it's too late.

Trying to impose our state's theme song on other believers never works well. Just remember that in your pilgrimage you have a finite period of time to investigate all that the Christian life has to offer, which is infinite in scope. At best you will settle in one state and visit others as time permits. However, when you cross state lines, the western jesus will search you at the border to see if you qualify to enter into their fellowship. Should any doctrinal contraband be found, you will be labeled *persona non grata.*

Each state has a verse they claim that defines the Christian life, and anyone who challenges their western jesus will meet with significant resistance. For example, if you visit the Prayer state, you might hear these sarcastic words from its residents: "Jesus said that his house was a house of prayer not a house of teaching or doctrine." As you travel and move into the state of Faith, this might be their cry: "The Scriptures tell us to walk by faith not by sight. They don't tell us to walk by prayer."

Still, others from another state will remind us that Jesus said it is better to give than to receive, not it is better to pray, study, or love each other. Such subtle sarcasm has little to do with the truth. Obviously we are to correct believers who have fallen prey to false doctrine, but that is rarely what we fight about. We do battle over making mountain theology out of molehill doctrine.

We can't possibly be a great prayer warrior, theologian, meditator, giver, evangelist, servant, and lover of grace in this lifetime. It just isn't going to happen. We are called to all of these, but there will only be time to cultivate a few; and what we find to be so refreshing was never meant to be used as a weapon to beat others up with by telling them they will never have victory if they don't reap where our state doctrine has sown. We are all called to be laborers in different parts of the Lord's vineyard.

When Culture, Tradition, and Scripture Collide

We are living in a day, and even more importantly, in a culture that has drifted far from biblical truth and the reality of church as defined in the New Testament. I have watched this happen with great concern but with the clear realization that we are fighting an uphill battle, which may not be possible to win short of a divine intervention of God. In the West, as stated in the introduction, we tend to look at Scripture through the lens of culture, tradition, and theological bias as opposed to looking at culture, tradition, and theological bias through the lens of Scripture.

Culture and tradition weigh in more heavily and with more authority than Scripture. We witness this daily in our churches throughout the land. Let's take a good hard look at this. We will start with *tradition*. Most of us have family traditions. They are often associated with birthdays, anniversaries, or special holidays that we share as a family. Perhaps there is a traditional meal that is served each year to celebrate the end of your son's basketball season, or you go out to a special restaurant for your wife's birthday. There are traditions within our nation that highlight historical events. The Fourth of July and Thanksgiving are such traditions. Churches also have traditions. Each year there may be a special event or series of messages that are given. The building itself may have a traditional look to it, such as a cross, stained-glass windows, or a large oak pulpit. None of these are violations of Scripture, but just try to change, replace, or do away with a tradition and see what happens. You will soon see that these traditions are often on the same level as sacred Scripture, if not usurping the Scriptures. Change the Bible so it is easier to read, make versions for all age groups, and even make it gender neutral, and you will not receive anywhere near the resistance as changing something in the sanctuary. Why? Because tradition runs deeper than Scripture for the western believer.

The next thing we need to address is *culture*. Culture reflects the values and interests of a society. There are many things in culture that are perfectly acceptable. Music, art, literature, dress, and food may very well be morally acceptable within a culture and Christianity. The problem arises when a societal change in culture is brought into the church building. It is often viewed by my generation as worldly, when in fact it may be completely neutral. It may not be my preference or yours, but it must not be labeled as worldly just because we don't like it. Worldly implies a contemporary value system that violates Scripture, such as immodest dress, movie clips from immoral movies, or ungodly lyrics in worship. However, this is a far cry from removing stained-glassed windows and putting in a more contemporary look that is more appealing to the surrounding culture. Stained-glass windows, pews, and oak pulpits are not biblical requirements but are traditional cosmetics that often clash with the cultural.

Would it offend? Yes. Why? Because of tradition clashing with culture. It might be culturally relevant but traditionally out of line. How do we blend the two?

The underground church in China and the persecuted in India have little in the way of church tradition. They don't complain about music, comfort, parking spaces, or the temperature in the sanctuary. There is no sanctuary.

The church, in order to be effective, must get past the cosmetic issues and face head-on the reality of advancing the kingdom of God. We must learn to function as a community of believers.

A Cultural Contradiction

I will let you in on a little secret about our western jesus. I discovered this many years ago. After I had given a sermon on a particular doctrine, a man who had been attending our church for a while came up to me and said, "You don't really believe that." I told him most assuredly that I did believe it. He left the church and went across town to a church that cherished this doctrine even more than I did. I couldn't help but think how strange it was until another incident followed shortly thereafter. A church not far from us decided to go from congregational-led to elder-led. The pastor called me in advance to find out how we had handled this. I told him that we had started with elders and thus never had to make such a transition. They made the change. Guess what? Many of his people left and started attending our church, which is elder-led. What I learned from all this is that people don't like change in their own church, but they have no problem going to another church that is already functioning that way. I have seen this in music, philosophy of ministry, doctrine, and a host of other issues. People simply don't like change.

This only solidifies in my mind how deeply we have bought into a western jesus. Such minutiae don't exist in third-world churches. These aren't even issues in many respects. I went to a little Spanish church in South America one Sunday morning. It was brutally hot and the church only had a roof. There were no doors or windows. There was no children's ministry or nursery. The pastor preached a message on the Second Coming while the children played on the dirt floor in front of the pulpit. There were probably one hundred people in attendance, yet no one seemed distracted by all that was going on around them. Dogs were barking, babies crying, and the wind stirred up the dust as it blew through the sanctuary. (Of course, the western jesus would not have called it a sanctuary.) One thing was clear. The people praised God and rejoiced. They were friendly to me even though we were separated by language and culture. Who in America would attend such a church? I couldn't help but think how alive the Spirit of Christ was in that little setting and how often the sterile, clean, air-conditioned, and perfectly choreographed worship of our own culture may very well be led by a western jesus. You see, they were the church, and being the church is a far cry from putting on a worship service. Executing a worship service may be nothing more than a veneer of holiness. It looks good on the outside, but the Lord looks under the hood. He had much to say to the Pharisees about this in Matthew 23:25: "Woe to you, scribes and Pharisees, hypocrites! You clean the outside of the cup and dish, but inside they are full of greed and self-indulgence!"

This is why I don't experience apoplexy when I see a pastor in jeans standing behind a Plexiglas pulpit. I'm not interested in all the holy hardware. A formal choir and well-tuned orchestra can be just as much a performance as a worship band. Let's be careful not to judge. It cannot be stated too often that "the Lord sees the heart" (1 Sam. 16:7).

I am well aware of why many pass judgment on new church buildings that look like office complexes. I know why they are concerned with plastic pulpits. I know why they don't like chairs in the sanctuary. These things are a concern because attendant with many of these changes has been a watered-down pulpit ministry. Rather than passing judgment, why can't both sides learn from each other? The more formal crowd should be concerned with one thing, and it is not what the building looks like. They should be concerned that a genuine reverence is being paid to Almighty God in true worship (which may have many styles) and solid biblical exposition. The less formal and more contemporary church should not be concerned about how old styles lack relational ministry, but whether or not Christ is glorified. God is big enough to accommodate both ways.

God can be worshipped in many settings. He knows that some prefer one style over the other. What is essential is that the true God is being worshipped in heart and substance. Who is this God we call Lord? What is he like? What does he demand from his followers? How is he to be worshipped? What does he want us to know? What doctrines are important? These are the crucial questions. The setting in which they are answered is unimportant.

The western jesus can be quite stubborn, extremely biased, and doctrinal in theology while departing from the transcendent Christ whose truth covers all time and all cultures. Frankly I think that my generation should accept the fact that music, worship styles, and philosophy of ministry will change. Rather than run to another church, they could stick around and help disciple the younger generation by making sure that in all their change they keep doctrine pure and Christ central.

We might be surprised at what God can reveal to us if we open our minds to different styles of worship. One of the greatest and most well-known expositors in our nation was the host pastor of a conference that I attended a number of years ago. The conference was limited in size, so the visiting pastors were placed in various homes of the people who belonged to the church. I happened to be staying with one of the pastoral staff. Though I appreciated the excellent teaching, I noted the host pastor's strong anticharismatic view. That evening I engaged the staff member I was staying with in some good theological discussion. As it turned out, he had just returned from a mission trip to South

Korea. While there, he attended the largest church in the world, which was Pentecostal in doctrine. He informed me that he was just there out of curiosity. As our dialogue unfolded and as he became a bit more comfortable with me, I saw his doctrinal shield come down. "Ya know, Mike," he said, "I decided to attend their Friday night prayer meeting to see how they pulled it off. There were thousands of people in this vast auditorium crying out to God." He became more animated as he recalled his visit. "After about an hour, I was exhausted and couldn't think of anything else to pray about. What I didn't realize," he said, "was that this prayer meeting lasted all night, and I was already exhausted." His parting comment I will never forget. "What our doctrinally sound church here in the States preaches, they live out." He told me how convicted he was by their zeal for God. "I have all the doctrine," he said, "but they're living what I claim to believe."

I knew exactly what he meant. Call for a prayer meeting and people stay away in droves. Most western prayer gatherings can be held in a phone booth with room to spare. The western jesus who leads most of our churches today has all the doctrine down pat. Every service is slick and can rival most Hollywood productions. But call upon the masses to come and pray, or give to missions, or walk the narrow road, and you will soon find out who really believes. Remember: "we believe only what we act on; all the rest is just religious talk."

We might be surprised to see how clouded our perspective of the church is were we to take off the western glasses and see the church as Christ sees it and as revealed by the apostle Paul. I'm not suggesting that formal services become informal or vice versa. I am suggesting tolerance. Now I know the word *tolerance* strikes fear into our hearts because the world wants the church to be more tolerant. Their desire for tolerance, however, is in the moral and doctrinal arenas whereas mine is in the philosophy of ministry arena. There is a big difference. The Lord has left us with absolute truth concerning morality and ethics, but Scripture is very open ended concerning how the church should gather and conduct its service. There is true freedom in Christ in this area.

Expository Preaching

I had the privilege of meeting John Stott at a pastors' lunch about a year ago. Someone asked him about expository preaching. He said that all preaching was expository if the Scriptures were used. Here again I think we have taken on a cultural western mind-set. I couldn't have agreed with him more. I believe that the Scriptures should always be taught, but does that necessarily mean a verse-by-verse study of a book? Those who hold to this argument often refer to Paul's teaching "the whole plan of God" as mentioned in Acts 20:27. Now let's think this through. Since he only stayed for a year or two in most of the cities, how could he have covered all the Old Testament in a verse-by-verse study? Though I deeply admire the fine exegetes we have today, I'm not sure that taking five or six years to go through a book is all that beneficial. If this were applied to the entire Bible, it would take several hundred years to teach the whole counsel. For the first twenty years of my pulpit ministry, I did book studies and often took several years to go through one book. By the time I finished I would jokingly ask the congregation, "How many of you are old enough to remember when we started?"

Culture also plays into this to some degree. The church I pastor is located just west of Washington, D.C. Most of the people work for the government, military, or big business, which simply means they will be in and out in the twinkling of an eye. It seems as if there is barely time to learn their last names. Because of this fluidity, a little more than five years ago I decided to teach through the entire Bible by taking large snapshots of each book. I just completed the Old Testament. This gives our people an overview of how the Bible is put together. I call the series "From Creation to Glory," and I am relentless in keeping before them the pilgrim theme.

I'm not opposed to spending five years studying a single book. I just say that Scripture does not tell us to do that, and a western mind-set may creep in that is not always the best in this case. If it takes three hundred years to go through the Bible at that speed, then I hope all congregations are made up of people with the last name Methuselah.

CHAPTER 4

How God Views the Pilgrim

PICK UP ANY NEWSPAPER and the headlines will more often than not highlight major decisions of world leaders. News is certainly important and tells us what is going on around the world. We read about our president and the heads of state in various nations. We read about multimillion-dollar contracts of sports heroes and movie stars changing partners like a mother changing diapers.

When we read Scripture, however, the big names get second billing. It's Joseph, not Pharaoh; it's Daniel, not Nebuchadnezzar; it's Paul, not Agrippa; it's John the Baptist, not Herod. If we had lived during those days, the reverse would be true. The *Babylonian Times* would certainly not feature Daniel over Nebuchadnezzar. The king would be the center of attention, and all of his decisions regarding his kingdom would be the headlines.

A number of years ago I began to see Scripture in light of who and what God saw as important. I couldn't help but notice that the big shots were casually mentioned, if not marginalized, which could only mean that who and what God sees as a priority is very different from what we see. This should cause us to take note of his priorities. For example, we read in

Acts 1 of a prayer meeting that took place just prior to Pentecost. In Acts 12 we read of another prayer meeting that was in a home. The answer to their prayers was Peter's release from prison. Certainly there were more important political issues going on at the time that could have been highlighted. Some may argue that the Bible is a spiritual book and didn't focus on the politics of its day. I think such a dismissal is a bit presumptuous. God sees all events and certainly doesn't leave out the power brokers of history. He mentions the pharaohs, the kings, and the Herods, but always to show how puny they are in comparison to his faithful followers, such as Joseph or Daniel.

God often compares the shallow wisdom of the world with the wisdom of godly people. It is said of Stephen as he stood before the Sanhedrin: "They were unable to stand up against the wisdom and the Spirit by whom he spoke" (Acts 6:10). It is recorded that Pharaoh said of Joseph, "Can we find such a one as this, a man in whom is the spirit of God?" (Gen. 41:38 NKJV). Daniel was recognized by Darius as having an "excellent spirit" (Dan. 6:3 NKJV). Scripture is filled with other examples that show God did not focus only on spiritual issues, but also showed us from his perspective whom he had sovereignly placed in charge of the major events in history.

There is much to learn from this. Our western culture places a great deal of emphasis on celebrity status, both in the secular arena and the spiritual arena. We are often mesmerized by the size of a ministry or by a speaker's skill. Now, I don't wish to imply that large ministries are based on celebrities. Many large ministries do a great job in the area of preaching and serving the handicapped and poor. My point is that we may not know what God is doing behind the scenes in small ministries or prayer gatherings. Perhaps the greatest preacher in the world is ministering in a house church in Nepal.

Suppose you see in the paper a huge full-page ad inviting you to hear a gifted evangelist. His qualifications are impeccable. As a matter of fact, he is so powerful that he reached an entire city with the gospel. You call to make reservations only to find that the event is sold out. A few weeks later another ad appears inviting believers to hear another evangelist. His credentials are just the opposite. He has been preaching for a long time, but there are no converts. Curious, you call to see about reservations only to find out that the event had been cancelled due to lack of interest. Those who responded to the first ad went to hear Jonah, a rebellious, bitter, reluctant prophet. Because the second event was cancelled all who wanted to go missed the opportunity to hear Noah, a preacher of righteousness and one of only two men Scripture records as having walked with God.

Almost all pastors' conferences today focus on how to have a bigger church. There are few conferences focusing on Bible teaching. "Feed my sheep" (see John 21:15), Jesus said, and "I will build the church" (see Matt. 16:18). The masses are drawn to the leadership conferences only to return home with a myriad of "how to" handouts but no ability to carry it out. Here again I want to be careful and balanced. I have no problem with large leadership conferences. I have been to them. My point is that we tend to exalt the big and put on the back burner those things that God considers important. How many would go to a prayer conference or a seminar on holiness? Such gatherings are not usually well attended, yet these are the very truths the Lord mentions so often in Scripture. I'm concerned that in the West we have been told that big means success and big somehow taps into our pride.

About twenty-five years ago I went into the jungles of Bolivia to visit a mission station comprised of just five families. I flew in on a single-engine plane and was warmly greeted by this little community of believers. I could hardly believe the setting. Here were five little homes in the middle of nowhere. They were trying to contact a nomadic tribe. Out of ignorance I asked the field leader if they had presented the gospel to the tribe yet. With tears in his eyes he said, "We have been here three years and have only seen them once." I realized that I had struck a nerve.

Later I was asked to give the devotional at their Tuesday night Bible study. I thought, *No problem.* All pastors have many devotionals and sermons in their back pocket. I could always give my sermon on commitment. *Oh yeah,* I thought, *they have given their lives to the Lord.* Scrap that idea. I'll give the one on "love not the world," but they are a thousand miles from any civilization. I could preach on the subject of moral discernment. . . . It wasn't long before I was in a panic. *What could I possibly tell these godly, committed saints?*

When Tuesday night arrived, I spoke out of 1 Corinthians 4:2: "In this regard, it is expected of managers that each one be found faithful." I encouraged them in the fact that results aren't the issue, but faithfulness is. Perhaps this is why Noah and not Jonah is mentioned in Hebrews 11. Noah's results were zero, but his faithfulness was praised by God.

Of course, this is not western thinking. I pastor a fairly large church, and I meet regularly with a group of pastors who have considerably smaller flocks. Sometimes I leave our prayer time considering why that is. These men are every bit as faithful, and perhaps more so. Some are clearly more knowledgeable than I. What is it about us that is so focused on numbers? Someone once told me that men love to create, count, and control. A healthy church should grow, but there are often extenuating circumstances that may limit growth. A western mind-set has lost the virtue of faithfulness and replaced it with tangible results. Look at all those in Scripture who never had big ministries but were recorded in heavenly chronicles as impacting eternity. If we spend our lives always comparing and looking at results, we will come up short. We need a biblical perspective that looks behind the scenes to see what is really going on.

Consider the account in Genesis 40–41. Here we have Joseph in prison with two men who had worked for Pharaoh. One was a butler and the other a baker. Pharaoh was angry with them and had them put in jail. They both had dreams and were saddened by the fact that there was no one to interpret them. Although they did not volunteer this information to Joseph, he noticed how sad they looked and inquired as to why. This simple act of faithfulness gave Joseph the opportunity to interpret their dreams. The butler was soon released and went back to work for Pharaoh. (This is exactly what Joseph had told him would happen according to the interpretation of the dream.) Joseph also asked the butler to tell Pharaoh about him so that he could also be released. The butler, however, failed to carry out Joseph's request, and two years elapsed before Pharaoh also had a dream. Since no one could interpret it, the butler remembered Joseph and informed Pharaoh about his abilities in this area of interpreting dreams. Pharaoh sent for Joseph, and redemptive history continued on its uninterrupted path.

As you know, Joseph is eventually placed second in command of Egypt and has 20 percent of the grain put in storage to prepare for the famine that Pharaoh had dreamed would come. As a result of this, the twelve tribes of Israel are established and the Messiah comes through the line of Judah. Suppose Joseph had not asked why the two fellow prisoners were so sad? Can you see how all of redemptive history rested on this simple but faithful inquiry?

Many significant events are occurring at this moment because of the faithfulness of people who will never be heard of this side of heaven, but a western jesus may tell you that you are not measuring up. You may feel like a failure as a pastor or Sunday school teacher. You may not be seeing the results you would like to see. We all from time to time fall back on western thinking, which feeds off our pride. Yes, there are many faithful pastors who have reached celebrity status, but not out of pride or a desire to be famous. Others may have a larger Sunday school class or Bible study than you have, but that is not your concern. Your concern is to be found faithful.

Christ was faithful, but according to western standards he looks like a failure. The pilgrimage can get hard if we spend our time examining our sojourn through western glasses. One of the main reasons Scripture was written is for us to have our natural thinking changed. Our fallen bent is to make comparisons.

A number of years ago I gave a message titled "Calculating the Average." Here is the gist of what I said. At about the age of four or five, we begin to calculate the average. Little boys start to compete without even realizing it. Someone spots a dollar bill blowing in the wind, and twelve kids at a birthday party all go running after it. The boy who gets to the dollar first, without knowing what *calculate* or *average* means, calculates the average and realizes that he is the fastest. Those close behind know they are faster than all those behind them. Those who are way behind realize they are not in the same league with the speedsters. Those in the middle feel safe but not great. A certain embarrassment comes with being the slowest. He may even be laughed at or called "slowpoke." That child never wants to be put in that position again.

Throughout our lives we calculate the average in almost every situation. We do it without thinking. Looks, athletics, intelligence, music, wealth, personality, humor, lineage, neighborhood, and the list goes on as we size up where we fit. Unfortunately, we also do it in the spiritual arena. There is a sense of one-upmanship all around us. In the midst of a social gathering, we might maneuver the conversation in the direction where we tend to excel in order to test the waters to find out just how good we are in relation to those around us. Parents especially like to tell of their children's accomplishments. "My little Johnny is running wind sprints, and he is only seven months old," says a proud mother. You were just ready to chime in and tell of your precocious little nine-month-old who just took his first step, but having calculated the average and been found wanting, you change the subject to the weather.

Those who boast in one setting may be very quiet in another. How childish to compare church sizes and numbers of baptisms. Jonathan Edwards may have been the greatest theologian this nation has produced, yet his congregation was never more than a few hundred people. A. W. Tozer also had a relatively small church, but look at the continuing influence these two men have had over the years well after they departed this world. There was depth to their teaching. The Lord doesn't measure success on the same scales as the western jesus does. Kingdom living is often reversed from the natural way. We need to stop calculating the average and rejoice that our names are written in heaven.

Pride is always lurking in the background when we make comparisons. This reminds me of the young couple who got married and entered into the ministry. The young preacher had just taken his first church and life was looking up. Soon after they began their ministry, the wife told her husband that there was a shoebox in her closet. She said she always wanted to have a transparent relationship, but the shoebox was off limits. "You will just have to trust me," she said. "I don't ever want you looking into it." He agreed. One day, after having been married for twenty-five years, he went into her closet to put something away and there was the shoebox staring him right in the face. Overwhelmed with curiosity, he couldn't take it any longer. He opened the box and to his surprise he saw three eggs resting on top of a great deal of cash. *What could this possibly mean?* he thought. That night at dinner he confessed what he had done. "I know I was wrong," he said, "but I just couldn't stand it." He then inquired about the eggs and the cash. She decided to tell him her little secret. "When we got married, I decided that every time you gave a bad sermon, I would put an egg in the shoebox." He couldn't help but feel very proud to know that in twenty-five years he had only given three bad sermons. "So that explains the eggs," he said, "but what about all that cash?" She replied, "Every time I collect a dozen, I sell them."

We must be careful not to prize what God doesn't prize. The transcendent Christ and the centrality of his message will always be the main issue. When we as believers are devastated by failure using world-system measuring sticks, it simply shows that Christ is not our satisfaction.

In John 6, Jesus said some hard things that resulted in reduced attendance: "From that moment many of His disciples turned back and no longer accompanied Him" (v. 66). I wonder how big our churches would be today if Jesus were the pastor? I wonder how many would be inclined to tell him he needs to get real and stop the narrow legalistic view of life? I wonder how many would tell him to be more relational? I suspect that the size of our churches, including the one I pastor, would drop dramatically in attendance. A few years back we had a man who was very serious and very direct about what he thought regarding the Christian life. One day he came up to me after a service and said, " I know you are concerned about the overcrowding and having to preach several times over the weekend. I have a solution. Preach like Jesus and it won't be long before you go to one service and you won't need the sanctuary. One of the small classrooms will do."

Though I didn't appreciate his statement, I did take to heart how fearful we are to say the hard things. Jesus didn't seem terribly concerned about those who left. He didn't run after them and apologize for being too hard. He didn't ask them to reconsider. He did turn to those remaining and ask, "You don't want to go away too, do you?" (John 6:67). We must learn to see how God views the life of a pilgrim.

CHAPTER 5

Reason versus Revelation

■■ ■■ ■■

But the natural man does not welcome what comes from God's Spirit, because it is foolishness to him; he is not able to know it since it is evaluated spiritually.

1 Corinthians 2:14

HUMAN REASON AND BIBLICAL revelation are fascinating subjects that if not properly kept in balance can keep us off balance. We can't move forward without first defining our terms. *Reason* is the natural human ability to negotiate the issues of life by employing logic and intellect. We use reason to decide what car to buy and where we can get the best value for the dollar. We reason out the best time to take a vacation or mow the lawn. Reason is a gift from God given to unbelievers as well as believers, and without it, life would not only be hard, it would be impossible.

Reason is often based on wisdom or intuition. We draw from past experiences. However, reason is strictly a human ability, and all people have the ability to reason at varying levels depending on their intellectual capacity. Logic is the science of the principles of reason, having its own set of laws. We use logic to sift through arguments where contradictions may lie.

Revelation, however, takes us into another world. Scripture abounds with the message of revelation. It has been defined as "what God wants man to know that he could not know otherwise." The Bible is a book of revelation in that it tells us what human reason could never tell us, namely where we came from, why we are here, and where we are going. No microscope or telescope can reveal such truth. Without revelation, man is left wandering around the globe trying to figure out the mysteries of life with his reason, but reason does not take us into this realm. It's off-limits for the human mind.

The Word of God takes us into another world and allows us to see beyond our natural horizons. We use reason and logic to discern when the oil in the car needs changing. The Bible does not address such issues. Reason and logic on the other hand cannot address issues of the soul, eternity, creation, future events, and the eternal kingdom. This brings up another western problem. The church employs reason where only revelation can give us the answer. The western church doesn't challenge many issues because it is intimidated by logic and intellectual arguments. We bow to the god of evolution, western morality, ethics, and materialism. We have become so adept at reasoning that divine revelation takes a backseat and is rarely consulted.

The central passage on this matter in the Old Testament is Proverbs 3:5–6; in the New Testament, it is 1 Corinthians 2:14. Note carefully that we are warned in Proverbs 3 not to lean on our own understanding. We are not to be wise in our own eyes, but in all our ways we are to acknowledge him (KJV). Paul takes us a step further when he separates the unregenerate man from the believer. He tells us by divine revelation that the natural mind cannot understand spiritual truth. It will actually appear to be foolishness to him (KJV). He is blinded to the truth of the gospel. Pastors and scholars often use this verse to show the inability of the natural mind to grasp the gospel. Yes, this is true, but it goes much further than just the gospel. It applies to the whole of the Christian life. It is not just the gospel that needs to be spiritually discerned. The entire Bible needs to be discerned for us by the Spirit of God. This is where things get sticky. Can I hear from God today? Can he instruct me from his Word regarding the deeper issues of life? Can he reveal through his Word personal direction for my life? If I am not a scholar, can I still know what God is saying, or do I need a seminary degree and original language study? These are monumental issues that the church has debated through the centuries, resulting in much confusion.

God Has Revealed Them unto Us

In the first three chapters of Paul's first letter to the Corinthians he has much to say about divine revelation. In chapter 2, Paul uses a human illustration in order to drive home spiritual truth when he says, "For who among men knows the concerns of a man except the spirit of the man that is in him? In the same way, no one knows the concerns of God except the Spirit of God" (1 Cor. 2:11). Yet, I fear that we in our western culture have come to pride ourselves on knowing exactly what the Scriptures teach. We have come to believe that if we can exegete a text through careful study in the original languages, then we can surface from our study with the assurance that we know the mind of God. I'm not at all sure that Paul would agree. Liberal scholars can tell you what the text says every bit as well as a conservative scholar can. So what does Paul mean when he says it must be spiritually discerned? What does he mean when he tells us that we cannot know the things of God without the Spirit?

Hearing from God

We now enter into one of the most controversial areas of western Christendom. Can a believer hear from God? First of all let me say that I have the highest regard and respect for biblical scholarship. I always consult commentaries to make sure that I am not missing something that may be better highlighted in the original language, and though I have no seminary training or original language study, I have never felt that God cannot reveal His deeper truths to me, nor do I feel that those who are blessed with scholarly minds are just slaves of intellect. Many godly scholars rely on the Spirit of God for deeper insight than they do their formal training.

Next I believe we need to define some terms. Exactly what do we mean when we talk about hearing from God? Some may define this as an audible voice from heaven. Some may use the Bible to make it say what they want it to say and then tell others that God told them "such and such." Though I don't rule out the possibility that God could speak audibly, I do not consider this the norm. What I do believe—and please hear me out before you shut me out—is that *all genuine believers hear from God*, even those who say he no longer speaks today. How can I make such a statement? Because I listen closely to the terminology of those who deny that God speaks today, and, according to Jesus, "the mouth speaks from the overflow of the heart" (Matt. 12:34). Those pastors and scholars who rail against hearing from God often tip their hand without realizing it. Here is what I mean. When someone says God spoke to me, one of the cute counterarguments goes something like this: "When he spoke, did he speak in a bass or baritone voice?" Clever, huh? If someone said that to me, I would respond by saying, "Apparently you have never heard from God, for he doesn't speak with a bass or baritone voice but a spiritual voice, which can only be spiritually discerned" (see 1 Cor. 2:14). Their cute rejoinder is based on what they perceive is the extreme view. The person who rejects hearing from God disguises his personal experience in this area by using other phrases such as, "I got a great insight from Scripture today." To which I want to ask, "Was the insight in blue or green?"

They also use expressions such as "The Lord tugged at my heart." Well, did he use a cable or strings in the tugging? "The Lord laid it on my heart." Did what he lay on your heart weigh five or twenty-five pounds? These terms are merely code words for "hearing from God." Saying "God pulled at my heart" doesn't have quite as much of an authoritative ring, but in reality it says the same thing. "Insight," "tugged at," and "laid on my heart," are merely euphemistic expressions for hearing from God. Remember that extremists are marginalized and don't represent the majority view of either side.

Another concern from the doctrinal side is that if you claim to have heard from God, you are adding to the closed canon of Scripture. Not so! To add to the canon would be to add universal doctrine for all believers, whereas to hear from God is a personal revelation regarding your own life. "Your word is a lamp for my feet and a light on my path" (Ps. 119:105). Justification, sanctification, and propitiation are not a lamp for *my* feet but for *all* feet.

Western scholarship, in an attempt to keep the church doctrinally pure, often puts itself in a straightjacket. There is no flex, no room for the still small voice of God. Everything must be explained. Mystery is not welcome in the western world of academia. I fully understand the reasoning, but the fear of opening Pandora's box to the floodgates of heresy is no reason to shut down the voice of God.

I personally consider myself as doctrinally evangelical and conservative. I teach expositionally most of the time. The spiritual milieu from which I have come is a bit eclectic. I read voraciously, though a bit slowly. I read all I can by John Piper, and I consult MacArthur commentaries. I listen incessantly to Tim Keller, who I think really gets it. I have had much of my thinking shaped by R. C. Sproul, J. I. Packer, and Ravi Zacharias. But I have never believed that any group or system of theology could possibly have a corner on all truth. I have been blessed by Henry Blackaby, Chuck Colson, and Dallas Willard. These men don't all agree, even on the issue at hand regarding hearing from God, but they all have influenced my study.

Still, no one so touches my soul as A. W. Tozer. That's right, I like the mystics, provided they stay within the bounds of Scripture. Tozer's writings have a long shelf life because what he teaches are eternal truths that transcend all culture and all time, which is always the test of good writing. Tozer's works will be around many years after his departure because they don't address felt needs and a niche market.

So what about hearing from God? Many years ago my oldest daughter, Kelly, was in the eighth grade at a local Christian school. We began to see her struggling. I don't mean morally or ethically; she was just very unhappy and her basic chemistry seemed to clash with the school. I don't put any blame on either side. My wife and I did not know what to do. Since the Bible does not address the subject of what school your child should attend, how were we to find God's will in this matter?

Like many subjects, believers have their favorite verses to support a particular philosophy. Those who believe the Bible teaches in favor of Christian schools often quote Psalm 1, where we are warned not to walk in the counsel of the ungodly. The counterargument to that is, what will we do the rest of our lives regarding where we work? We will always be working for or under the counsel of ungodly people. In actuality the verse tells us not to *walk* in ungodly counsel, but it does not say to *remove* ourselves from ungodly counsel. It is all around us, and we will be exposed to it in the schools, military, sports, big business, and yes, even Christian schools.

Those who support putting their children in public schools employ such verses as, "Go into all the world and preach the gospel to the whole creation" (Mark 16:15). Keep in mind, the Bible is not a road map but a compass. It doesn't always tell you exactly what to do in every situation. So how can we know? Reason and simple logic may often be used, but when you feel the issue is of great import, you want a word from God.

One day when Kelly came home after a particularly bad day, I decided a decision had to be made. I told my wife, Kay, that we needed to hear from God. The next morning during my devotional time I read these words: "The LORD our God spoke to us at Horeb, 'You have stayed at this mountain long enough. Resume your journey and go to the hill country of the Amorites and their neighbors in the Arabah, the hill country, the lowlands, the Negev and the sea coast—to the land of the Canaanites and to Lebanon as far as the Euphrates River" (Deut. 1:6–7). On the surface, these words have absolutely nothing to do with where to send your children to school. The context has nothing to do with school, but when I read the words "You have stayed at this mountain long enough," I knew it was time to go to the Amorites—it was time to leave the protective mount of the Christian environment and go into the world. I called my wife immediately and told her I had a word from God. She was quick to inform me that she had also heard from God. (I couldn't help but think we had better agree.) She had been reading in Genesis about Joseph demanding that his brothers return to their father, Jacob, and bring back Benjamin. Jacob is grieved by such a request, but in Genesis 43:9, Judah guarantees his father that Benjamin will be safe. My wife felt deep within her spirit that it was time to take Kelly out of the land of Canaan and she would be protected.

Let me share another example when the Lord clearly spoke to me from his Word. A number of years ago my family and I were renting a house from a deceitful young man who asked us to leave and refused to return our security deposit. In my devotional time that day, I came across this passage: "If anyone hits you on the cheek, offer the other also. And if anyone takes away your coat, don't hold back your shirt either. Give to everyone who asks from you, and from one who takes away your things, don't ask for them back" (Luke 6:29–30). That Scripture penetrated deeply into my soul and it was unmistakably clear that I was not to fight for my security deposit, even though we were left with no money to move into our next home. Yet within a week's time, I had three thousand dollars in the bank, a second car, a nicer home (which we eventually purchased), and a washer and dryer. I saw the hand of God at work in a way that I had never experienced. If these events had unfolded over a year's time, I would never have made the connection of the Lord speaking to me and his blessings that followed immediately.

Would I ever tell someone else in the same situation to do what I did? No! Would they have every right to use our legal system to stay in the house where they had a two-year lease? Certainly. But sometimes the Lord speaks to us in a way that it is unmistakably clear. Listen to the words of our Lord's disciples on the road to Emmaus: "So they said to each other, "Weren't our hearts ablaze within us while He was talking with us on the road and explaining the Scriptures to us?" (Luke 24:32). This sense of "burning" may be a parallel expression to Hebrews 4:12, where it tells us that the Word "penetrates" into the core of our moral and spiritual life.

I do not encourage believers to seek strange meanings beyond the clear intended meaning of the Word. However, I also do not want to muffle the voice of God during times of meditation, study, and prayer, where he may speak at a personal level and reveal direction for the believer's life.

Do I advocate this as a daily way to perceive the will of God? No. This is not the norm, and I realize that much foolishness can arise when people play footloose and fancy free with Scripture. But I also put as much stock in this as I do from those who reject this as dangerous but put confidence in such statements as "The Lord laid on my heart" or "I felt a heaviness from the Lord." Such statements are equally subjective as to what I just described about how I knew God had spoken about our daughter's schooling.

What I find most interesting regarding how the Lord spoke to both me and my wife is that we were in different books of the Bible in totally different contexts but with similar revelation: leave the protective arena and go into the world. I have had such encounters with God on several occasions, but they are rare. When others tell me of such encounters, I watch to see if their lives reflect a consistency of sound doctrine. One man said to me that God had told him to divorce his wife. Guess what? He had been clearly led by the "spirit," but not the Spirit of God.

One irony in all this is that those who lament such heresy creeping into the church quote from their theological heroes of the past whose writings are replete with such experiences. Spurgeon, Edwards, Moody, Whitfield, Wesley, and a host of great missionary statesmen of whom the world is not worthy have all testified to certain times in their lives and ministry when God spoke to them. Why could it not happen today? Perhaps the church could use a fresh dose of God's prophetic voice. The western church has bathed itself in right doctrine to the point of washing away the experience that right doctrine may lead to.

I have never heard the audible voice of God nor have I ever had a dream or vision in which God guided me, but many others have had such encounters at major turning points in their lives. I in no way wish to promote such things, and I'm not on a campaign to resurrect every first-century experience. No one needs to seek such experiences. When we do, the chances of seeing a vision or hearing an audible voice increase greatly because we can be guided by emotion. On the other hand, as we live godly lives immersed in the Word and prayer, God may choose to speak however he wishes.

May I recommend Noel Piper's book, *Faithful Women and Their Extraordinary God*. She has selected seven women who have impacted the world of missions in a way that almost seems hard to believe. All the women are quoted as having been given direct guidance from God in most unusual ways. Are we to deny such experiences? Were they lying about what happened? Their lives give evidence of divine encounters that called some of them into missionary service that bypassed the normal procedures of going through a mission agency. The protection they received from God and the fruits of their labors are unparalleled. I do have a way that I judge such experiences. Usually a direct call from God requires risk and doesn't fit our natural human inclination, such as giving up my security deposit or removing our child from a protective environment.

Doctrine versus Intimacy

He has made us competent to be ministers of a new covenant, not of the letter, but of the Spirit; for the letter kills, but the Spirit produces life.

2 Corinthians 3:6

There has been a longstanding war in Christian circles that once again leaves Christ's people with a black eye. This war is not a declared war but one that subtly rages between pastors, theologians, and individual believers. On the one side are those who profess to know God based on sound doctrine; on the other side are those who claim to know him through revelation, which leads to intimacy. So, you ask what is the difference. *Doctrine* is the collection of truth that when systematized defines the fundamental beliefs of the Christian faith. The deity of Christ, justification, sanctification, the Trinity, and a host of other teachings complete the foundation upon which the church is built. Without doctrine you can drift into heresy, which is the fertile soil where cults take root. *Intimacy,* however, is the belief that doctrine in and of itself is incomplete in giving us daily guidance. *Revelation* is the Holy Spirit opening our minds and hearts to hear personally from God in such a way that we do not violate doctrine, but go beyond the facts, thereby experiencing a more intimate and personal encounter with God.

The war exists based on the fear of what the other side is teaching and what negative effect it may have on Christianity. If you are of the more doctrinal persuasion, you fear that those who claim to hear from God will be driven by emotion, feelings, hallucination, visions, dreams, and the like. If you lean to the side that claims intimacy, you fear that doctrinal purists will spread a gospel that is sterile, intellectual, and bookish. The truth is that both sides have plenty of Scriptural and experiential ammo with which to blast the other side. The Bible is quite clear that doctrine is important; otherwise the church morphs into a mass of confusion and everyone does that which is right in his own eyes. We see this from Scripture as well as church history. Equally true is dead theology that leads the church into head knowledge but no real life in Christ.

So how do we solve this problem? Much like other issues in life, the truth often lies somewhere in between. Before someone yells, "Compromise," hear me out. Many times one side points to flawed extremist views of the other side. Those who claim to hear from God have a longstanding history of false prophets, doctrinal error, and experiences that counter biblical truth. Not to be outdone, the doctrinal purists have a history of fighting over every nuance of Greek verb structure (including execution if you don't see things my way) and boring people to tears over intellectual studies reserved only for those with 170 IQ or higher. They often answer questions nobody is asking. Doctrinal purists tend to sacrifice experience on the altar of theology, while those who cherish intimacy tend to sacrifice theology on the altar of experience.

The truth is that both sides are most clearly represented in Scripture *with boundaries*. Scripture warns against cold intellectual teaching, referred to as the "letter of the law," but adds a counterbalance to those who will not "endure sound doctrine." Just because each side can point to "nut cases" on the other side does not nullify the scriptural truth to which that side adheres.

Those who claim intimacy often tend to throw doctrinal caution to the wind. Yet, the reformers, Puritans, and church fathers gave their lives to protect the church from heresy. Scholars and theologians are to be commended for standing as sentinels at the doorway of the church, keeping the heretics at bay. They have acted as shepherds to drive the wolves back into the hills where they belong. Thank God for doctrinal purists who have kept the truth the truth. Those who draw from intimate revelation need to walk close with the purist who will help keep them in bounds. Likewise, purists need to walk with the mystic who finds Christ to be personal and will help the purist to experience life.

The purist is afraid to leave his doctrinal moorings for fear of spooky mysticism, while the intimate crowd fears being tethered to narrow teaching that might restrict their free spirit in sailing spiritual seas unrestrained. Will the former miss the voice of God while the latter is tossed to and fro with every wind of doctrine? Doctrine is a protective fence around the church to keep her pure and untainted from worldliness and heresy. Once inside her walls the personal Christ leads his sheep through intimate revelation based on sound doctrine and obedience to his Word.

There will always be those few who misrepresent both sides. Dead intellectual orthodoxy pitted against wild claims of "God told me" will always be with us. In the meantime, "Be diligent to present yourself approved to God" (2 Tim. 2:15). Learn to "contend for the faith that was delivered to the saints once for all" (Jude 3). Be careful to listen to God's voice, which will never contradict his written Word. Doctrine and intimacy should never be at odds. Doctrine is the glove. Intimacy is the hand that fits snugly therein.

Logic versus Revelation

The law of noncontradiction is one of the fundamental doctrines in the laws of logic. I have used it when debating unbelievers with regard to absolute truth and other issues. However, logic does not always transcend into the spiritual realm. For example, it is not logical that "Whoever tries to make his life secure will lose it, and whoever loses his life will preserve it" (Luke 17:33). It is not logical that "Whoever exalts himself will be humbled, and whoever humbles himself will be exalted" (Matt. 23:12). It is not logical to "give, and it will be given to you" (Luke 6:38). It is not logical that "when I am weak, then I am strong" (2 Cor. 12:10). It is not logical to "love your enemies" (Matt. 5:44). The entire Christian life makes no sense at all. We are called to make an illogical U-turn, but the world is quick with "yea hath God said," and we find ourselves eating from the tree of knowledge rather than the tree of life. We leave no stone unturned when it comes to biblical interpretation.

Logic and careful exposition can help us arrive at doctrinal soundness, but they can never transcend into knowing the personal will of God for every believer. Consider prayer, for example. Let's say you are a purist in your understanding of doctrine; and since the canon of Scripture is closed, God no longer speaks. Would you ever ask for prayer in making a major decision to move from Maine to Texas? If God no longer speaks, how would you know what he wants you to do? Is this just a wisdom decision where you break out a legal pad and draw a line down the center with pros on the left and cons on the right? I'm not saying this would be wrong, but I would want more clarity than that. Since God no longer speaks and since Texas isn't in the Bible (sorry Longhorns), why would you bother asking for prayer to make the right decision? How would God answer the prayer if he no longer speaks? What is even more disturbing is that most who feel God has no direct communication with his children outside of the written Word do believe that Satan can put thoughts in our minds. Are we willing to say that Satan has more direct communication with us than God? That is a bit sobering.

Adding to the Canon

One argument from the doctrinal purist is that a believer claiming to have a word from God is adding to the closed canon of Scripture. Not so. Adding to the canon would be getting a word from God that is for *all* believers. This would be a new *doctrine* as opposed to a personal word for direction in your life. Using my daughter's schooling situation, for example, would be adding to the Scriptures if I told everyone to leave the Christian school and enter into the world of the public school system.

When I read the Word, I am not one who while reading about Joshua and the battle of Jericho asks, "What walls need to come down in your life?" The reason for not doing this is that the walls coming down have nothing to do with a difficulty in your life any more than the story of David and Goliath has anything to do with the giants in your life. To build a message in this manner is to apply a universal principle or doctrine where it is not found. You might then ask what allowed me to read about Moses leaving a mountain and then decide that my daughter should enter the public school? The difference is that in my preaching I would never say to my congregation, "Now what mountains do you need to descend?" There is a big difference between a personal word from God that is alive and powerful, and making that personal word a universal doctrine. That would be adding to the canon.

Strange Doctrine

Is what I am saying an aberrant view of orthodox Christianity? The truth is that this is found all throughout church history. Spurgeon had some rather unusual experiences in this realm. Martin Lloyd Jones had a mystical side to his theology that few want to challenge because of Jones's great contribution to the Christian faith.

I am not into "health and wealth," "name it and claim it" theology, nor do I dwell in the realm of extreme mysticism, but I do believe that a great sovereign God can reveal himself to us apart from his written Word. As dangerous as this may sound, the Word itself tells us that God speaks outside of written revelation. In Psalm 119:71, we are told that God speaks through affliction. In Proverbs he tells us we can learn through the reproofs of life (see Prov. 15:31). Nature tells us of God's existence (see Ps. 19:1–2 and Rom. 1:20). Answer to prayer is another way God speaks. His grace is an instructor according to Titus 2:11–12. His peace can rule in our hearts (see Col. 3:15). His Spirit speaks to our spirit telling us that we are his children (see Rom. 8). None of these ways are written revelation, but they are used of God to communicate to us.

In all this we must make sure that when we believe God speaks, we test the message with his written Word where possible. Does it contradict his Word? Is it consistent with his moral and ethical truth? I am in no way suggesting wild God-told-me-so theology. I have been around plenty of that, and the rotten fruit in the lives of such people is soon evident. I have also been around those who are very solid in their theology who also hear from God at major turning points in their lives.

Jesus and Doctrine

We all know that Jesus warned against cold orthodoxy. The Pharisees were blasted (see Matt. 23), as were legal scholars (see Luke 10). He warned against knowing the Scriptures but missing the person that Scripture reveals (see Luke 24; John 5:39). He talked about those who have ears to hear. My concern in our western culture is that we can produce great scholarship yet still miss the person. A western jesus can be studied, while the transcendent Christ can be known. A western jesus dispenses doctrine, while the transcendent Christ dispenses life.

Even the word *doctrine* has a western definition. We immediately think of systematic theology, the deity of Christ, or issues regarding his second coming. Yes, these are the fundamental doctrines, but the word simply means "teaching." Have you ever heard of the doctrine of child rearing, marriage, kindness, giving, and such? You would be hard-pressed to find the term *doctrine* associated with these subjects because they do not fit into our carefully organized theologies. Have you ever heard of the doctrine of sober men? Here is what Scripture teaches: "But speak thou the things which become sound doctrine: That the aged men be sober, grave, temperate, sound in faith, in charity, in patience" (Titus 2:1–2 KJV). Alan Redpath, former pastor of the great Moody Bible Church, has these words to say about intimacy with God: "To so many people, the Lord is in danger of being no more than a patron of our systematic theology instead of the Christ who is our life."

The Da Vinci Mode

When Dan Brown's book *The Da Vinci Code* arrived on the scene and began to make waves literally all over the world—to the point of increasing tourism in Paris and other related locations mentioned in the book—evangelical scholars and pastors began to defend the "faith that was delivered to the saints once for all" (Jude 3). The books and articles along with sermon series really took Brown to task regarding inaccuracies both theological and historical. I read much of what was out there, and it proved most helpful. I am thankful to those who exposed the errors and brought the truth out into the open. My concern, however, was that we glutted the market with redundant information to the point of overkill. One or two books would have sufficed. Here again, I think human reason became the weapon of choice, and we tried to fight a spiritual battle stripped of our spiritual resources. "The weapons of our warfare are not fleshly, but are powerful through God for the demolition of strongholds" (2 Cor. 10:4). Is there a place to shed light on the truth? Most assuredly. But we must go below the surface and seek the counsel of God as to why Dan Brown wrote the book. If we can reveal why the world acts and does what it does, they just might wonder how we could know the condition of their heart, even if they deny it.

In the book, Robert Langdon is the key character through which Dan Brown expresses his views. On page 321 Langdon, who is a Harvard professor, tells his students that through sex we find God. Why did Brown have his character say this? One of the great benefits of Scripture is its ability to look deep into the soul of man and root out his motives. I often tell people that if you can master Romans 1:16–32, you will know all you will ever need to know about the human race.

There are four Scriptures that, in my opinion, tell the truth about Brown's blatant attack on Christianity and the divinity of Jesus. In John 3:19–20 we read these words: "This, then, is the judgment: the light has come into the world, and people loved darkness rather than the light because their deeds were evil. For everyone who practices wicked things hates the light and avoids it, so that his deeds may not be exposed." Note carefully what Jesus says about why people refuse to come to the light. They love darkness, and they don't want their deeds brought into light because those deeds are evil. Like many doctrinal issues in Scripture, there is often an unfolding revelation. This is true of man's rejection of truth. In Romans 1:18 we are told that men suppress or hold down the truth. Why? Because of unrighteousness. No one rejects truth for no reason. No one rejects truth with their intellect; they reject truth with their morality.

We then find in 2 Peter 3 that men deny the promise of Christ's coming. Why? Because they are walking after their own lusts. Last, in Jude it says mockers will come in the last days who are sensual and have not the Spirit. When we put all these passages together, we see a love for evil, a suppression of what we know to be true because of the evil, a rejection of Christ's return or a denial of his divinity based on sensual desires, and a mocking of the things of God by those who walk after their own lust. By the way, all four of these are in *The Da Vinci Code*.

I don't wish to trivialize the needed scholarship that holds Dan Brown accountable for his falsification of historical facts, but we must know why. We in the West tend to intellectualize much of our concerns. Jesus, to the best of my knowledge, never argued with his opponents but went right to the issues of the heart. He avoided using human reasoning and rested in the Father's direction. Note how many times the religious and political leaders tried to trap him, but his responses always revealed motive. Again I wish to reiterate that apologetics has its place. We need to use scientific studies to reveal the fallacies of evolution and the like. There is a place for this. However, we must help the world admit to what they have suppressed. At the base of their rejection is a moral problem, and they know it: "For though they knew God" (Rom. 1:21) and "The law is written on their hearts" (Rom. 2:15). When we help them see the real reason, they can't help but wonder how we can speak with such authority. To some degree, the words "never a man spoke like this man" should be said of us as it was of Jesus since we have the mind of Christ and his written revelation.

The Easter Parade

As stated earlier, people never deny truth with their intellect but through a morally depraved nature. Depravity and intellectual arguments do not mix. Jesus met with many intellectual debaters but dismissed their arguments and pointed them to their signature sin. The Pharisees were made to look at their hypocrisy, the woman at the well faced her immorality, and the rich young ruler was confronted with his love of money. When we leave the company of intellectual debaters and point to their signature sin, they should run to their friends and say, "Come and see a Christian who told me all things that I have ever done" (John 4:29).

Let's take another look at western reasoning. Every year at Easter out come a plethora of medical stats on how much Jesus suffered. The gruesome details leave many weeping. I don't wish to minimize the pain, but my father years ago asked me why there was so much hype over Jesus' sufferings. He said, "I don't want to be sacrilegious, but I have friends in the military who were captured and tortured for years." He always felt a little guilty for not joining the western crowd in bemoaning the sufferings of Christ. I told him that there were no Scriptures that indicate Christ's physical suffering was the worst that any man had ever experienced. When we read Psalm 22:1, we get a different picture. Jesus cried out, "My God, my God, why have You forsaken me?" He didn't cry out about the physical pain, but about the emotional pain of separation from the Father. Can you see how this deeply affects how we look at the crucifixion? If we miss the point here, we miss the point altogether. If we go racing off with human reasoning regarding the pain of nails in the feet and hands but miss the great theological import of what was accomplished at Calvary, we lose the intended blessing. Again I add a disclaimer. The crucifixion of Christ was horribly painful and the Scriptures certainly point this out. This however is not the central theme in the Gospel accounts. Since the Father and the Son have an infinite love for one another, the separation was infinitely painful. This is where the real pain was placed.

Simba and Mickey

The Scriptures reveal to us the full scope of time in eternity past to time in eternity future. There are four stages of history that cover all known time—creation, the fall, redemption, and restoration. There are many great works that examine this subject. Edmond Clowney was one who highlighted it in his writings and teachings at Westminster Seminary. When I first was introduced to these stages, I began to notice that fallen man attempts to live them out in entertainment, writings, and life in general. Though the natural man is in a separated state from his Creator, he seems to have these four stages built into his makeup. He distorts them, but they are nonetheless there. Take our romances for example. Boy meets girl (creation of a relationship), they have a falling out (the fall or breach in the relationship), he pursues her (redemption—trying to win her back), and they live happily ever after (restoration—the relationship is restored).

In *The Lion King*, the cub Simba looks in a pool of water, but he sees a king. Mickey Mouse looks in a mirror and paints not himself but Walt Disney, his creator. These scenarios are played out all through life as man seeks redemption. His problem is not that he is unaware of his need for redemption but in the fact that he sees himself as his own redeemer. As believers, we see life through divine revelation, but often we drift back into the ways of human reasoning. We must never lose sight of our pilgrimage. As we pass through life, we are called to be vigilant and discerning about everything around us. If we fail to see ourselves in this light, we fall into the world's trap of thinking that human ingenuity will lead us into Utopia. Looking for a city that has foundations, whose builder and maker is God, gets replaced by creating a Utopia whose builder and maker is man.

CHAPTER 6

A Western Jesus and Theology

TROUBLE IS USUALLY JUST around the corner when theology is put on the table for discussion. If we play the word association game, the words that flow from the hearts of people regarding this topic will be quite varied. Some will pause and say that theology is nothing but cold facts about God, while others will rise to the defense of this noble science and say without theology you won't know the God you claim to worship. I wish to strike a delicate balance and help both sides in the argument come to the table with an open mind. I'm very concerned that a western jesus has infected each of these opposing parties and is doing damage to the church.

Few, if any, believers in Siberia have had systematic theology training, yet many live more vibrant victorious lives than those in the western church who have been well trained in this discipline. The *Westminster Confession of Faith* asks the question, "What is the chief end of man?" The answer is, "To glorify God and enjoy Him forever." I love that question and the answer as well. However, if you grabbed twenty theologians who had never heard this question, would they arrive at the same answer? Probably not. Any group of people who get together and systemize God or write out creeds and confessions still have just the opinions of fallible man.

Have you ever anticipated meeting someone because they have been described to you by close friends as someone you would enjoy getting to know? After the long-awaited meeting, however, you walk away mumbling to yourself, "He was not at all what I expected." If you think it is hard to describe a person, just think how hard it is to describe God. That is what theology tries to do. Scholars throughout the centuries have systematized God and his attributes. Though I love theology and have numerous books in my library that I often consult from time to time, I wonder what I will say to Jesus when I meet him face-to-face. Will I say, "You are not at all what I expected"? My guess is that many pastors and theologians will find themselves wide of the mark. If we have grown to know him, we will say, "You are all that I expected and infinitely more." This is exactly what the Queen of Sheba tells Solomon when she meets him: "She said to the king, "The report I heard in my own country about your words and about your wisdom is true. But I didn't believe the reports until I came and saw with my own eyes. Indeed, I was not even told half. Your wisdom and prosperity far exceed the report I heard" (1 Kings 10:6–7).

I consistently run across people who throw monkey wrenches into my well-defined theology. In Bible college and seminary we learn certain tools for analyzing Scripture. We study hermeneutics (the science of interpreting Scripture) and exegesis (the critical explanation or analysis of a text) only to come across people who can't even pronounce these terms, yet who live profoundly vibrant Christian lives. Some have had dreams come to pass or have had unexplained visitations from God that are unexplained by western theology. We try to tell them their experiences are not valid and may even be satanically induced because God no longer speaks this way. Yet we begin to realize that some of these people are not weirdos but are well-grounded in the faith though lacking formal education. They possess an indwelling boldness and, much like Jesus, they seem to speak with authority and not as many pastors and theologians. We become intrigued and begin to wonder why our conservative, time-tested theology hasn't brought us to the same place of intimacy. Maybe we aren't the problem; maybe it is our theology. This is not to be construed as an endorsement for dreams and visions but a challenge to our unbiblical and biased western mind-set that tells God who he can and can't talk to and when and where he will return.

For those of us who are called by God to teach the Word, we often tell our people, "Never interpret Scripture based on experience, but interpret experience based on Scripture." Generally speaking this is a good rule of thumb when studying the Word. However, we may run into some speed bumps if we are not careful.

Many years ago I picked up a commentary on the book of Acts written by a wonderful old pastor who has long since passed away. I loved his writings, but his comments on the following text were troublesome. Acts 17:26 says, "From one man He has made every nation of men to live all over the earth and has determined their appointed times and the boundaries of where they live." In commenting on this, he told his readers that man would never go to the moon because the Bible had made it clear that man is bound to this habitation. We are faced with three possibilities: 1) The Bible is inaccurate; 2) NASA has lied to us and no one has ever set foot on the moon; or 3) The passage was wrongly interpreted. I think I'll go with number 3. How often do we hear that God no longer speaks in dreams or visions. So what do we do with the thousands of testimonies of Muslims finding Christ in their dreams? We are faced with three possibilities: 1) The Bible is inaccurate; 2) These testimonies are all lies; or 3) Our theology has been westernized. I think I'll go with number 3. Remember our original statement: Never interpret the Bible by your experience but your experience by the Bible. As I said, generally speaking this is good advice, but sometimes my experience trumps my interpretation. It does not trump Scripture, just my western understanding of it. The transcendent Christ can slice through the theology of a western jesus. Just to let you know, I don't think this is normative, but to restrict God based on western theology is not a doctrine but a phobia.

I am very conservative, and I see the Bible as the final authority on all matters. I don't think we should consult dreams or visions for our daily direction. Still, there are many cases that thwart the typical western mind-set.

Our western jesus can lead us to act in a hypocritical fashion if we are not careful. Depending on your theological persuasion, if honest, you will probably admit to some inconsistencies. For example, if you hold to a particular prophetic view, you tend to read books and listen to messages that support what your prophetic leaning is. Now here is where the hypocrisy can surface. You read one scholar who interprets a prophetic passage in favor of your already biased view. You then read another scholar who exegetes the same passage and also arrives at the same conclusion as the first scholar. The problem is that the second man contradicts the first in his interpretation of the text yet both arrive at the same conclusion. You really don't care as long as both land where you want them to land. How well would this go over in a college math class? A problem solved in the wrong way is still marked wrong even if the answer is correct. Does the secular college math class have a higher standard than the theology classroom? Yet we distance ourselves from those of a different persuasion but link arms with those who support our view even though they arrive at it in a contradictory fashion.

Past Heroes

I am concerned for the western church and its integrity regarding the great Christian leaders of the past. Why, for instance, do we exalt Christian leaders of yesteryear while neglecting their major moral and theological flaws but malign present-day leaders if they don't measure up to our theological standards? We exalt Martin Luther knowing full well that he was considered crude in his speech, anti-Semitic, and had denied the veracity of James and Revelation. The very people who blast present-day pastors while showcasing Luther as the standard would never allow Luther to hold a leadership position in their church if he were alive today. And what shall we say of John Calvin, who had people burned at the stake because of disagreement over doctrine? Isaac Watts had some aberrant views on the deity of Christ. Spurgeon smoked cigars and C. S. Lewis's theology was wide of the conservative mark. All are men who have played great roles in advancing the kingdom of God but are held to a lesser standard than contemporary leaders. If any of these men were alive today and had a daily radio program, they would be called heretics by many of todays leading pastors and theologicans who presently exalt them. Time has a way of exaggerating their strengths and downplaying their frailties. Perhaps that is why we grade dead men on a curve and raise the bar on our contemporaries. Although I actually have profound respect for Luther, Calvin, Zwingly, the Puritans, and Jonathan Edwards, I think the western jesus has called us to an inconsistent standard. As pilgrims, we must be careful in all of our assessments. This is not to say that we shouldn't warn the flock of so-called Christian leaders who deny orthodoxy such as the virgin birth or salvation by grace alone through Christ alone. My concern is the lack of consistency. These men have often been referred to as the great Redwoods of church history, and rightly so; but let us not forget that even the greatest of trees have some fungus in the bark.

A New Start

I suspect that many people have taken a hard look at life and wondered what would happen if the planet were to start all over again with two fallen people. Would houses look the same? Would industry look the same? Would man invent basketball, baseball, football, and golf? How about cars and planes? No doubt, all things being equal, there would be homes, industry, and sports. The chances of things looking exactly the same are highly unlikely, if not impossible. Just look at how the nations do things very differently. They have come up with different forms of government. Their economic and political systems are different.

In much the same way, if a hidden people-group were found and given a Bible in their language, with all necessary resources to study Hebrew and Greek, what would their doctrinal statements say if they were in no way influenced by the West? What would a church service look like, or would there even be a service? How would they dress? How might they worship? Would they have a senior pastor (a term not found in Scripture)? Do you believe that a thousand years from now they would build buildings with steeples, stained-glass windows, and pews? If your answer is yes, upon what logic do you base your answer? It certainly doesn't come from Scripture. Do you think their scholars would say, "The chief end of man is to glorify God and enjoy Him forever," as the *Westminster Confession* says? Personally, I think this is *a* chief end of man. We take confessions and statements of faith as divinely inspired. No group of people no matter how learned can arrive at a final and definitive statement about Almighty God. We often are challenged to view life from a biblical perspective. As true as this is, I would like to add a little something to the challenge. It is one thing to see life through the lens of Scripture, but what if the lens we view Scripture with is distorted? In other words, if I look at Scripture with a cultural bias, will that not affect how I interpret the sacred writings and will this not ultimately affect my worldview that Scripture is supposed to reveal to me?

How often we read or hear that all we believe, say, and do must be motivated by "thus saith the Lord." All sides of any theological argument claim Scripture to be their authority. This seems to lend immediate credibility to one side and subtly implies a lack of biblical support for the other side. For example, the music wars that continue to rage within our churches are rarely interpreted in the light of Scripture; they are interpreted in light of a generational or cultural lens from which Scripture is now viewed. If you don't like drums, then just put on a pair of generational glasses, pick up your Bible, and voilà—drums are of the devil. A number of years ago I went to a conference in which the teacher warned us against contemporary Christian music. One of his arguments was that drums originated in Africa among animists who used them to bring up evil spirits. I couldn't help but wonder about the flute that is used in India to charm snakes out of a basket. If the drums go, the flutes must go. The Bible warns us not to twist Scripture. Let's return to our question. Would we do church the same way if there were no western influence?

My guess is that it would not even mildly relate to what we do today. I'm not implying that what we do is wrong; it is simply a western view of worship and theology. How we see the Lord is driven by a culture that has fed upon its own bias and theological bent. It becomes like an ingrown toenail that festers. This is why so much is being written today about the church trying to find itself. Maverick writers have put pen to parchment with edgy push-the-envelope books trying to get the church to be the church—relevant and relational. In the process, doctrine has been sacrificed on the altar of pragmatism. Yet if we are not careful, we will sacrifice pragmatism on the altar of western theology.

We must all take a hard look at what we do and see if it is derived from tradition, culture, or Scripture. It is hard to take off the cultural glasses that remove the color and depth of field found in true Bible study. The western jesus has obscured the mighty Christ.

Believe it or not, we all approach Scripture with a theological bias. We have been influenced to think a certain way about the Bible. We may be reformed, Pentecostal, charismatic, dispensational, or not even familiar with all four terms, but we still enter our time of devotion with a desired outcome. The desired outcome is usually threatened by "difficult" verses that thwart that desire, if not demolish it. Some difficulties in Scripture are more than speed bumps; they are roadblocks that defy interpretation as viewed through the lens of our theological bias. In such situations we disassemble the verse through careful exegesis and then reassemble it to fit neatly into our theology, when in fact it may be the theological system that needs to be disassembled.

The theology of most of us in the West has been formed in various ways. If you have had formal training, then you are likely a product of what you have been told the Bible says. Perhaps you sat under great teachers who steered you through a set of verses that prove a particular theology—after leaving out or explaining away passages that didn't support the theology of that institution. I am most grateful for the Bible training I received, but once I left Bible college and entered full-time ministry, I came across many people throughout the years who presented a different perspective and challenged my theology. We often have trouble admitting that we just might be wrong. I am not talking about the fundamentals of the faith but about those doctrinal issues that are more tangential to the major issues.

I read a great deal and am familiar with what most of the well-known theologians and pastors believe about various issues, that is, prophecy, baptism, predestination, sign gifts, and so forth. I have often seen the clear butchering of a text to make it say what they want it to say in order to support their point. Like it or not we are fallible people trying to interpret God's infallible Word. The interpretation of any passage will first go through the grid of personality; your personality has much to say about how you view a text. For example, if you are a reserved, somewhat private person, then verses like "Iron sharpens iron" (Prov. 27:17) or "Confess your sins to one another" (James 5:16) will be viewed very differently from someone who is an extrovert and whose life is an open book. I have sat in on several thousand staff and elder meetings throughout the years, and I can tell you well in advance of a meeting how each person will react to a theological subject just because of what I know about their personality.

I in no way say this is absolute, but "generally speaking," it has been my observation that most believers who hold to reformed theology are highly intellectual. I read many reformed writers and have been blessed by their great intellect. However, great intellect coupled with logic does not necessarily render a proper interpretation. I am not saying their interpretation is wrong. I only wish to point out that great intellectual minds tend to gravitate to this system of theology. Yet God never exalts intellect; he exalts spiritual discernment. "God has chosen the world's foolish things to shame the wise, and God has chosen the world's weak things to shame the strong" (1 Cor. 1:27).

On the other hand, we have those who are in the charismatic or Pentecostal camp, who are often (but not always) led by emotion. So which is right, intellect or emotion? The Bible addresses both. We are to love God with our whole heart (emotion) and mind (intellect). In studying the Word, I can intellectually arrive at a conclusion and often miss the emotive element behind the text. Each week at our staff meetings I have a different pastor lead us in devotions. Some will do a careful exposition of the text quoting great theologians of the past, such as Edwards or the Puritans. Others have never read anything by Edwards but bring a more practical devotional. The personality is reflected in the actual style of the devotion.

One is not necessarily right and the other wrong. They are just different and reflect different facets of the great diamond of theology. Does this mean that highly intelligent people should be ignored? By no means. God has gifted the church with such people who help the rest of us mortals understand the text with greater detail.

The second grid that interpretation goes through is fear. That's right, fear. Many fine expositors turn to original language as an escape in order to avoid the clear teaching of a text for fear that another view will open the door to wild heresy, but this should never be the reason for wrongly dividing the Word. I am thinking specifically of the sign gifts. (As an aside, I am not trying to take a particular theological stand on any particular issue. I just want us to force ourselves to be honest with the text and remove the fear factor.) I have never healed anyone nor do I speak in tongues, but there is no clear verse anywhere in Scripture that tells us the miraculous gifts passed away in the first century. In fact, many great theologians and scholars who are not in the charismatic camp would agree with what I just stated. However, much interpretation is out of fear that if we still hold to this, then wild heresy is sure to follow. This is no reason to make the text say something that it doesn't say.

A few years ago I was seated next to a great scholar. He was very conservative and reformed in his theology. He also happens to be an expert in the Koran and has evangelized many Muslims. During our conversation, I quietly leaned over so no one else could hear and asked him what his position was on tongues, fully expecting to have him tell me they passed away after the last apostle died. He carefully looked around to make sure he was not within listening distance of anyone else and told me the following story. One night before addressing a large crowd of Muslims at an evangelistic crusade, a close friend encouraged him to spend an extra amount of time in prayer, which he did. In the midst of deep, passionate, and lengthy prayer, his friend later commented that this scholar was speaking in an unknown tongue. The next day he had the greatest amount of genuine conversions he had ever experienced. He told me this happened one other time in his fifty years of preaching. The problem he faces is that he doesn't know how to fit it into his theology. He does not go around endorsing tongues, nor does he play down what actually happened. His is just one of countless stories that illustrate the speed bumps in our theological framework. Theology based on fear will always marginalize such experiences.

The third grid has to do with how you were raised or what theological system you were taught in Bible college or seminary. This naturally plays a profound role in what you believe and how you examine a text. Many friends of mine have gone to seminary to get advanced degrees and have intentionally chosen schools with a different theology from what they were raised with. By different, I don't mean liberal. If they were raised in a dispensational setting, they often chose to go to a reformed seminary. Their purpose was to see if the other side had a good argument—which it always does. The Bible is a complex book, and most theological systems can present a pretty good case for what they believe. My concern is not with what supports their view but with the disingenuous interpretation of texts that don't support their view.

The fourth grid is what you want the text to say. There is a passage in 2 Corinthians that tells us to become all things to all men. This is a favorite with those in the seeker service movement. (Here again I am not supporting a view but trying to show what we do with texts we don't like.) Those who oppose the seeker services will take this text, and by the time they are through, it is literally unrecognizable, which only frustrates the layperson who has no formal training. The reformed and Arminian camps do wonders mangling verses that don't fit their theological position. I have read a great deal on both sides, and I know of what I speak.

The last grid has to do with sinful bias. If we harbor sinful habits, we will take the clear teaching of God's Word and distort it. The ugly face of sin raises its head particularly in the arena of morality. "Flee from youthful passions" (2 Tim. 2:22) is archaic and gets in the way of my movie and TV diet. Since the text isn't clear, maybe it means flee to and not from. "I will not set anything godless before my eyes" (Ps. 101:3) couldn't really mean that in light of our present culture. Believers also suppress the truth in unrighteousness (see Rom. 1:18).

As you can see, there is a great deal that affects how we interpret Scripture. I don't want this to discourage you by having you think there must be no point in reading the Bible if each of these grids so deeply affects the outcome of how we interpret it. God is fully aware of our frailties and can make the necessary adjustment provided we remain teachable. Jesus said in the Gospel of John, "If anyone wants to do His will, he will understand" (John 7:17). The Holy Spirit is the final interpreter. Some of the most deeply spiritual and discerning people I know have read the Bible many times through and have rarely visited a commentary, yet seem to possess a profound knowledge and clear direction from the Lord. When I was in Bible college, I had a professor who had read the Bible more than three hundred times from cover to cover. He used to tell us, "It's amazing how much light the Bible sheds on all those commentaries."

Having traveled a great deal (I'm in Romania as I write this chapter), I have come to see that our western theology has a built-in bias that we must learn to recognize and see Scripture as it really is. Those who have not had a great deal of formal training often see things more clearly because their minds have not been shaped by theological bias. We would all be very surprised to find out just how blinded we really are to other interpretations, which in fact may not be contradictory to ours but supplementary. Let me relate a rather humorous account of this very thing. While I was watching a televangelist on TV many years ago, my youngest daughter, Katie, walked into the room. I wanted to warn her of false teaching, which this man blatantly promotes, so I asked her to sit on my lap and watch for a few minutes. The evangelist blew on the vast crowd and everyone fell over. While I was thinking about how I would explain in simple theological terms the error of this man's ways, Katie looked up at me and asked why the cameramen didn't fall down. Out of the mouth of babes. At a very young age, with no doctrinal understanding, she could see right through the whole charade while I missed the obvious. We might all be surprised by the obvious. Bias and a predetermined outlook can cloud, if not disable, our ability to see what is right before us in the text.

When my second oldest daughter, Megan, was about seven, she told me that the wheel on her little scooter had fallen off. I looked down and saw that a tiny cap was missing and I would have to go to the store to get another one. She said, "Dad, why don't we pray and ask God to help us find it." She had traveled all over the neighborhood and the cap could be anywhere. I decided to be a good example and pray, knowing full well God was busy with other more important issues and we would never find this cap. We opened our eyes after praying, and there it was lying in the grass just a few feet away. Little people don't have any theology to cloud their view of God.

Potential Superstition

Are we not dangerously close to being superstitious when we get upset over praise songs (with good doctrine) replacing hymns, or chairs replacing pews, or wooden crosses removed from the sanctuary, or plastic versus wooden pulpits. Do we believe there is a type of magic that pews have over chairs? Does God's Word do a greater work when the expositor stands behind an oak pulpit than when he stands behind a music stand? Is there more power in invoking the presence of God if stained-glass windows surround us? Can you see how close to ritualism, legalism, and superstition all this comes? These are strictly western battles, and they drain energy from the body. The Scriptures are completely silent in such matters, but personal preference often overrules.

This naturally forces us to find some way around the difficulty. Certainly difficulties must be resolved, but never at the expense of honest interpretation. The finest of pastors and scholars are capable of being disingenuous in relating to such matters. I have come across countless interpretations motivated by a theological system, bias, or desired outcome that often seemed shameless. I no doubt have fallen prey to such schemes.

Here are six ways often used to get around a difficult text. They can be legitimate or illegitimate. Motive will determine legitimacy.

1. *Original Language.* Knowledge of Hebrew and Greek is of great value, but what layman hasn't been baffled by scholarly works that claim different meanings for words? I am always suspicious when the word is made to fit the author's doctrinal bias. It's a little like watching an instant replay. Half of the crowd says the player had possession of the ball, while the other half says he didn't. It is interpreted by a desired outcome. I was

reading some literature from a man who is a big promoter of homeschooling. He quoted a verse in Scripture that had the word *teaching* in it. He proceeded to tell his readers that the actual word for *teaching* in the Greek was "homeschooling." I laughed hysterically. Though I don't know Greek, I know in my heart that it doesn't mean homeschooling.

2. *Compare Scripture with Scripture.* This is an excellent way to find God's mind on a subject because a subject may be dealt with in many books of Scripture. The trouble occurs when we start looking for the exit ramp that will lead us to a Scripture that we can make serve our desired outcome, even if it is forced to fit.

3. *Context.* What could be more logical than considering the context? Yet I have read many commentaries where one scholar looks at the immediate context while another, who doesn't feel this will serve his purpose best, will say you need to consider the overall context of the book. If that doesn't work, he may say that the overall tenor of Scripture fits his view. Again, I wish to stress that this may very well be valid, but we must be careful in forcing an interpretation.

4. *Secular Sources.* Often if a word leads to a troubling outcome, pastors and scholars will scratch around secular literature of that era to see if the word could have a different meaning that would support their argument. Given enough time, they will probably come up with what they are looking for. Don't evolutionists do the same while looking for fossils that will support their theory?

5. *Translations.* This may be the most humorous of all. Many pastors say, "A better translation here is the KVJ, NIV, or NASB," when in fact they have no clue. They read in a commentary where some scholar told them this. Another commentary may pick another translation. Unless you are a textual critic, you really don't know and are at the mercy of your own best judgment. Rick Warren was hammered for this in his *Purpose Driven Life* by pastors and scholars who are guilty of doing the same thing but on a lesser scale.

6. *Original Manuscripts.* When all else fails, just say, "This verse isn't found in the most original manuscripts." How many times has that been used?

My purpose here is not to question Scripture, which I do believe is without error in its original autographs, but to encourage a genuine approach to the Word. The Holy Spirit is the ultimate interpreter. We certainly need sound scholarship. I always consult commentaries after I have listened to the Spirit of God through meditation and prayer. The Spirit can bring my attention to context, language, and comparing Scriptures with Scripture through a scholar. However, I am always on the lookout for a forced interpretation that brings about the author's desired outcome.

Seek the Spirit of God, who will guide us into all truth. The Word is true, the Spirit is true, but our desired outcome may tempt us to skew the truth.

Sticky Theology

I love theology. Spurgeon referred to it as the loftiest science. It gives us a firm foundation regarding what we believe. I sense, however, that we have taken it into realms where even angels fear to tread. If you belonged to an underground church in China, you would be forced to fellowship with people who may have a different take on some doctrinal issue than you. Only in the West do we have time to sit down and write out lengthy doctrinal statements, creeds, and confessions. Perhaps the western jesus has too much time on its hands.

Don't get me wrong, I have been teaching at a Bible church for many years. I love expository preaching and standing on sound doctrine, but I have also come to realize that not all of what we teach is clearly outlined in Scripture. If you took the biggest names in the evangelical world and asked them to start a church together, it would be doomed to fail at the outset. That church wouldn't last a minute. The founders would never arrive at an agreed upon doctrinal statement. This seems to be a sad reflection on the church.

Two friends of mine recently decided to start a church together. I knew that their personalities were strong, but of far greater concern was their view of theology. They felt so strongly about every conceivable doctrinal issue that I knew this relationship had the shelf life of a Hollywood marriage. Within the course of two months, they had parted company—over one verse of Scripture. The verse had nothing to do with salvation, nor was it even mildly tangential to anything relevant to the Christian life. The western jesus found his way in and destroyed any potential these men had for being co-laborers with each other or with Christ. Unfortunately, the western jesus has found his way into our western church as well, and we are broken and divided as a result.

Yet if this same church would come under persecution from foreign soil, we would rally and put Christ as central. If we were meeting in a warehouse with the pastor's Bible resting on an oil drum, no one would complain that it wasn't an oak pulpit. We would happily join in as someone strummed an old guitar, leading us in worship. There would be no complaints about what songs were chosen. The western jesus would be replaced by the transcendent Christ.

Christ as Central

One quiet Tuesday morning in early September, our staff meeting was interrupted by our receptionist: "A plane has flown into one of the twin towers in New York," she said. I thanked her for this information but was a bit perplexed by her interruption. After all, many small planes crash daily, and though this one may have hit a building in New York, was it worth disrupting a staff meeting? Would the next interruption be to tell me of a car wreck on the beltway? A few moments later she interrupted us again to say a second plane had hit the other tower. This was no coincidence I thought, so we all gathered around a little portable TV to find out what was happening.

That weekend we had more than seven hundred new faces show up on our church's doorstep. Since we are about twenty miles west of the Pentagon, and many of our people through the years have been secret service agents, admirals, generals, and CIA employees, we may have felt the impact more than most. After all, it was very close to home. Suddenly, minor doctrinal disputes were shelved. Eternal matters made their way to the front of the line, and we saw firsthand what the church ought to look like.

Hurricane Katrina had a similar influence. Denominational distinctions among genuine believers were buried. Caring for the poor and disenfranchised, preaching the gospel, and advancing the kingdom became the real issues. Prayer meetings abounded. What would happen to the church in the West if about every three to four months we had a Katrina or a 9/11? I tend to believe that secondary matters would vanish, for there is no time for secondary matters during times of war.

Hurricane Katrina and 9/11 are now only memories. Passion for God has once again ebbed since these tragedies. I'm reminded of Israel during the days of Judges, when every man did what was right in his own eyes (see Judg. 21:25) until God unleashed the power of heathen nations to act as a rod in his sovereign hand. The people would turn back to God—only to forget him again as time passed. The western church is in the same wilderness.

The western church is in desperate need of an overhaul. Do I have all the answers? Most certainly not, but many years of ministry have taught me a great deal, and I could have spared myself much pain if I had known at the outset what I know now.

A Doctrinal Paradox

Regarding the subject of theology we must ask ourselves some very hard questions. Why, with all the seminaries, Bible expositing seminars, books, videos, counseling centers, and fellowship groups, is the church in the West so weak? Something does not make sense. In the West, we are educated beyond our experience whereas the persecuted church is experienced beyond their education.

I would like to see someone gather a set of statistics. I would like him to take his research team into a large, finely tuned, doctrinally sound church that has an excellent expositor at the helm and test the spiritual waters. I would not want him to survey their Bible knowledge, but their spiritual walk. What entertainment do they frequent? What magazines do they read? What is the divorce rate? What percentage of the congregation struggles with Internet pornography? How are their children doing?

Then I would like the researcher to go to another large church that is not as sound theologically but is evangelical, and take the same survey. Would there be any difference in the spiritual temperatures? Since no such survey has been taken to my knowledge, I don't know what the outcome would be; but if I were a betting man, my money would be on a tie. I doubt seriously that doctrine, theology, and great teaching raise the spiritual temperature much. This is not to suggest that we should do away with sound teaching since it obviously makes no difference in people's spiritual growth. I simply want to suggest that the teaching must be supplemented by action. It must move from the pulpit to the public square. Luther said that one of the best instructors is affliction (see Ps. 119:71), which third-world churches experience daily. There is certainly much more that must take place besides sound teaching.

Jesus made two interesting statements regarding the Scriptures. In one place he told the Jews that they search the Scriptures because in them they think they have eternal life (see John 5:39). His point was that despite all their study, they missed the person of Christ. They couldn't see the forest (Christ) for the trees (doctrines). On another occasion, however, Jesus rebuked the religious leaders by telling them, "You are deceived, because you don't know the Scriptures or the power of God" (Matt. 22:29). They had questioned him concerning whether or not there is resurrection of the body. He took them to the Old Testament and built his argument around a careful analysis of Exodus 3:6 and the little word *am*. So as you can see, Jesus can warn us to not get so caught up in theology that we miss the person of Christ, while at the same time he acts like a theologian building a doctrinal case around the tense of a verb. Everything points to the person of Christ, and we must see theology and doctrine as the support system that brings to light the transcendent Jesus.

Right Doctrine and Right Living

Most of you have probably heard this statement: "Right doctrine leads to right living." As true as this statement is, there must be some clarity given to it or we will find ourselves trying to resolve a major contradiction. The contradiction that I speak of is that Mormons live exemplary lives, often well above Christian standards, but they certainly don't hold to sound doctrine. But if right doctrine leads to right living and Mormons live right, then they must have sound doctrine. At this point we must be careful. All cats are animals but not all animals are cats.

All those who obey right doctrine will live rightly, but not all who live rightly obey right doctrine. I bring this up because each theological system the West has developed claims that its doctrine is important for right living, yet I see many conservative believers from different theological camps who live upright lives. The big question is, is there one particular theological persuasion that historically has produced more right living than all other theological persuasions?

If I were moving into a farming community and wanted to know how to have a fruitful harvest, I don't think it would take much mental horsepower to figure out what I needed to know. I would travel around during the summer months and see which farmer had the best crop, then I would go to him for advice. But suppose all the farms were equal in production, and to make matters worse, after interviewing each farmer, all use different methods that they believe make them successful. If each man believes his way is the only way, and each of their ways is different but produces equal results, assuming the soil is consistent in that region, then I would need to find the common denominator employed by all. If I could find a successful farmer who didn't use any methods other than dropping seeds in the ground, then I could assume that the soil is the common denominator.

Don't we have something like this within the Christian community? Don't we all claim that our particular set of doctrines must be adhered to in order to please God? Don't our well-defined statements of faith express the irreducible minimum that one must believe to be a victorious Christian? And if right doctrine leads to right living, shouldn't we look for that theological system that is bearing the most God-honoring fruit? But much like the man interviewing the farmers, suppose our investigation shows that an equal number of victorious believers are found within each theological camp? What must one look for, the differences or the common denominator? Do we know of any set of doctrines that when believed produce the highest yield? In other words do reformed Baptists have fewer divorces than non-reformed Baptists? Do Charismatic premillennial immersionists have fewer eating disorders than evangelical postmillennial sprinklers? Do hyper-Calvinistic amillennial cessationists have less trouble surfing the dark side of the Internet than moderate Calvinistic premillennial tongue speakers?

Sadly, this is how westerners shop for a church. Some want contemporary Christian music but no praise singers up front because it is distracting and takes all the glory away from God. Others want contemporary Christian music led by a choir, while still others want the more formal piano/organ combo. Once you find the place that has your music style, you are then faced with the doctrinal issues. You end up with a mix-and-match set of doctrines, values, and music that a mathematician who specializes in matrix will need to help you sort out. It's too bad there isn't a consumers guide to churches, much like the Christian yellow pages. "Let's see what we have here. Oh yes, this looks like my kind of church. They have a singles ministry that plays video games after the contemporary service that is led by an amillenial charismatic reformed hyper-Calvinist who believes in baptism by immersion. Oh rats, I see that this service is at 8:15 a.m. on Sunday and I like to sleep until 10:00." Only in the West do we have time for such trivia.

Here is what I have found out about victorious believers by looking at what godly people have in common. First and foremost, they love Christ and have made him the supreme joy in their lives. And because of this they follow him: "If you love Me, you will keep My commandments" (John 14:15). His commandments are not doctrinal in nature but are sacrificial and moral. I have never known a Christian whom God has used to advance His kingdom who loved luxury. Second, victorious believers have an insatiable appetite for the Word of God, from which they draw their spiritual nourishment. Third, they have a devoted prayer life that is in sync with their love for the Word. Fourth, they have a care less attitude about the things of this world. Last, they have a non-judgmental attitude about those who disagree with them. I confess to you that I am not there yet. However, these are the type of people who have convinced me they understand this thing we call the Christian life.

We make a fuss about a lot of issues in our western culture. Does a person have a closer walk with God if he worships in formal attire at a church with stained-glass windows where the pastor stands behind an oak pulpit? Can a worshipper experience a close walk with the Lord if he meets in a converted warehouse, wears jeans, and listens to a pastor who preaches from behind a music stand? These are not small questions. The church has been held captive to such issues for about three decades, which has nullified the effectiveness of the church.

I know these are strong words coming from someone with very little formal training. However, I have engaged myself in thousands of hours of theological discussions with people all over the world from different theological, but not liberal, camps who are victorious believers.

CHAPTER 7

A Western Jesus and Prophecy

■ ■ ■

I have told you now before it happens so that when
it does happen you may believe.

John 14:29

THE FOLLOWING THOUGHTS ON biblical prophecy probably come
more from disillusionment than anything else. This was the driving force
that called me to see if Scripture really said what prophecy buffs tell us.
My intention is not to attack or ridicule. However, what I propose in this
chapter will go against the mainstream of almost all prophetic interpretation. By going against the mainstream, I do not mean that I have a new
prophetic scheme that will render the traditional views invalid. What
I do mean is that I think we are completely off track in the way we handle
prophetic interpretation. I have given this a great deal of thought over
many years. Perhaps my thinking comes from a biased mind, shaped by
scholars whose prophetic interpretations have been left threadbare with
the passing of time—what they led me to believe would come to pass,

never came to pass. The prophetic views are very western and come from too much downtime.

Prophetic interpretation is more than just a discipline. It's arriving at an interpretation of future events based on a limited amount of information. The Scriptures are prophetic to a large degree. The question, however, does not revolve around the issue of prophecy but how to interpret the prophetic Scriptures.

A Radical View

What I am about to say will come as a shock to many. My only request and prayer is that you read this with an open mind and then make your own decision:

> Prophecy can only be understood by those living during the time of its fulfillment, and the details were never intended for those living prior to it.

Obviously a statement as bold as this needs some explanation. Clearly there are some general truths in the prophetic scheme of things that we can understand; for example, Jesus is coming again. But I strongly contend that the divisive spirit that has arisen over the premillennial, postmillennial, pretribulation, posttribulation, and midtribulation view is what grieves the heart of God. This has brought disgrace to his holy name, has made the church a laughingstock to outsiders, and has left hundreds of biblical scholars with egg on their faces. If I take the time to quote from the prophetic commentaries of the last two decades that have led the church to believe the world could not possibly go on another five years because of the lack of oil in the Middle East, or because the planets in 1983 were lining up in such a way that the combined gravitational force would split the Mount of Olives, or that Russia will come down from the north and destroy Israel because Ezekiel 38 explicitly says it will happen, or that the common market fits Daniel's ten kings, I would need more than a chapter. I would need an entire book. We have shot ourselves in the foot a thousand times over these issues, which is one reason the church is limping along.

Believe it or not, the Scriptures themselves have a great deal to say about how difficult it is to sort through prophecy. In Daniel 12 we read: "I heard but did not understand. So I asked, 'My lord, what will be the outcome of these things?' He said, 'Go on your way, Daniel, for the words are secret and sealed until the time of the end'" (vv. 8–9). Note carefully that Daniel—who recorded prophecy under the inspiration of the Holy Spirit—didn't even understand what he had prophesied. This is in perfect harmony with a New Testament passage in 1 Peter 1:9–12:

You are receiving the goal of your faith, the salvation of your
souls. Concerning this salvation, the prophets who prophesied about
the grace that would come to you searched and carefully investigated.
They inquired into what time or what circumstances the Spirit of
Christ within them was indicating when He testified in advance
to the messianic sufferings and the glories that would follow. It was
revealed to them that they were not serving themselves but you con-
cerning things that have now been announced to you through those
who preached the gospel to you by the Holy Spirit sent from heaven.
Angels desire to look into these things.

Here the Lord is telling us that Old Testament prophets inquired about the details—what time or what circumstances—but verse 12 tells us that it was not for them to know.

In Acts 8:30–31, Philip asked the Ethiopian eunuch if he could understand the prophetic statements of Isaiah: "Do you understand what you are reading?" The eunuch responded, "How can I unless someone guides me?" If it was clear, why couldn't he understand? But now that the prophecy of the Messiah had come to pass, Philip could render a perfect interpretation.

Listen to these words in John 12:16: "His disciples did not understand these things at first. However, when Jesus was glorified, then they remembered that these things had been written about Him and that they had done these things to Him." Here again we have the word *understand.* In Luke 9:22 we read: "The Son of Man must suffer many things and be rejected by the elders, chief priests, and scribes, be killed, and be raised the third day." Yet in Luke 18:31–34 we read this: "Then He took the Twelve aside and told them, 'Listen! We are going up to Jerusalem. Everything that is written through the prophets about the Son of Man will be accomplished. For He will be handed over to the Gentiles, and He will be mocked, insulted, spit on; and after they flog Him, they will kill Him, and He will rise on the third day.' They understood none of these things. This saying was hidden from them, and they did not grasp what was said."

Daniel didn't understand, the eunuch didn't understand, the disciples didn't understand, the prophets of old didn't understand—until the prophecy had come to pass; then it all made sense, but only to those living during its fulfillment.

Consider the credentials of the prophets. They were holy men, moved by the Spirit of God (see 2 Peter 2). They actually penned prophecies, not commentaries, yet the divine record states they did not understand the future of which they prophesied. They clearly had a prophetic overview, but not all the details. Consider also that they were looking down the corridor of time through the prophetic lens of Scripture, as are we, but what seemed blurry to the inspired writer is crystal clear to us, the uninspired interpreter. We see into the future with perfect vision. How is it that we can sit in the shadow of these giants and declare in the minutest detail all future events, while they searched diligently only to find they looked through a glass dimly. The tables have turned. The amateurs are telling the pros what it's all about. If God intended for us to know all the details of future events, don't you think he would have included charts, diagrams, and inspired PowerPoint slides in the canon?

Some may wish to counter my argument with, "Yes, but much more time has elapsed since the days of Ezekiel." As true as that may be, as we have already seen, the disciples didn't even understand the cross, which was right in front of them. Still, Jesus did not rebuke them in Luke 18:31–34. However, once it came to pass they were rebuked for not recognizing the event. "He said to them, 'How unwise and slow you are to believe in your hearts all that the prophets have spoken! Didn't the Messiah have to suffer these things and enter into His glory?' Then beginning with Moses and all the Prophets, He interpreted for them the things concerning Himself in all the Scriptures" (Luke 24:25–27).

Time is not necessarily the issue. The events that come to pass will be unmistakably clear if we are well versed in his Word. Listen to the words of our Lord: "I have told you now before it happens so that when it does happen you may believe" (John 14:29).

Don't overlook the importance of the word *when*. It designates the fulfillment as being the time period for full understanding. Remember Peter's comments on the day of Pentecost: "On the contrary, this is what was spoken through the prophet Joel" (Acts 2:16). He goes on to describe Joel's inspired prophecy of how the Spirit of the Lord would be poured out and how there would be signs and wonders in the heavens, and how the sun would be darkened and the moon would turn to blood. Was the Spirit of the Lord poured out? Yes! Did the sun turn dark and the moon turn to blood? No! Was Joel wrong? Of course not. God simply hadn't told Joel there would be at least two thousand years of church history that would separate the two events, and I'm not sure this is necessarily the proper interpretation. It's a good thing our modern-day interpreters weren't on hand. They would have broken out the time-line charts and had a field day, only to be proven wrong again.

It is common knowledge that the people of the Old Testament were more than mildly confused regarding the coming Messiah. His first coming was prophesied as a lowly, suffering servant (see Isa. 53). His second coming shows him as a triumphant lion and king (see Joel 3). Some thought there were two Messiahs. Could anyone blame them? They were not aware of the time-lapse between the two advents. Scripture is replete with prophetic misunderstanding *until* the events come to pass.

Words, Words, and More Words

All prophetic schemes are hopelessly flawed and rely heavily upon the subtle nuances of words in their original language.

Another factor that makes prophecy difficult is the exact meaning of words. Words are obviously crucial to all biblical doctrine. However, unlike eschatology (the doctrine of last things), other doctrines do not hinge as much on words as they do on concepts and historical settings. Salvation, for example, could be perfectly understood without any knowledge of the terms *propitiation, justification, sanctification,* and so on. Salvation is seen in historical events such as the Red Sea, Abraham offering Isaac, Jonah, the parable of the publican and the Pharisee, and others. All flows neatly into the New Testament, where it is refined and distilled in the epistles for ultimate clarification. Illustrations and typology abound, making clear what one must do to be saved. However, in stark contrast, prophetic schemes rely solely on the meaning of a single word. In his book, *The Pre-wrath Rapture of the Church,* Marv Rosenthal builds much of his case for the timing of the rapture over Greek prepositions. This is a tenuous argument at best.

He does an equally capable job of showing how the term *coming,* which can be translated by three different Greek words, complements or destroys an entire prophetic scenario. Unlike other doctrines that show up in typology, history, allegory, parable, and progressive revelation, prophecy is still future with nothing to hang our arguments on but fine nuances in the meaning of words once removed from our own language. This is shaky ground at best from which to construct an argument as complex as detailed future events.

Forcing the Issue

*All prophetic schemes force, twist, distort
and manipulate Scripture to make the pieces fit
the espoused prophetic view.*

As I mentioned above, Marvin Rosenthal's *The Pre-wrath Rapture of the Church,* which came out a number of years ago, caused a real stir. I highly recommend this book, but not for reasons one might expect.

Mr. Rosenthal shows unequivocally how terribly faulty the various traditional prophetic views are, and he is right. He then espouses his own view, which I might add is very interesting, but still, in my opinion, violates the spirit of how prophecy is to be interpreted. What is so refreshing about the book is a) the author has done his homework; b) he is not sensational in his approach; c) he is delightfully honest; d) he is extremely humble; e) he does the best job of avoiding "forced interpretations." Despite all of these fine qualities, the book still lays out a neat time line of future events that, in my opinion, simply cannot be known at this hour of history. It is worth reading because it shows how forced prophetic scenarios are and how the Scriptures must be manipulated to arrive at an already biased conclusion. All books on prophecy set out to prove beyond a shadow of a doubt that their view is right. The writer never fails to remind us how neatly his argument fits Scripture. There are rarely any loose ends or difficult passages to deal with because they can all be explained by the prophetic theme heralded by the author. What is so "unique" is that every author is able to show that his prophetic view is in perfect accord with divine revelation. I have never seen so many square pegs fit so neatly into round holes.

Clanging of the Symbols

Every prophetic view must assign meaning
to highly questionable symbols in order to promote
the espoused view.

As a young, naive believer thirty-five years ago, while attending an evening class on prophecy, I was amazed to hear that the statue in Nebechednezzer's dream literally represented the future reigning kingdoms. *Wow!* I thought, *Here it is all spelled out—Babylon, Media Persia, Greece, Rome, and Russia.* What I didn't realize was that the Scriptures didn't spell it out, but my professor did. He just helped fill in a few of the missing blanks. After all, it is intuitively obvious to the most casual observer that the following passage so clearly represents the Soviet Union:

"In the days of those kings, the God of heaven will set up a kingdom that will never be destroyed, and this kingdom will not be left to another people. It will crush all these kingdoms and bring them to an end, but will itself endure forever" (Dan. 2:44). Another classic text is found in Matthew 24:32–34.

The traditional premillennial view is to arbitrarily assign the meaning of the fig tree to be Israel. Why not? It makes their 1948 return to the land a lot more meaningful, because if this text teaches that Israel will return and the generation living at that time will not pass away, then all we have to do is assign a time frame to the word *generation;* we then know when to expect the rapture (unless you don't believe in the rapture). Well, here we are almost sixty years later—which is outside normal time limits given to the word *generation.* And so on it goes—with computer capabilities to assign everyone the mark of the beast, to the ten kings in Daniel representing the common market, which doesn't exist anymore, to Rosh the chief prince of Meschech and Tubal in Ezekiel being the Soviet Union, which has also collapsed.

I am not saying all prophetic schemes are wrong. One of them might be right. The fig tree might represent Israel and maybe Ezekiel 38 is a description of the Soviet Union, but I wouldn't stake my life on it nor would I endorse an entire prophetic system that is based on such faulty assumptions. It certainly wouldn't be an issue of fellowship or church membership. Christians have been defrauded long enough over such issues. Disappointment and disillusionment reign when events don't fall neatly into place as one has been promised they would.

What Did the Prophets See?

Try to imagine having no New Testament revelation regarding the Lord Jesus Christ. Put aside all your knowledge of his birth, death, and resurrection (events that were prophesied and have come to pass). Now put yourself in the shoes of an Old Testament prophet, priest, or king. What could he have assumed about the future Messiah through the prophetic lens of Scripture?

- Genesis 3:15—seed
- Deuteronomy 18:15—prophet
- Job 19:25—redeemer
- Psalm 16:10—will not be left in hell
- Psalm 22:1—forsaken
- Psalm 24:9—king
- Isaiah 7:14—virgin born
- Isaiah 9:6—son born, mighty God
- Isaiah 53—suffer and die
- Daniel 9:26—cut off
- Zechariah 12:10—pierced

Admittedly, this is not an exhaustive listing of Messianic prophecies, but these are certainly the major ones. What could an Old Testament believer have surmised about this Messiah? First off, I'm not convinced that he would have seen all of these texts as relating to this future deliverer. The messianic psalms seem to be speaking about David. Peter in Acts 2:29 sheds light on what they must have previously believed when he said, "Brothers, I can confidently speak to you about the patriarch David: he is both dead and buried, and his tomb is with us to this day." Peter's point is that a reading of this prophecy in the Old Testament was not clear. But now that it is has been fulfilled, it is very clear to whom David was referring. Paul indicates the same thing in Acts 13:35–36.

The clear indication here is that many must have thought Psalm 16:10 was referring to David. Was it clear that the prophet in Deuteronomy 18 of which Moses spoke and the Messiah of which Daniel spoke were in fact one and the same? Here again, let Scripture give testimony: "When some from the crowd heard these words, they said, 'This really is the Prophet!' Others said, 'This is the Messiah!'" (John 7:40–41).

Can you imagine the number of possible prophetic interpretations that could have arisen out of these verses? There may have been an *amessiah* view (the prefix "a" meaning "no"). This could have come out of a wrong interpretation of Zechariah 12:10, where Jehovah is pierced. Since Jehovah is God, and God is a spirit, and spirits can't be pierced, then this must not be literal terminology. But when God took on human flesh and was pierced at the cross, then the prophetic Scriptures made sense: "For these things happened so that the Scripture would be fulfilled: Not one of His bones will be broken. Also, another Scripture says: They will look at the One they pierced" (John 19:36–37).

The number of potential combinations of prophetic views could have been innumerable. The questions of how, when, and why must have been most perplexing. But that wasn't the issue. The issue was simply to know that a deliverer would someday come for his people, and when he did, *then* the prophetic word would come to full light and bless those living during the time of fulfillment. Those living prior to the fulfillment were to be obedient to what they knew and not try to second-guess the Scriptures.

Once future events take their place in history, those living will be able to say (if prepared and knowledgeable in the Word), "So that's who the witnesses are in Revelation 11. Now it all makes sense, these seals, trumpets, elders, spirits, dragons, and so forth. This is not what I had anticipated at all."

But our present-day western pride and insatiable appetite for future details will not allow us to learn from the experience of those before us who simply didn't understand. We will not be content until we have forced, manipulated, distorted, jammed, mashed, and shoved every symbol and verb tense into our prophetic scheme. And if others don't agree, then we will split from those heretics and treat them as heathens and publicans.

The fact is, Daniel was not a pretribulationist, for the Bible says he didn't understand. Moses was not a premillennialist, for the Bible says he didn't understand. Isaiah was not an amillennialist, for the Bible says he didn't understand. It seems that only twenty-first century Christians understand. But look at what we have "understood": we understood that the social security number was the mark of the beast; we understood that the six-day war was a sign of the end; we understood that the Jupiter effect would split the Mount of Olives; we understood that the Middle East oil would cause war with Russia. Yet here we are knee-deep in our own understanding and buried in unfulfillment. In essence, many have been "taken for a ride" on the prophetic railroad that has led to mass confusion, church splits, and hurt feelings. Multitudes have been left in the wake of prophetic interpretation that we really never understood. Underground churches in China are not concerned with such matters.

A Call to Holiness

All prophetic views are promoted by those
who espouse them as essential for holy living.

What could be more important than a close walk with the Lord? Holy living is what the Christian life is all about. When asked "What difference does it make how I feel about the future?" the standard reply is, "It will affect how you conduct your daily life." Again, I pause to say how much I appreciate this as a motivation, but in all honesty I have never faced a new day saying, "I had better obey the Lord today because I'm amillennial or premillennial, and he may come back at any moment." I am motivated by the following: "I love him because he first loved me" (see 1 John 4:19). If I love him, I will keep his commandments (see John 15:10). For the love of Christ constrains me (see 2 Cor. 5:14). "But the Day of the Lord will come like a thief; on that day the heavens will pass away with a loud noise, the elements will burn and be dissolved, and the earth and the works on it will be disclosed. Since all these things are to be destroyed in this way, it is clear what sort of people you should be in holy conduct and godliness as you wait for and earnestly desire the coming of the day of God, because of which the heavens will be on fire and be dissolved, and the elements will melt with the heat" (2 Pet. 3:10–12).

The above verses could be held up as an argument to support the fact that prophecy will drive one to a holy life. Note carefully that I have never said we can't know anything about the future. I simply contend that we can't know all the details, especially the timing. This passage in 2 Peter does not deal with details but causes us to focus on the truth that one day everything will burn up. Therefore why put stock in a temporal value system? Clearly I am motivated to have a holy life because I fear

God and know that all will eventually come to an end. But to say that, if I am not amillennial, pretribulation, posttribulation, midtribulation, or some other prophetic flavor then my life will not reflect God's holiness, this again becomes another tactic to force prophetic interpretation. Joseph lived a godly life without the aid of millennial time-line charts put on PowerPoint.

And of course all those who endorse a particular prophetic theme claim the early church held to their view. Here again we can't even agree on what happened in the past much less interpret what will happen in the future. These issues must be left to the Lord in his sovereign plan to carry out. It can be exciting to study the Scripture and arrive at personal views, but it should never be to the point of dividing God's people.

Only in the West do we labor over such trivia. Just tell someone who is being persecuted for their faith that you have good news for them: we don't go through the tribulation. Bring in your favorite time-line chart to believers in an underground church in Iraq and tell them you have the date of Christ's return, which happens to be tomorrow at 6:00 a.m. Again I think we have too much time on our hands as a western jesus guides us with precision through the future with no prophetic stone left unturned.

When I hear of missionaries who can't get support from western churches because they can't sign the church's doctrinal statement on end times, I grieve. When godly people are denied church membership over eschatological issues, I'm deeply hurt. The energy, time, and money wasted on this cannot be calculated. We need to follow the transcendent Christ, who is coming again in all his glory, and forsake the western jesus, who is more confused than ever. I do not say that it is wrong to have a prophetic view. Just don't put it on the same shelf as the gospel.

CHAPTER 8

The Pilgrim and His Gospel

"ARE YOU SURE YOU are right about that?" "I promise—it's the gospel truth." We often try to verify how sure we are of some bit of news floating around by telling people it's the gospel truth. I'm not certain where this term was born, but it probably came out of our Christian witness regarding the gospel.

The gospel has been defined as the death and resurrection from the grave of our Lord Jesus Christ. This is certainly a correct definition, as it is given to us in 1 Corinthians 15:1–3. Though correct, we find as we examine the use of the word *gospel* as it is found in Scripture that there is much more to it than just a ticket to heaven. The term is often used in contexts such as "Does he preach a clear gospel?" or "Have they heard the gospel yet?" By such terminology, the word is used in its most limited and narrow definition. Those of bygone years used this term to describe the Christian life: "Are they living according to the gospel?" or "Is that church consistent with the gospel?" Such expressions indicate that the gospel has a daily impact and is not just used to describe someone who is saved. Consider the usage by the apostle Paul in Philippians 1:27: "Just one thing: live your life in a manner worthy of the gospel of Christ. Then, whether I come and see you or am absent, I will hear about you that you are standing firm in one spirit, with one mind, working side by side for the faith of the gospel." Here we are told that our very lives should reflect the gospel. Obviously the way we conduct ourselves does not display the account of the resurrection, but the impact of this message on our lives should motivate us to live in such a way that someone just might ask us of a reason for the hope that is in us (see 1 Pet. 3:15).

In this chapter I would like to examine several major dimensions of our lives that tell us just how much we really believe the gospel. I am not implying that if we do not reflect various facets of the gospel's power that we are not believers. What I want us to understand is that there is much more to this message than our western mind-set has allowed us to believe. No one perfectly lives out all that I will share in this chapter, but I do hope that it encourages you to see how much more there is to the gospel than just going to heaven when you die.

The Gospel Gives Boldness

When they observed the boldness of Peter and
John and realized that they were uneducated
and untrained men, they were amazed and knew
that they had been with Jesus.

Acts 4:13

This passage is unique in that it has contained within it a nice little three-point outline. The religious leaders couldn't help but notice the boldness of the apostles, the ignorance of the apostles, and the fact that they had been with Jesus. The very reason for their boldness was born out of the fact that they had been with Christ. They really saw the gospel in light of telling others, even if it meant persecution.

This boldness was not only seen in New Testament times. Shadrach, Meshach, and Abednego refused to bow down to the golden image. Their

THE PILGRIM AND HIS GOSPEL ■ 109

bold statement to the king was based on an eternal perspective: "If the God we serve exists, then He can rescue us from the furnace of blazing fire, and He can rescue us from the power of you, the king" (Dan. 3:17). Note carefully their service and boldness for God was not contingent upon God doing their bidding. It made no difference whether or not God delivered them because they knew that ultimately they would be delivered.

We see this boldness even more clearly in the last part of Hebrews 11, which can be divided into two parts. From verse 32 through the first part of verse 35, we have the happy victorious fruit of great faith. These men and women of faith conquered kingdoms, shut the mouths of lions, quenched the violence of fire, escaped the edge of the sword, had weakness turned to strength, routed the enemy, and had children raised from the dead. Quite impressive, to say the least. The second half of Hebrews 11 describes others who were tortured, flogged, jeered, chained, put into prison, stoned, and sawed in two. "All these were approved through their faith, but they did not receive what was promised" (v. 39). The first set of faithful saints gained what was promised, while the second set of faithful saints did not get what was promised. The question that we ask ourselves is, what was promised, and why did some receive it and others didn't? This is no small matter. Many years ago two young boys in our church were diagnosed with leukemia. Both were named Tim. One survived and one didn't. What are we to make of such situations?

The subject of promise is what determines boldness. When we read that some received the promise, we need to understand that these were temporal promises that were given. For example, David on occasion was promised victory over an enemy. When victory came, it could be said that he gained what was promised. Those who didn't receive what was promised were all who died without experiencing the heavenly city because this was not a temporal promise but an eternal one. People of great faith know that many difficulties are to be faced in this life. Some may escape and some may not, but we will all be taken to the new heavens and the new Earth. Peter reminds us in his second epistle: "But based on His promise, we wait for new heavens and a new earth, where righteousness will dwell" (2 Pet. 3:13). This is the same Peter who showed boldness before the religious and political leaders who threatened his life if he preached the gospel.

If you have been a believer for any length of time and have never shared your faith, you don't understand the gospel. I didn't say you are not saved; I simply said that you probably hold to a western jesus. You have your ticket punched and are on your way to heaven, but that truth has not impacted your witness. The gospel isn't just about you or me but about those who have yet to hear.

The Gospel Makes Forgiving Others Not an Option

> *Then he knelt down and cried out with a loud*
> *voice, "Lord, do not charge them with this sin!"*
> *And saying this, he fell asleep.*
>
> Acts 7:60

Forgiveness is one of the most difficult things to do whether we are believers or unbelievers. We have all been the subject of gossip, sarcasm, or mistreatment at some time. Many still hold onto bitterness because of a father or mother who spoke harsh words. Some remain angry at a coworker who was wrongly promoted, the anger and hurt refreshed at each pay period when the "undeserving" coworker gets a bigger slice of the financial pie.

Paul tells us in Colossians 3 that we are to forgive just as we have been forgiven. Let me tell you why forgiveness is so difficult. When we can't forgive, it is because deep down we believe that we had fewer sins that needed to be forgiven at the cross than those who have offended us. By nature we see ourselves as just a little bit better. The West contributes to this kind of thinking. The exaltation of self is big business for America, and believers have fallen for it in a major way.

If we can't forgive, it is because we really don't understand the gospel. The gospel is all about forgiveness. We are told in Romans 3:22–23: "That is, God's righteousness through faith in Jesus Christ, to all who believe, since there is no distinction. For all have sinned and fall short of the glory of God." Note carefully that there is no difference—all have sinned. There is a level playing field at the cross. When we really understand how much we have been forgiven, then forgiveness flows more freely to others who have deeply hurt us.

Stephen, rather than being bitter toward those who stoned him, requested that this not be laid to their account. How could he draw so deeply from God's grace to forgive at such a time? He understood the gospel as it is revealed in Scripture. He conducted his life and faced death in a manner worthy of the gospel.

If we were to judge ourselves by our own standards, we wouldn't make it. To illustrate, take the following tests. There is no one watching, no grades will be given, and you can grade your own paper.

1. Have you ever honked at someone in front of you because they didn't move when the light turned green, but got upset a week later when someone honked at you because you didn't move when the light turned green?

2. Have you ever secretly rejoiced when your enemy got sick or in an accident and said to yourself, "This is God's judgment"? But when you were sick or in an accident, it was Satan attacking you.

3. Have you ever been upset because no one called you when you were sick, but soon realized that you rarely, if ever, call to see how someone is doing?

4. Have you ever told someone, "You're defensive and really have no excuse for what you did," but soon find yourself in a similar set of circumstances trying to explain your actions and then getting upset because your accuser said you were defensive?

5. Have you ever been critical of someone's poor performance and then wondered why people don't cut you some slack when your performance is poor?

6. Have you ever wanted to justify your actions because you knew there were extenuating circumstances that, if known, would help people understand, but when others try to justify their actions, you say they are making up excuses?

7. Have you ever yelled at someone in order to tell them to calm down?

8. Have you ever been furious because someone invaded your privacy, but later enjoyed reading someone else's diary without permission?

9. Have you ever been angered because the bumper sticker on the car in front of you showed the fish symbol with Darwin written on the inside, while your bumper sticker says, "God will make a monkey out of Darwin"?

10. Have you ever felt that others were hypocritical?

We're a strange breed, aren't we? Can you see that if we judged ourselves by our own standard, we would be found wanting. We would come up short. To live with an unforgiving heart is to miss out on life in a big way. When we understand the gospel in its greater context, it will impact our understanding of forgiveness.

To Understand the Gospel Is to Have Peace

He sent the message to the sons of Israel,
proclaiming the good news of peace through
Jesus Christ—He is Lord of all.

Acts 10:36

Peace I leave with you. My peace I give to you.
I do not give to you as the world gives.
Your heart must not be troubled or fearful.

John 14:27

Perhaps there is no place that a western gospel appears in all its shallowness more than when the subject of peace surfaces. We are promised long life in the West. We are promised a carefree life in the West. Medicine and technology are the gods who make such promises. Here again the Christian falls prey to such anemic guarantees.

There are two types of peace found in the New Testament. Romans 5:1 tells us we have peace with God through our Lord Jesus Christ. This means that through the gospel we have been made right with God. We were enemies, but we now have been reconciled to God: "Therefore, no condemnation now exists for those in Christ Jesus" (Rom. 8:1). Simply put, we are now on our way to heaven. However, because of this great truth we should also experience the second peace talked about—the peace of God as mentioned in Philippians 4:7. The western culture in which we are immersed destroys such peace. There is a standard for good looks in the West; if you don't measure up, then low self-esteem (a nonbiblical term) sets in. We are reminded to fear everything. There are health scares, financial fears, looks to worry about, and the never-ending saga of trying to keep up with the Joneses. Moving next to the Smiths will not solve the problem.

The western mind feeds off of worry generated by a culture with a false bottom. The midlife crisis seems to be a major player in our western culture. The United States keeps accurate records regarding the life expectancy of its people. For the sake of argument let's say the average person in America can expect to live to be eighty. This means that when we reach forty, we have hit the midpoint. There is now more sand at the bottom of the hourglass than at the top, and we realize that life is half over. Suppose you lived in a culture where people only live to be about forty, but they had no statistics on life expectancy. When would you have your midlife crisis? When should you begin to worry? Suppose you lived in a culture where people live to be one hundred but there are no statistics on life expectancy. How would you know when to have a midlife crisis? Or let's add another scenario. Suppose you could find a culture or group of people who would live forever, where would the midpoint be? If I'm not mistaken, our gospel promises us eternal life, which begins not when we die but the moment we believe. Since there is no midpoint in eternal life, why do we as believers have a midlife crisis? The answer is simple. We have a western jesus. We don't understand the gospel. Paul, unlike many of us, had great peace when he said, "For me, living is Christ and dying is gain" (Phil. 1:21).

Genuine peace comes from knowing we have been forgiven. Many of us walk around with a heavy load of guilt because of past failures and sins. Here again we should draw from the example of Paul, who admitted in his first letter to Timothy that he was chief among sinners. He openly admitted that he was a blasphemer and a persecutor. He then shared that he had received grace and mercy. He was not plagued by his past. When we can't seem to forgive ourselves, we are falling back into a works righteousness. Our natural religious bent of trying to atone for our sins begins to creep in. Go to the cross and, as Martyn Lloyd Jones used to say, preach the gospel to yourself daily.

The Gospel Sets Us Free from Want

The wild world of the West is on a never-ending pursuit to draw us into the clutches of materialism. A true understanding of the gospel and all its implications will set us free from such desires. In 2 Corinthians 8:9 we read Paul's words regarding the gospel and how it relates to natural wealth: "For you know the grace of our Lord Jesus Christ: although He was rich, for your sake He became poor, so that by His poverty you might become rich." We are told here that we have become rich; but if we are not careful, the western jesus will convince us that the riches are material. Paul is explaining the fact that to have Christ is to have it all. We are rich in our spiritual wealth and future inheritance.

Can you see how western thinking has diluted the impact of the gospel and made us discontented? Being envious over what someone else owns shows that we believe that what they have is of more value than being content in Christ. We show the idols of our heart. A few years ago I was in Latvia and met a sweet godly woman who lived in rather poor housing, at least by western standards. She pulled me aside and said that a particular Christian organization wanted her to come to the United States for a leadership meeting. She was told that she would be staying in the Hyatt Regency in the Washington, D.C. area. She was appalled at what such luxury cost and told me that she in good conscience could not see money wasted like that when she could stay in someone's home. I counseled her to accept this as a gift from God and enjoy herself, but deep down I envied the strength of her love for God over the good life.

The Replacement Gospel

The above heading has probably signaled to you that I am getting ready to launch into some vitriolic diatribe about a shallow gospel. That is not where I'm headed. I do, however, want the reader to see that the aforementioned realities of the true gospel have been replaced. Ever since I have been a believer, I have noticed, and been guilty of, the evangelizing of other *believers.* Since they already have the gospel, we preach our favorite new discovery. Western believers have a never-ending array of formulas and theological systems that we think everyone else must adhere to in order to find real joy in the Lord. We push the gospel of homeschooling, the gospel of premillennialism or amillennialism, the gospel of counseling technique (which is always some new way of getting into a person's soul), the gospel of weight loss, the gospel of biblical eating, the gospel of worship styles, the gospel of fellowship groups, and the gospel of Christians and politics. (Now is there anyone left whom I have not offended?)

There is an interesting parallel between Christians who have found a spiritual formula that has supposedly changed their life and health-food devotees who have a recipe for longevity. Both usually prove to be nothing more than a placebo.

Anyone living in a western culture has been exposed to dramatic claims about all aspects of our health. Our western culture is formula-driven for nearly everything. Like snake oil salesmen, there is a cure for every ill. The dialogue usually goes something like this:

"George, I think that one of the reasons you feel tired all the time is due to your eating habits."

"Tom, I'm inclined to disagree with you. I get up every morning and have a bowl of fresh fruit, a light salad for lunch, and organically fed fish for dinner topped with sesame seeds shipped in from Zanzibar."

"Yes, that all sounds great, George, but if you have the morning fruit before you exercise, it turns into protein, which then turns into glucose, which when mixed with the salad for lunch dissolves and slows down your metabolism, which then converts what you eat into trans fats, which is nothing more than raw sewage, which nullifies the value of the fiber in the fruit. And if the seeds from Zanzibar were not first sun dried in Arizona and eaten three hours before you go to bed, unless of course you live west of the Mississippi, then your digestive tract works overtime, canceling the value of the organically fed fish, and in essence means that the net result of your daily intake is equivalent to downing four Big Macs, three hot fudge sundaes, and a Snickers bar. No wonder you're so tired."

Not to be outdone, the western jesus makes equal claims in the spiritual realm. The dialogue usually goes something like this:

"Sally, I think the reason you don't feel close to God is directly related to your spiritual diet."

"Judy, I'm inclined to disagree with you. I rise early every morning, read the Word for thirty minutes, and pray for thirty minutes. At noon I meditate on the Word, and in the evening I memorize two verses of Scripture."

"Yes, that all sounds great, Sally, but if you don't confess all known sin and cleanse each room in your house of demons, then this nullifies the value of your prayers and actually turns them into tools of the enemy to make you spiritually lethargic, not to mention the fact that your time in prayer must precede your time in the Word, otherwise the Word will have no power and will be as dry as dust, which cancels the value of the Word, and in essence, means the net result of your daily spiritual intake is equivalent to sleeping till noon and then gorging on three hours of soap operas. No wonder you feel spiritually depleted."

The western jesus is a formula jesus. He is a legalist and specializes in keeping you frustrated with rules and doctrinal minutiae. Every difficulty in your life can be readily explained because you didn't keep the rules perfectly. Job's friends were disciples of a western jesus. He suffered because there must have been some sin in his life. There are countless millions throughout the ages who have never heard of a protein, a carbohydrate, or the metabolic process but have listened to their bodies and have eaten sensibly and lived long productive lives. There are an equal number of believers who have never heard the words *justification*, *propitiation*, or *sanctification* but have listened to the indwelling Spirit and have gone on to live rich victorious lives in Christ.

It saddens me when formulas are tossed around, if not thrown at each other. For example, here is one that is floating around the church these days. If I say that I am a sinner saved by grace, I may be rebuked and told that we are no longer sinners but saints. The truth is that both of these expressions can be defended by Scripture. If the former helps you see yourself as a sinner who is now saved, then rejoice. If the latter helps you focus on being a saint, then rejoice. But, for the love of God, do not tell someone they can't have a victorious life if they don't hold to your favorite expression.

In the West we tend to campaign for those things that have really blessed our lives, and we are so passionate that we have trouble believing that anyone could be blessed if they do not practice what we are enjoying. These things then become the gospel—the way, the truth, and the life.

I have experienced a continuous flow of this-will-change-your-life preaching. A consistent barrage of new Christian how-tos pass in review, and we are told that this new thing will revolutionize our lives. This is a replacement gospel.

In 1976 a wonderful African American lady started attending our church. She had just come to know the Lord by listening to Jay Vernon McGee on the radio, who encouraged his listeners to get into a good

Bible-teaching church. We were just getting started when Rose entered our lives. As I learned about her life, I realized she had been through some very tough times. She never got past the eighth grade and would never hold a high school diploma in her hands. But Jesus was now very real to her and, as a new believer, she had great confidence in him. Rose is now in her eighties. She is more than a powerful witness. Christ fills her life and she reads only the King James Bible. She spends long periods in prayer and in the Word and is saturated with the love of Christ. To be frank, I envy her consistently joyful spirit. I have visited her in the hospital on three different occasions, and she typically says something like this: "Pastor Mike, I done told all the nurses and da doctors about Jeezus, but they just don't know him. Would you talk to them when they come in?"

I have often wondered how much theology Rose has packed away. She never seems to have any other agenda but "Jeezus." She has never preached to me the latest counseling technique or homeschooling curriculum. I don't know what she feels about reformed theology or if she knows what it is. I do know this—she has a profound love for Christ that has never been diluted by other gospels.

Let's go back and look at the life of Jesus for a moment. How much did he expect those he encountered with the gospel to believe? When he met Nicodemus, he gave bad news to a good man: "You must be born again" (John 3:7). Being a Pharisee will not save you. When He met the woman at the well, he gave good news to a bad woman: "In fact, the water I will give him will become a well of water springing up within him for eternal life" (John 4:14). To the blind man, he asked if he believed on the Son of God. The blind man responded by saying he didn't know who he was. Jesus revealed himself as the Son of God. The blind man responded by saying, "'I believe, Lord!' . . . and he worshiped Him" (John 9:38). Just prior to the raising of Lazarus, Jesus spoke to Mary and Martha, the sisters of Lazarus, and said: "'I am the resurrection and the life. The one who believes in Me, even if he dies, will live. Everyone who lives and believes in Me will never die—ever. Do you believe this?' 'Yes, Lord,' she told Him, 'I believe You are the Messiah, the Son of God, who was to come into the world'" (John 11:25–27). You might have noticed the simplicity in each encounter, yet the same message was not given. Nicodemus saw Jesus as the person who could give you new birth. The woman at the well understood his omniscience when she said: "Come, see a man who told me everything I ever did! Could this be the Messiah?" (John 4:29). The blind man saw him as the Son of God, and the sisters of Lazarus understood him as the resurrection and the life. They each witnessed a different facet of his divine nature and saw him as the Savior. He was not a doctrine or a theological concept. He was not a creed, statement of faith, or confession. He was the Son of the living God. This simplicity not only brings us into the kingdom, it is all that is needed to live in the kingdom. While theology and doctrine are orthodox expressions of what we believe about him that may help us to have a deeper understanding, genuine fellowship in Christ comes only through meditation upon his Word and a consistent obedience to his will.

Here again we return to one of our subthemes. We have too much time on our hands. Issues that we feel passionate about in the West are luxuries. By *luxury* I mean that we have the luxury to sit around and debate these issues that would never even surface in other cultures. The older I get, the more issues I dump into the category of "Each one must be fully convinced in his own mind" (Rom. 14:5). This is not some kind of compromise; I just believe that we are very dogmatic where Scripture is often silent or unclear. We need to ask ourselves if we are more passionate about homeschooling or prophetic scenarios than we are about the gospel that Paul passionately proclaimed. By the way, I have no problem with homeschooling, different methods of worship, or prophetic scenarios, unless they become the gospel.

CHAPTER 9

A Western Jesus and the Ultimate Contradiction

IN ORDER TO BE an effective witness, we need to know something about the culture in which we live. The gospel will always be the power of God unto salvation, but how it is dispensed may change with culture and time. Paul reasoned with the Jews out of the Scripture, but he reasoned with the Gentiles out of natural revelation. The western world of the twenty-first century needs the church to bring its gospel to their rescue, but we first must know what we are up against.

Worldviews and new philosophies incessantly blow across the intellectual landscape seeking public recognition in the marketplace of ideas. Such winds of thought rarely bend the ear of society, but those that command attention enter with gale-force velocity. Postmodern thought is no exception. It not only captures the attention of academia, but also chairs nearly every department from public schools to postgraduate institutions. It has crept into law, medicine, education, technology, and the most critical disciplines of life. The term *postmodern* is very elusive and very western.

Postmodernism is a worldview that denies the concept of absolute truth, craves community, questions authority, and practices toleration. According to postmodernism, the validity of an experience or statement is generally determined by its perceived authenticity rather than the logic behind it.

I have watched a significant change develop in the thinking patterns of emerging generations. No longer do people have a set of values, either ethical or moral, that direct their culture as a whole. Instead, whatever one feels is right for himself is right. Moral absolutes are passé. No one can claim he has the truth because truth has solved nothing.

Postmodernists are not to be put into the category of some cult. They don't have some charismatic leader or claim divine revelation. There is no headquarters passing down the next assignment or subscription to a certain set of doctrines. They don't knock on doors or wear a uniform. They can be Christian or non-Christian. What postmodernists generally have in common is a sincere desire to be heard as opposed to always having to listen. They don't bow to the gods of facts, figures, and statistics, but they tend to be more relational. A common question a postmodernist would ask is, "Do you care about me and what I think, or do you have an agenda that you want me to follow?" Jesus listened with compassion and saw people as without a guide to care for them and lead them: "When He saw the crowds, He felt compassion for them, because they were weary and worn out, like sheep without a shepherd" (Matt. 9:36). Today our society also seems hopeless and helpless, more than I have ever witnessed in my lifetime.

The Renaissance and Enlightenment periods may pale in comparison with the global impact of postmodern thought. Having pastored for nearly thirty-two years, I have developed a genuine heart for people who find themselves trapped in a false belief system. Jesus said, "Then you will know the truth, and the truth will set you free" (John 8:32). The clear implication is that if you don't know the truth, then you are in bondage. Jesus had a sincere concern for those who believed a lie, and we should follow his example by caring enough to rescue them.

I spend a great deal of time with the younger generation. They keep me honest and force me to realize that my generation is not "the way, the truth, and the life." I am not pressured to compromise my biblical worldview, but I am challenged to see with an eye of compassion why so many are disillusioned, both with Christianity and the secular worldview. Unfortunately, the church sometimes isolates itself from new thought and points a condemning finger at those who have fallen prey to world-system thinking. (The term *world system* comes from the Greek word *kosmos* meaning "order." It is normally used in Scripture to define a system of thinking that is contrary to biblical revelation.) We have become an island unto ourselves, fearful of rubbing shoulders with those who do not share our view of life. A western jesus encourages us to avoid those of a different stripe. We separate from the younger generation and declare with rigid authority how wrong they are.

Emerging postmodern generations are driving their stake in the ground and are claiming an otherwise unexplored piece of intellectual real estate. They present an honest assessment of life and the history of thought. This new breed of thinkers has set up shop in the world of education, technology, and science and does not readily accept the worldview of previous generations. As believers in Christ, we must be aware of postmodern thought and those who question truth at every turn and even wonder if truth exists. They ask hard questions and turn their backs on clichés and cookie-cutter responses to the difficult issues of life. Being somewhat philosophical in their mind-set, postmodernists will challenge answers that have historically proven to be threadbare. What the western church has been hiding for years is now out of the closet, giving soft answers to hard questions.

Postmoderns are frustrated because of what I will refer to throughout this chapter as the *ultimate contradiction*, which simply stated is: man is increasing exponentially in knowledge but the inner quality of life never changes. The postmodernist has therefore rightly diagnosed the problem but has arrived at a false conclusion—surmising that if truth and knowledge are designed to improve life, and life is not improving, then truth must not be absolute, but relative. The purpose of this chapter is to explore the logic behind postmodern thinking, expose the fatal error which, when corrected, is the key to solving the ultimate contradiction, and help the western church get on board before the train leaves the station.

The Logic behind Postmodern Thinking

The mind-set behind any new invention, medical discovery, or pursuit of leisure is to make life on planet Earth compatible with human desire. We want life to be pleasurable, conflict free, and without difficulty. Thus, we pursue knowledge with a vengeance because we believe it is the gateway to a better life. We believe knowledge will become our servant, plot our course, and fulfill our dreams. We will call upon it during times of distress, and it will come to our rescue and deliver us from trouble.

Knowledge is good, and we spend billions each year on research and development in pursuit of it. Many look forward to the day when we will possess all knowledge, thus making mankind sovereign in every area of life. But there is a fly in the ointment, a cruel twist in the logic of it all. Satan keeps the mind in bondage to human reasoning and offers compelling arguments to believe a lie. "You are of your father the Devil, and you want to carry out your father's desires. He was a murderer from the beginning and has not stood in the truth, because there is no truth in him. When he tells a lie, he speaks from his own nature, because he is a liar and the father of liars" (John 8:44). Satan is the author of the ultimate contradiction. History shows that the problems of life have increased with the increase in knowledge. How can this be, since knowledge is supposed to solve problems?

Though I am not an expert in the history of thought, I can think of no generation that has distanced itself from previous generations as postmoderns have from their predecessors. They have become distrustful and are a generation that wants to experience reality. "Don't tell me about truth, show me" has become their cry. Since knowledge is designed to solve problems, and we are increasing in knowledge at an exponential rate, then why isn't life working? Why are homes shattered and relationships broken? Why is divorce so prevalent when we have a glut of marriage counselors? Why is white-collar crime on the rise? What is the culprit—ignorance or education?

Science penetrates the microworld of the atom and the macroworld of the universe, but such knowledge never seems to bring us closer to world peace, not to mention peace within our own hearts. Technology advances daily, but who leaves the office earlier as the result of a faster computer? As C. S. Lewis said, "Education merely makes man a more clever devil" (Dennis McCallum, *The Death of Truth*, Bethany House Publishers, 1996, 242). Just ask anyone who worked for Enron or Worldcom. Education stole their retirement. So what good are truth and knowledge if our problems seemingly increase with an increase in these wells of wisdom? We have either not yet arrived at truth, which perhaps is just around the corner, or truth is not absolute but relative. As pilgrims, we must be aware of this type of thinking or we will make little headway in reaching the lost.

Two Boxes

Humanly speaking, postmodern logic and reasoning is good. However, is the reasoning of man adequate in solving the problem? I want you to imagine a large box with the label *human wisdom* printed on the outside. This box represents all the truth that man has discovered throughout the past five thousand years of recorded human history. Hereafter this concept will be referred to as Box 1. Opinions and hypotheses don't belong in this box, only proven truth. In one sense life has improved, but in another sense nothing has changed. Just consider all the vast sums of knowledge benefiting man that we have learned in the realm of science. How could anyone deny that we live better than our forefathers? Look at what we have done with education. Masses of people have been educated and have sought to uncover new truths. Technology is beyond comprehension. What previously took days now takes seconds, thanks to computers. Because of medical advances, people are living longer and diseases are being cured. All of these disciplines fit in Box 1. They are wonderful advances, but they never seem to scratch the internal itch. We seem to be on a treadmill that moves faster with every increase in human wisdom, but as with all treadmills, there is no advance no matter how fast the RPMs. Could this be what God meant when he gave Daniel the following command? "But you, Daniel, keep these words secret and seal the book until the time of the end. Many will roam about, and knowledge will increase" (Dan. 12:4).

There is a second box labeled *divine wisdom,* which we will call Box 2. This box removes the veil of confusion and unlocks the mystery behind this ultimate contradiction. This is the box containing biblical revelation. (General or natural revelation is how God manifests himself through the design and order of the universe [see Ps. 19:1–2]. Biblical revelation is how God reveals his personal character to genuine believers.) God now enters the picture and sheds his light on the subject at hand. If you are postmodern in your thinking, please don't tune out at this crucial point. I think you will find that the Scriptures agree with much of what your generation has discovered—namely, that an increase in knowledge does not solve man's problems.

The beauty of Scripture lies in its consistent revelation from Old Testament to New Testament. There are many threads of truth that run parallel to one another throughout God's Word. The purpose of biblical revelation is to take man beyond *human wisdom* into a world of *divine wisdom* that he would otherwise know nothing about. Telescopes and microscopes can never peer into this world. It is hidden from man's natural senses and is only revealed by God himself. In addition, progressive truth in Scripture is not only consistent but unfolds greater degrees of revelation from Genesis to Revelation. (Progressive truth in Scripture is the slow revelation of a truth or subject matter, as we move from one end of the Bible to the other. For example, certain truths about marriage are revealed in the early chapters of Genesis and are built upon in other books, culminating in Ephesians 5.)

Progressive Truth about the Nature of Man

Contrary to popular opinion and wishful thinking, man has an evil nature, which we as believers refer to as *depravity.* This is clear not only from Scripture but from observation and experience. All people have an equal capacity to do wrong. Just prior to the flood, we read these words in Genesis 6:5: "The LORD saw that man's wickedness was widespread on the earth and that every scheme his mind thought of was nothing but evil all the time." The world had become so evil and violent that God destroyed it with a flood. Just after the flood, we find these words in Genesis 8:21: "When the LORD smelled the pleasing aroma, He said to Himself, 'I will never again curse the ground because of man, even though man's inclination is evil from his youth. And I will never again strike down every living thing as I have done.'" The Scriptures reveal in the early stages of civilization that man has a heart problem.

If you and I were living in approximately 2500 BC, we would predict that as time progresses, man would learn more about education, technology, science, and medicine. This would improve life and eventually usher in a utopian society. If the Scriptures were based on human reason, then progressive revelation would reveal and predict that man would eventually solve his heart problem and the world would live happily ever after. Returning to Scripture and fast-forwarding to about 600 BC, we come to the book of Jeremiah with joyful anticipation that man is getting better than the first diagnosis pronounced in Genesis. But the prophet Jeremiah gives no slack and says, "The heart is more deceitful than anything else and desperately sick—who can understand it?" (Jer. 17:9). This doesn't sound too promising. We now find that our hearts are incurably wicked. Does this mean that all of us are murderers? No. It means that we have a sinful nature that we can't seem to overcome. We are angry, bitter, fearful, resentful, hateful, jealous, and so on. Sometimes we loathe ourselves because we can't cure this disease of the soul. Perhaps if we move away from the Old Testament, we will find some good news about ourselves in the New Testament. By advancing six hundred years, certainly man will have improved his lot in life and be a more refined and caring person.

Let's read the words from the gentle, loving Jesus found in Mark 7:18–23, "'Are you also as lacking in understanding? Don't you realize that nothing going into a man from the outside can defile him? For it doesn't go into his heart but into the stomach and is eliminated.' (As a result, He made all foods clean.) Then He said, 'What comes out of a person—that defiles him. For from within, out of people's hearts, come evil thoughts, sexual immoralities, thefts, murders, adulteries, greed, evil actions, deceit, lewdness, stinginess, blasphemy, pride, and foolishness. All these evil things come from within and defile a person.'" More bad news about man's heart! Basic logic tells us this can't be true. Man is intelligent and has the capacity to learn from past mistakes. Certainly as he studies history he can see the error of his way and persuade himself to do better. Such midcourse corrections have failed miserably with the test of time. The world, however, was a mess in the days of Christ, much like it was during the days of Noah.

Perhaps the apostle Paul, who comes after Christ, can predict a better future for man. Paul was a highly educated individual. Certainly he can introduce some reason to this otherwise insane assessment of man's evil heart and conclude that future generations will extricate themselves from this mess. Let's see what he predicts: "But know this: difficult times will come in the last days. For people will be lovers of self, lovers of money, boastful, proud, blasphemers, disobedient to parents, ungrateful, unholy, unloving, irreconcilable, slanderers, without self-control, brutal, without love for what is good, traitors, reckless, conceited, lovers of pleasure rather than lovers of God" (2 Tim. 3:1–4). Keep in mind that Paul is looking down the pipeline of the future. He didn't go with conventional wisdom but with biblical revelation. Paul didn't listen to human wisdom but to divine wisdom. He made no prediction that human knowledge was the key to solving world problems. Paul was consistently bold, and he prophetically proclaimed what his biblical predecessors had said. Who could possibly argue that the Scriptures do not have the upper hand? In the United States, a western jesus has fallen for the worldview that we will improve. The church is trying to lift itself up by its own bootstraps.

Moses, Jeremiah, Jesus, and Paul all agree with the postmodern assessment of human wisdom—it hasn't changed the human heart. The Bible would be an unreliable source if man's condition had improved over time by applying human wisdom. But Scripture never changes course, nor does it apologize for its harsh predictions. It is relentless in revealing man's condition. He can't fix it. He's stuck. Yet a western jesus promises a new life. We have become postmodern in our own thinking. How many believers actually consult Scripture for direction? Pop psychology is woven into the fabric of the western church, and to pull the string may unravel the whole pattern. We have been drawn away by the world around us so that clear thinking from a biblical mind-set is all but a thing of the past.

Cosmetic Perjury

Man has learned about human wisdom for centuries. Does it work? Sure it works, but not on the human heart. Human wisdom improves man cosmetically, but it will never fix one's heart. All of psychiatry and psychology will never fix the evil nature of man. There will always be wars and rumors of wars as long as man occupies this globe. "You are going to hear of wars and rumors of wars. See that you are not alarmed, because these things must take place, but the end is not yet" (Matt. 24:6). Human wisdom will give you a facelift. Divine wisdom, on the other hand, will give you a new heart.

Is Scripture true regarding the condition of man as it relates to self-correction? By looking at society, has man through human reason, wisdom, and logic been able to quell the evil forces of his inner being? The postmodernist might say that he is civil, and if more people were like him, this world would be a better place. Has he ever hated anyone? Ever been in a jealous rage even if outward signs were not present? Ever had an evil thought, told a lie, or gossiped? This is our nature. You can clean up a pig and bring it into your house, but as soon as the pig escapes, it will return to the muck and mire from which it came. It is the same with man.

Postmodernists get the big picture. They have looked at life, studied history, and made an assessment that humanity is in the same condition that it has always been. However, though their assessment is true, their ultimate conclusion is false. They keep operating from human wisdom, which restricts their view of life. Truth is in fact absolute, but applying human wisdom to the human heart is like putting a bandage on a fatal disease. Human wisdom is cosmetic and will make life a lot easier, but it will not change the inner man. If we as believers don't understand this, how can we put our arm around the shoulder of this culture and lead it to the gospel truth?

Paul was quite astute to what he faced in his day. He tells us in 1 Corinthians 1:22, "The Jews ask for signs and the Greeks seek wisdom." Why such a statement? He was revealing the nature of different forms of thought, even though their message didn't change. "But we preach Christ crucified, a stumbling block to the Jews and foolishness to the Gentiles" (1 Cor. 1:23). Paul was concerned with the thinking of those at Corinth and sent them a letter in response to his understanding of their logic. Much of what Paul wrote to the churches was written to help correct some type of problem in their reasoning. God recorded this for us, knowing that we would face similar problems. He knew the power of the world to shape our thinking and wean us from biblical truth. The church today is so far removed from a scriptural mind-set that the very issues we are to set straight have made us crooked in our thinking.

Destination Nowhere

As an aside, I believe there is something of great import that needs to be inserted at this point. Though I hope to write on this in the future, it will suffice at this time to give you a taste of what I call the *ultimate apologetic* or defense of the faith. In order for scientists to label something as scientific, it must be observable and repeatable. If it doesn't measure up to these stringent criteria, then it fails to be a scientific truth. The following three verses that are woven through this book reveal a most interesting observable and repeatable truth about the nature of fallen man. Human reason and logic, however, says this can't be. That's what makes them so significant. Man so desperately wants to prove these verses are wrong and thus battles with them daily, but he always loses. It should not be observable and repeatable that "the eyes of man are never satisfied" (Prov. 27:20 KJV). Our quest to be satisfied is promised by every product on the market. "Fully satisfied or your money back" is the slogan of Madison Avenue. However, one year later that same promise is applied to a new and improved version of last year's product that claimed full satisfaction. It should not be observable and repeatable that the heart of man is incurably wicked (see Jer. 17:9). He has been waiting a long time to fix this, but

Scripture lays claim to the observable and repeatable fact that he can't. It should not be observable and repeatable that God will take man in his own craftiness (see 1 Cor. 3:19). This does not fit into our western plan for life. Our craftiness will in fact set the course for a golden age to soon make its grand appearance. But God will not be mocked and it is observable and repeatable on a daily basis that when man declares his independence from God based on his crafty ways, he will in fact reap what he sows. Just look around and make a careful observation of humanity's craftiness and where it has taken us. Tomorrow's headlines will testify to man's depravity and so will the headlines the day after that.

Nothing accents human wisdom more than technology, and nothing accents technology more than the field of travel. Speeding up travel is designed to make life less stressful. Waiting breeds impatience, and we think that getting from point A to point B faster should solve this feeling of angst. Let's see if we can prove the futility of human reason by something we observe daily. Two hundred years ago if a man missed a stage coach and was informed by the ticket agent that the next one would be in two weeks, he would rant and rave and curse a blue streak as he marched back home. His grandson, however, has the benefit of technology in his favor and travels in trains. He heads down to the station and finds he just missed it. He inquires as to when the next one will leave. The ticket agent tells him that the next train will leave in two days. Upon hearing such news, he rants and raves and curses a blue streak as he heads for home. His son is most privileged because he lives in the jet age. He heads to the airport and just misses his flight. The lady behind the counter assures him he can get on the next flight that leaves in two hours. He rants and raves and curses a blue streak as he heads for a Starbucks to get a café latté while he reads the latest *Sports Illustrated* and watches a movie on his laptop. His son, however, does not have to put up with such inconvenience. He rolls out of bed and sits in his swivel chair while he downloads work from the office. His computer registers that the download will take two minutes. He rants and raves and curses a blue streak about how slow his computer is and plays a video game on his cell phone to kill time and relieve the boredom. Technology has shrunk the time from two weeks to two days to two hours to two minutes but failed to shrink the anger and impatience of the human heart. Ah yes, "the heart is incurable."

Impatience is part of the fallen nature of man and cannot be corrected by technology. History shows that the anger that accompanies impatience keeps pace with every new discovery, no matter how much time it saves. Why? Because "Death and Destruction are never satisfied, and neither are the eyes of man" (Prov. 27:20 niv). The heart reaction remains the same. We just can't fix it. This is observable and repeatable. These are fixed laws that man refuses to accept. The prophets of old testified to these truths. The church must not be led astray. This is where we help the world see its error.

In the cosmetic nature of education, much like technology, education has its place. Being educated is certainly better than remaining ignorant. Education helps us navigate through the changing tides of life, but it promises far more than it can deliver because it is separate from biblical revelation. The familiar promise that "what the mind can conceive, it can achieve" is nothing more than a pipe dream from the positive-thinking crowd. Educating our society to believe that "I'm the master of my fate and the captain of my soul" only tells man that he is sovereign over all. As long as he thinks he is in charge because he is highly educated, new problems will continue to arise. However, such futility only spurs on the academic community. Education gurus surface like tulips in spring, waving the banner of "salvation through education."

In the field of medicine, I delight in the fact that I live in an age of penicillin, aspirin, laser surgery, novocaine, anesthesia, and MRIs. What I don't delight in is the belief that we will overcome death through the marvels of medicine. Biblical revelation tells me that medicine is only a cosmetic for the aging process, which may keep me on this planet a little longer than my forefathers but will never overcome the wages of sin, which is death (see Rom. 3:23). Cosmetics do wonders for the face but nothing for the soul. We see the believer falling for the world's wisdom.

Finally, the cosmetic nature of science is appealing because it deals with objective, measurable truth. Science itself is the study of knowledge gained through experimentation and experience. Human wisdom limits man's application of science. He will apply scientific methods in areas that lead to futility. Space exploration is wonderful if we are seeking to explore the greatness of God and his creation. But if we are spending billions trying to figure out how the universe came into being, we could save lots of money by consulting the Bible, which says, "In the beginning God created the heavens and the earth" (Gen. 1:1). The western jesus has us believing there is life on other planets, and evolutionary thought is making headway in the evangelical western church.

The world forever promises a new invention or technological breakthrough, but we will forever remain in the desert with our souls parched from the dry, dusty winds of empty promises. Human wisdom is a veneer covering the pain, making it look like the pain is not there. That's what cosmetics do best. They cover the wrinkles and age spots of life. They restore a youthful look although the body knows better. The cosmetic nature of human wisdom only masks the problem. It makes things appear better than they are. A large home and a nice car may be nothing more than an attempt to camouflage the emptiness in our soul. Is it any wonder that people feel they have been lied to? This is what I love about postmodern thinkers. They are brutally honest with their assessment of life and they are holding my generation's feet to the fire for lying to them.

Man has such a confidence in himself that he clings to the hope that the next generation will pull it all together. How many times have we heard a commencement speech or political address seasoned with positive rhetoric about the hopeful future ahead for our nation and the world because man with his great intellect will eventually harness it for world peace? How many times have we heard the words "You're the generation upon which the future rests"? Countless speeches have been given over the centuries with this same theme, only to find that nothing changes—not even the speeches.

The Gospel and Human Wisdom

When a postmodernist is confronted with the gospel or the claims of Christ, he immediately puts this truth in Box 1, human wisdom, and sees it as just another claim that is not absolute and is therefore irrelevant.

This is a fatal mistake. Jesus doesn't fit into human wisdom. He is, by his very nature, Box 2—the embodiment of divine wisdom. He said, "I am the way, the truth, and the life. No one comes to the Father except through me" (John 14:6). He claims to be the truth. He is the revelation of all truth. In Colossians 2:3 Paul says, "In Him all the treasures of wisdom and knowledge are hidden."

It is a critical mistake to mix the two boxes or to apply them to a realm in which they are doomed to fail. For example, the absolute truth of biblical revelation was never intended to improve cosmetic issues in life. God has not revealed how to make a better microwave because he knows man is capable of discovering how to do this on his own. On the other hand, human wisdom was never intended to tackle the spiritual nature of man. Why? Because human wisdom is incapable of penetrating into the spiritual arena. The gap between the two boxes is infinite. Once we grasp this truth, then the ultimate contradiction is resolved. There remains no more confusion or frustration since we now have a divine perspective.

A western jesus proclaims a gospel of the good life, and his followers try to convince unbelievers that coming to Christ will solve all their problems. An unbeliever examines the Christian's life and finds that a believer also gets sick, loses his job, experiences financial trouble; thus he doesn't see any real difference from his own life. The Scriptures are quite clear that we don't come to Christ to get a bigger house or better job. We come to Christ to get healing in the soul, forgiveness of sin, and to be declared righteous.

How God Draws People to Himself

Every believer must be a student of how lost people think. New philosophies of life come and go. We need to be sensitive to the cultural mind-set of unbelievers and how they process truth, but more importantly, we must know what Scripture reveals about their minds. The issue is no longer modern or postmodern, atheistic or agnostic, religious or sacrilegious. It is God's infallible assessment of why man rejects truth. Knowing this, coupled with our understanding of postmodern thought, should give us the proper tools for reaching out with the gospel to this generation and to those that will follow. Romans 1:16–32 is one of the greatest revelations as it probes deeply into how man thinks in his natural, fallen state. This passage includes God's infallible argument regarding the downward spiral of man and civilization as we know it:

> For I am not ashamed of the gospel, because it is God's
> power for salvation to everyone who believes, first to the Jew,
> and also to the Greek. (Rom. 1:16)

Here, the apostle Paul, the author of Romans, explains that the gospel (good news) of Jesus Christ is the power of God that purchased our salvation. In this verse Paul tells us that the gospel is the power of God unto salvation. God's power to save is found in the good news of Christ as our liberator.

> For in it God's righteousness is revealed from faith to faith,
> just as it is written: The righteous will live by faith. (Rom. 1:17)

In the verse above, the righteous nature of God is revealed in the person of Christ. This is the righteousness that man needs in order to enter heaven. Man's righteousness is tainted with sin. Since sin will not be tolerated in heaven, we must enter clothed in another righteousness—the righteousness of Christ himself. This is given freely to all who believe in Christ.

The ultimate answer to the ultimate contradiction is found in the gospel. This is the good news that Christ came to set men free. We find a fascinating piece of revelation on how God draws man and why man resists. Through my many years of ministry, I have never seen Romans 1 effectively refuted by anyone. There is simply no way out. A person can be a sincere skeptic as he enters into the deep waters of Romans, but once he emerges, he will either stop being sincere about his condition or cease being a skeptic.

> For God's wrath is revealed from heaven against all godless-
> ness and unrighteousness of people who by their unrighteous-
> ness suppress the truth. (Rom. 1:18)

We now come to the pivotal verse of Romans 1. Our first insight into the darkened soul of man is found in this verse. He does not have a mind that is illuminated for understanding. First Corinthians 2:14 also describes man's condition: "But the natural man does not welcome what comes from God's Spirit, because it is foolishness to him; he is not able to know it since it is evaluated spiritually." It would be rare for anyone to push away truth that benefited him. People only suppress truth if it interferes with their pleasure. People resist the gospel because it will impact the nature of how they live. Pornography, lying, cheating, stealing, and adultery are dealt with in the gospel. You come to the gospel to be freed from this bondage. Jesus said, "This, then, is the judgment: the light has come into the world, and people loved darkness rather than the light because their deeds were evil" (John 3:19). Romans 1 reveals what we all know to be true about ourselves. Man will often accept vague and unreliable statistics when they affect his health or life expectancy and reject clear and unmistakable evidence when it affects his pleasure. A man's morality is dictated by his theology.

The postmodernist has a good, honest assessment of life. However, he sees a serious flaw in our society in providing the ultimate solution as it relates to human wisdom.

> Since what can be known about God is evident among them, because God has shown it to them. (Rom. 1:19)

The very nature of God has been revealed to man according to verse 19. Paul continues to play the role of prosecuting attorney. His case is airtight. Man's defense attorney will soon be out of breath. There will be no place to turn.

> From the creation of the world His invisible attributes, that is, His eternal power and divine nature, have been clearly seen, being understood through what He has made. As a result, people are without excuse. (Rom. 1:20)

The apostle Paul defines natural revelation in this verse. Those who suppress the truth of God's existence through pride of intellect and offer up so-called scientific proof that there is no God will be left without excuse. God will expose all logic, intellectual arguments, and reason on Judgment Day. God's creation reflects his existence. Natural revelation prepares the heart for biblical revelation, which is the Word of God. This is divine truth.

> For though they knew God, they did not glorify Him as God or show gratitude. Instead, their thinking became nonsense, and their senseless minds were darkened. (Rom. 1:21)

Paul is clear that these people at one time knew God or were aware of his existence. They were not thankful and refused to acknowledge his glory. This has led to a darkened heart and imaginations that are empty of spiritual reality. Man tries to fill in the blanks with New Age philosophies, Eastern religions, human achievement, and other theories. From here on, Scripture reveals both humanism and the moral depravity of man. They alternate, as one seems to give strength to the other.

> Claiming to be wise, they became fools and exchanged the glory of the immortal God for images resembling mortal man, birds, four-footed animals, and reptiles. (Rom. 1:22–23)

This is humanism—the ultimate in pride, when a man professes himself to be wiser than his Creator. As the downward spiral continues, man takes God's glory and gives it to his idols. This allows man to make a god in his image and to become whatever he wants the god to be. This god is fashioned after man's own thinking and plays out a role that allows man to do whatever he pleases. This god holds no one accountable. Sadly, the believer does this as well as the unbeliever. We often don't want to gather with believers or read Scripture because of what it may demand of us. God, however, will have the final word.

> Therefore God delivered them over in the cravings of their hearts to sexual impurity, so that their bodies were degraded among themselves [moral depravity]. They exchanged the truth of God for a lie, and worshiped and served something created [humanism] instead of the Creator, who is blessed forever. Amen. (Rom. 1:24–25)

This is the height of humanism, which is birthed from moral degrada-tion. Why would man exchange or change the truth for a lie? Why would man exchange divine wisdom for human wisdom? Man's nature rejects the thought of God telling him how to live. He refuses to have a moral authority holding him accountable. He wants to run his own life and thus rejects what he knows to be true. Man has a natural bent towards worship, and if he doesn't worship God, he will worship himself or something else, which is humanism.

> This is why God delivered them over to degrading passions
> [moral depravity]. For even their females exchanged natural
> sexual intercourse for what is unnatural. The males in the
> same way also left natural sexual intercourse with females and
> were inflamed in their lust for one another. Males committed
> shameless acts with males and received in their own persons the
> appropriate penalty for their perversion. (Rom. 1:26–27)

Here again we see the sin of homosexuality, which falls under the cat-egory of moral depravity. Though a hotly debated subject, the Scriptures do not skirt the issue.

> And because they did not think it worthwhile to have God
> in their knowledge [humanism], God delivered them over to a
> worthless mind to do what is morally wrong [moral depravity].
> (Rom. 1:28)

This leads to the intellectual rejection of God, which is humanism. Paul finishes with a laundry list of sins, ending with the ultimate indict-ment in Romans 1:32: "Although they know full well God's just sen-tence—that those who practice such things deserve to die—they not only do them, but even applaud others who practice them." When man gets to the level of approving the sin in the lives of others because he so enjoys it himself, society is on the verge of decay. Has anything really changed after five thousand years?

Relative Truth

What does *relative truth* mean? The subject of relative truth will invariably look for an argument as soon as the gospel is presented. Postmodernists will not all react the same way. Some might agree that life never changes, not due to the failure of truth, but the absence of truth. We think we have truth, but we are in error. The problem is that we know categorically that we have observable, repeatable truth in all disciplines of life. However, these truths have not brought us closer to taming the self-centered nature of man. Other postmodernists have arrived at the conclusion that truth has done little, if anything, to bring peace to the world, not to mention their neighborhood. Therefore, truth is relative.

Relativism is another way to suppress the truth. People are not truly relativistic in their view of life. They use absolute truth daily to start their car, make a cake, or throw a football. What they don't want to call absolute is found in the moral or ethical arena. "Adultery may be right for me but wrong for you" is the cry of relativism. There are no moral absolutes. This defines much of postmodern thought.

Analyzing the World's Thinking

U Thant was the secretary general of the United Nations from 1961 to 1971. He was a Buddhist. His lament describes the human condition: "What element is lacking so that with all our skill and our knowledge we still find ourselves in the dark valley of discord and enmity? What is it that inhibits us from going forward together to enjoy the fruits of human endeavor and to reap the harvest of human experience? Why is it that, for all our professed ideals, our hopes, and our skills, peace on earth is still a distant objective seen only dimly through the storms and turmoils of our present difficulties?" (Ray Stedman, *Spiritual Warfare,* Word Books, 1978, 21). He seemed to be a forerunner for postmodern thinking. This lament was delivered before 2,500 statesmen and scholars pleading with them to give him an answer to the ultimate contradiction. "Why with all our . . . can't we live in peace?" Human wisdom will not help. It is impotent as it tries to alter the human condition. Genetic engineering can alter the gene but only the gospel can alter the soul. IQ, wealth, and power are not the issue, as Jeremiah warns: "This is what the LORD says: The wise must not boast in his wisdom; the mighty must not boast in his might; the rich must not boast in his riches. But the one who boasts should boast in this, that he understands and knows Me—that I am the LORD, showing faithful love, justice, and righteousness on the earth, for I delight in these things. This is the LORD's declaration" (Jer. 9:23–24).

As long as man professes himself to be wise, he will increasingly become a fool. An increase in human wisdom when applied to the soul will only exacerbate the problem and increase his desperate attempt to resolve the contradiction. "For the wisdom of this world is foolishness with God, since it is written: He catches the wise in their craftiness" (1 Cor. 3:19). The cycle is endless.

We are again reminded, "Don't be deceived: God is not mocked. For whatever a man sows he will also reap, because the one who sows to his flesh will reap corruption from the flesh, but the one who sows to the Spirit will reap eternal life from the Spirit" (Gal. 6:7–8). Sowing to the flesh is nothing more than a humanistic approach to escaping the inescapable. This is why we reap corruption when we continue to apply human wisdom to the incurable heart of man. An increase in knowledge will bring on an increase in frustration because the contradiction is directly proportional to man's rejection of divine wisdom in exchange for human wisdom.

I find the quote from U Thant fascinating as it allows us to enter into the mind of a bright man who was troubled by the ultimate contradiction. He couldn't, by way of reason, figure out why human wisdom would not solve the problems of the human race. As we examine his quote, I will parenthetically insert the answer to his question. Note carefully his plea. "What element is lacking [biblical revelation] so that with all our skill [human ability] and all our knowledge [human wisdom] we still find our-selves in the dark valley of discord and enmity [the ultimate contradiction]? What is it [biblical revelation] that inhibits us from going forward together to enjoy the fruits of human endeavor [human wisdom] and to reap the harvest of human experience? Why is it that, for all our professed ideals [human wisdom], our hopes [desired results from human wisdom], and our skills [human ability], peace on earth is still a distant objective seen only dimly through the storms and turmoil of our present difficulties [the ultimate contradiction]?"

What U Thant was asking is what we have posed throughout this chapter—how can man increase in knowledge yet never solve his problems? Without biblical revelation (divine wisdom) there is no hope for an answer, and "delayed hope makes the heart sick" (Prov. 13:12).

What was U Thant's lament? It can be summed up in one word—*frustration*. He was frustrated with the contradiction. It wouldn't leave him alone, and so in front of twenty-five hundred people, many of whom were scholars, he vented his frustration and begged for an answer. But no answers will be forthcoming until divine wisdom is consulted.

God devotes considerable space in Romans 8 to providing an answer to U Thant's frustration. Paul writes:

> For I consider that the sufferings of this present time are not worth comparing with the glory that is going to be revealed to us. For the creation eagerly waits with anticipation for God's sons to be revealed. For the creation was subjected to futility—not willingly, but because of Him who subjected it—in the hope that the creation itself will also be set free from the bondage of corruption into the glorious freedom of God's children. For we know that the whole creation has been groaning together with labor pains until now. And not only that, but we ourselves who have the Spirit as the firstfruits—we also groan within ourselves, eagerly waiting for adoption, the redemption of our bodies. (Rom. 8:18–23)

Paul addresses the issue of suffering and confirms the fact that suffering in this present world is eclipsed by the glory that awaits us in heaven. The creation itself is groaning to be released from its bondage and decay. Sin was the culprit that introduced frustration to the world. As long as there is sin, there will be frustration. Paul compares this frustration to a woman in labor, who longs to be freed from the pain even though she knows something better awaits her. Paul then describes a believer who awaits heaven and a new body free from pain, suffering, sickness, and frustration. Frustration is a reminder to humanity that we were not made for this present evil world. Something is wrong because we were created for eternity. This is where we come to a fork in the road. The unbeliever feels frustrated with life and tries desperately to escape the frustration by looking to human wisdom. As U Thant said, "We have harnessed human skill, knowledge, and wisdom so that we might enjoy the fruits of these endeavors, but all has been for naught." As an aside, it has been well over three decades since U Thant made his plea. Technology and human endeavor have increased exponetially since then, yet frustration still has the upper hand and his question still is unanswered. Thus, frustration prevails as man tries to extricate himself from this bondage of corruption.

The believer, however, chooses a different path. He knows through biblical revelation that frustration is designed by God to sharpen our focus on eternity. We await, as Paul says, "the redemption of our bodies" (Rom. 8:23). In other words, we long for another home. We know that we are "aliens and temporary residents" in this world (1 Pet. 2:11). We look as Abraham did, "For he was looking forward to the city that has foundations, whose architect and builder is God" (Heb. 11:10).

The believer is not exempt from pain and frustration; he simply sees it in a different light. He isn't fooled by the next invention, medical discovery, or technological advance as the savior of mankind. He knows through biblical revelation that "there is a way that seems right to a man, but its end is the way to death" (Prov. 14:12). The believer fully enjoys his new computer, laser surgery, and novocaine when the dreaded drill enters his mouth, and he is thankful for heat in the winter and air conditioning in the summer.

For the unbeliever, everything seems to be within his reach but never within his grasp. Human wisdom toys with his mind and plays nasty tricks with his emotions. Its promised joy turns out to be an illusion in the end. Human wisdom mocks him as a fool who wasted many years. The question, however, is how many have followed the western jesus in this venture? How many have been seduced into believing the postmodern philosophy?

Approaching the Postmodernist

The church cannot bury its head in the sand and hope that this kind of thinking will evaporate in the next few years. It is here to stay. It is firmly implanted in our culture, and we need to be prepared to engage in honest dialogue. So how do we approach this generation?

First, we must see postmodernists as products of false thinking. Cunning as he is, Satan appeals to man's sense of pride. In John 8:44 Christ referred to Satan as "a liar and the father of liars." Philosophical systems are tested over time and eventually burn out; thus men introduce new lies to keep society in a hopeful state of mind. Without consulting biblical revelation, man will continually look for some answer in human wisdom. New religions and philosophies will emerge, and this faulty thinking will be pervasive because man apart from the gospel is restricted in solving his own problems. We have seen the futility of such attempts, which are attested by history, personal experience, and biblical revelation.

Passing out a tract or using apologetics with the postmodernist doesn't work as effectively as it did in the past. Microwave evangelism is out and Crock-Pot evangelism is in. I'm not espousing that we wait to present the gospel after we have known someone for five years. However, postmodernism is a new way of thinking that the enemy has introduced, and it hardens the heart to truth. The view of truth is extremely different now, so facts and figures don't compute the same way they once did.

Second, the postmodernists want to know that people care about them. They relate more to experience than facts. Believers should listen openly so postmodernists will not feel rejected. Remember, they do understand the problem; they just don't understand the solution. We must gently lead them from human wisdom to divine wisdom and explain the difference. Once postmodernists realize that Scripture agrees with their assessment of man, the door will open for them to seriously examine the claims of Christ. Living with an unresolved contradiction brings about great frustration and stress, and many who live with this mind-set soon lose hope.

Another way to reach postmodernists is by learning to think the way they think. This is why Paul so carefully reveals the true nature of man in Romans 1. He knows that new philosophies will come and go with time. We must be sensitive to the cultural view in our day, realizing that all new worldviews are still excuses for living our lives independent of God. Postmodernism is another way to suppress the truth; however, we must not lose sight of the fact that there is a degree of sincerity as they look at the contradiction of knowledge versus problems. This must be our starting point.

- Recognize the legitimate frustration. See it as an intellectual block to the gospel. It becomes a barrier that shuts down apologetics. It leaves our gospel witness on a pile of a thousand other belief systems. It is discarded on the basis that there is no absolute truth. Jesus is seen as just another Mohammed or Buddha.
- Commend postmodernists for seeing life as it really is—a senseless treadmill. Their honesty is refreshing, but their hearts are still deceived.
- Introduce postmodernists to human wisdom. Show them how man has increased in knowledge. Remember the impatience illustration of the man missing the stagecoach. Show them how human wisdom is merely cosmetic. Review the history of man and allow them to see that nothing has really changed. There is a fundamental flaw in man's character.
- Introduce postmodernists to biblical revelation regarding the heart of man. Can this really be refuted? Does this not answer the contradiction? Hasn't Scripture proven to be true in spite of the fact that all the writers went against the grain of human logic?
- Introduce the gospel as the only hope for mankind.
- Look into your own heart and see if this thinking hasn't impacted you. It is very hard to influence people with that which you are not personally experiencing.

The western church, in order to win postmoderns, has blended with their thinking. We now see doctrine as relative truth. Orthodox truth is now disposable. This is no small compromise.

Without Excuse

It is important to note here that God will not be moved by excuses for rejecting him on Judgment Day. He will not say, "I really understand your dilemma. This contradiction confused your thinking and I can understand why you rejected me." This will not happen for the following reasons:

1. God has placed eternity in the hearts of men. "He has made everything appropriate in its time. He has also put eternity in their hearts, but man cannot discover the work God has done from beginning to end" (Eccles. 3:11). This means that all people are aware of their immortality. The body is mortal and will die, but the spirit will live on in heaven or hell. The Lord uses this to hold men accountable to seek after truth.

2. God speaks to man through nature in order to reveal himself and his power. "The heavens declare the glory of God, and the sky proclaims the work of His hands. Day after day they pour out speech; night after night they communicate knowledge" (Ps. 19:1–2).

3. According to Romans 2, the Law of God is written in the heart of man and he has a conscience that will accuse or excuse his actions. He knows right from wrong in a general sense. The word *conscience* means "to know with." To violate the conscience brings guilt to the soul. Man senses he needs forgiveness. If there is no God, where does the guilt come from? What standard has been violated to cause the guilt? Who created such a standard?

4. In John 16, the Lord tells us that the Holy Spirit convicts the world of "sin, righteousness, and judgment" (v. 8). The eternal nature of the soul is touched by God. Man has a sense of guilt but often chooses to rid himself of this guilt by suppressing truth or adopting a philosophy or religion that will soothe his conscience.

5. God subjects man to futility and frustration. In Romans 8:23, we have this testimony: "And not only that, but we ourselves who have the Spirit as the firstfruits—we also groan within ourselves, eagerly waiting for adoption, the redemption of our bodies."

In 1 Corinthians 3:19 we have these corroborating words: "For the wisdom of this world is foolishness with God, since it is written: He catches the wise in their craftiness." He does this so that man will sense that he was created for a better place. There is a sense of longing to be released from the bondage of frustration. However, God will keep the pressure on as long as man feeds from human wisdom.

We must learn to listen to the postmodernist. We must have compassion for his soul. Cramming the gospel down his throat will only add support to his objection—that no one is willing to listen to his heart. These people need first to be heard, and then we will gain the right to present the truth that will set them free. A western jesus will only distort the truth. We must be biblical in order to be effective.

CHAPTER 10

The Eyes of a Pilgrim

Death and Destruction are never satisfied,
and neither are the eyes of man.

Proverbs 27:20 NIV

THE SCRIPTURES HAVE MUCH to say about our five physical senses: "Taste and see that the LORD is good (Ps. 34:8). "Let your eyes look forward; fix your gaze straight ahead" (Prov. 4:25). "No eye has seen and no ear has heard" (1 Cor. 2:9). "Therefore, come out from among them and be separate, says the Lord; do not touch any unclean thing" (2 Cor. 6:17). A "fragrant offering" (Eph. 5:2). There is a particular emphasis on the eye and what it takes in. As a plebe at the Naval Academy, there was one hard and fast rule: *Keep your eyes in the boat.* A simple translation is, don't look around. Stay fixed on what you are doing. As a lowly freshman, you were not to be checking out what was going on around you. This was strictly enforced at mealtime. Twelve men sat at one rectangular table for each meal. At one end were two seniors. At the other end were two juniors. On the sides facing each other were four plebes being carefully watched by four sophomores.

Plebes were not allowed to look anywhere but straight ahead, and any glance in another direction would be met with "KEEP YOUR EYES IN THE BOAT, MISTER" at an audible level I cannot describe in writing.

This illustration has proved to be a fitting example for the eyes of a pilgrim. We are called to look upon many things in life. Our eyes should certainly capture the beauty of the world around us. The warnings are never about the beauty of life and all that God has called us to enjoy but are given as protection about what our eyes should not seek. The Lord knows the makeup of every pilgrim. He knows that we are but dust. He knows the temptations of life and the harm that lies in wait for the wayfarer.

When the Scriptures tell us "people's eyes are never satisfied" (see Prov. 27:20), they are revealing the very nature of man in his fallen state. He cannot fix the problem but is a slave to his never-ending lust for more. He simply can't bring this monster under control. If this proverb were not true, Madison Avenue and Wall Street would be out of business before sunset. The pilgrim will always have before him the same temptations the world has before it. We, however, are called to restraint. Paul warned Timothy with these words: "No one serving as a soldier gets entangled in the concerns of everyday life" (2 Tim. 2:4). This is no small statement. Here again we are not only called pilgrims, but soldiers. There is a battle, and by definition and calling, every true believer is in this war. The illustration is taken from the physical wars that are all around us.

As I write, we are engaged in a war with Iraq. Those soldiers who have been sent did not bring their golf clubs and giant-screen TVs. They travel lightly. Paul's point is that though our warfare is a spiritual one, the principle remains the same. We will be ineffective if we become entangled with all that life has to offer. John Piper often reminds his readers about what we will present to God when we meet him face to face. Will it be our seashell collection? Will it be our low handicap in golf? Even though I like seashells and play golf whenever I get the chance, my point is that these are not to be all-consuming. So often the pilgrims who retire think that retirement from the job is also spiritual retirement. They can kick back and relax. They have worked hard. They deserve it. Yet these are the very people who are needed to help bring along the next generation of warriors.

If the truth be known, those who have been in battle are the ones who usually stay in the battle well after retirement, and those who have been uninvolved usually remain so until their final departure from this world.

I know that I see much of this through the eyes of a pastor, but Scripture doesn't delineate. We are all called to advance the kingdom. "Therefore, my dear brothers, be steadfast, immovable, always excelling in the Lord's work, knowing that your labor in the Lord is not in vain" (1 Cor. 15:58). Yes, we need rest, but so often the rest is needed because we have been consumed with trying to make a ton of money, or get the next boat or car. The weariness should come from kingdom work. "So we must not get tired of doing good, for we will reap at the proper time if we don't give up" (Gal. 6:9). There seems to be no eternal perspective. What little there is has been blurred by a lust for the good life. Psalm 73 tells of the heart of a man who lost his way but later regained his pilgrim status. Perhaps you can identify with him. I am talking about Asaph, who was sidetracked as he observed the prosperity of the wicked.

If we look at the big picture of Psalm 73, we see that it is masterfully constructed and may very well represent a lengthy period in Asaph's life. Not unlike some of the other psalms, Psalm 73 goes from an emotional low to an emotional high, from despair to joy, from temporal to eternal, from native to alien, from fairness to justice, and from human reasoning to God's revelation. Many years ago there was a TV show called *This Is Your Life*. That would be a fit title for this psalm. It opens with a conclusion: "God is indeed good to Israel, to the pure in heart." It then proceeds into a downward spiral as the psalmist reveals how he views the unfairness of life. There is then a turning point in verse 17 and fairness is no longer the issue, but justice is. That's the big picture. Now let's take this psalm apart and apply it to our sojourn.

Disgust

You just put down the morning newspaper in disgust. The headlines of the high society section read, "Rock Group Sings to Sellout Crowd." They cruise through town for a one-night stand and pocket a cool million, not to mention T-shirt sales, albums, and all the endorsements that go along with such insanity. Not all rock groups are bad, but those who push sex and drugs are the ones that cause you to question why God doesn't deal with them.

So what's so upsetting? "These people are raking it in, living life to its fullest as they peddle their perversion." Secretly you're upset with God because you're having trouble with this month's car payment as you try to make an honest living. Where is God anyway? How can he bless sinful lifestyles? The bottom line of your observation is that life isn't fair, therefore God isn't fair—and a western jesus brings his temporal view of life into sharp focus.

The fact is, you can't tread in these waters too long without getting angry and bitter. If you think life should be fair, you'll be blasted from the saddle ten times a day. It won't be long before you start demanding fairness, and the only way to get it is to do what the world does in order to get your fair share. It's sort of an I'll-get-back-at-God attitude. After all, since God blesses the wicked people, you might as well join their team.

The Lord was not caught off guard regarding this potential fleshly response to life. He saw it coming. He also knew that people would struggle with this issue of fairness, so he left us an entire chapter in the Bible in order for us to step out of the western world of fairness and into a world of justice. Psalm 73 is clearly one of my favorite portions of Scripture. With every reading, this psalm explores new territory of my walk of faith. It takes captive attitudes that I have not dealt with in the area of fairness. I, too, struggle as I watch the world prosper. Life is not fair. No, but it is just, and we will see why in a moment.

The Pits

The writer, most likely a man by the name of Asaph, invites us into his personal chamber of depression as he contrasts his lot in life with the wicked people of the world who have rejected God. "But as for me, my feet almost slipped; my steps nearly went astray. For I envied the arrogant; I saw the prosperity of the wicked" (Ps. 73:2–3). Can you relate?

We are introduced immediately to the problem—Asaph thinks life should be fair and openly admits at the outset that this belief just about did him in. Life should have nice, neat explanations—no loose ends. Everything should fit neatly into a package with a ribbon on the top, and all who serve God should be blessed.

If you and I view life through the lens of fairness, we will inevitably sink deeper and deeper into self-pity as we view the prosperity of the wicked. Why should a drug dealer live in a mansion and enjoy the good life when my bills pile up and the kids are sick? Why do these potheads eat steak, drink to excess, and wallow in the penthouse of perversion? Is God asleep? It's not fair! No, but it is just, and we will see why in just a moment.

The Success of Pride

They are not in trouble like others; they are not afflicted like most people. Therefore, pride is their necklace, and violence covers them like a garment.

Psalm 73:5–6

I thought pride came before a fall. Life certainly doesn't seem to bear witness to that. Look at the arrogance of Hollywood, and what about the big name athletes who have pride written all over their muscular frames?

A few years back, while riding on one of the airlines, I read about a famous tennis player who made unbelievable sums of money for using a certain make of racket or wearing a certain type of tennis shoe. His total endorsement package was several million. He made three hundred thousand dollars per exhibition match. I couldn't help but think to myself, *Wow, three hundred thousand dollars for two hours of work—I barely make that in a week.* (Knowing the racket that much of Christianity has become, I should tell you that I'm just kidding.) We have all observed ungodly behavior in famous people who seem to mock God and live lives that exalt arrogance.

So why does God allow them to get away with it—and become filthy rich on the side. It's just not fair. No, but it is just, and we will see why in a moment.

Chili on the Side

Their eyes bulge out from fatness; the imaginations of their hearts run wild.

Psalm 73:7

Two well-known movie stars were at a dinner party one evening, and the topic of chili came up. Both claimed they knew where the best chili in the world was made. The only way to settle the dispute was to have a firsthand taste test.

Since one of the stars' favorite chili was served in a restaurant several states away, it was necessary to hire a pilot and a Lear Jet to pick it up and bring it back that evening for a sampling. The total cost for the chili was in the neighborhood of ten thousand dollars.

Are you outraged to find that people can afford to spend thousands on a bowl of chili as multitudes starve across the face of the earth? Do you feel that God should have poisoned the chili as a reminder that wasteful spending is immoral and those who indulge in such waste will be punished? Are you angered because that's what it cost to put braces on your child's crooked teeth, when in fact the only thing crooked in all this was the expense of the chili? Do you find yourself wondering when they will get their just reward? Are you upset because it doesn't seem to logically work out the way you feel it should? Are you coming to the conclusion that life is not fair? If you are, you're not alone, because life isn't fair. But it is just, and we will see why in a moment.

Mocking God

*They say, "How can God know? Does the
Most High know everything?"*

Psalm 73:11

A few years back I had a most unique privilege of speaking to a group of high school biology teachers. They were all candidates for a master's degree and were being taught by a professor from a local university. He had asked me to come and address the issue of "The Theology of Creation." Though the teachers were clearly well-schooled in the philosophy of evolution, they wanted to know what the other side thought because they knew this had become a really hot issue and wished to be sensitive to it.

I was quite pleased with their attitude. However, in every crowd there is always a scoffer, someone who just loves the sport of debate. In this particular case, it was an elderly woman who was obviously atheistic to the core. She mocked God in the most awful way. She finally made a statement that sent my blood over the boiling point. She said, "Every time you creationists can't answer a question, you throw God into the formula as a convenient cop-out." I responded, red face and all, "Yes, and every time you evolutionists can't answer a question, you throw in more time and chance; I guess we both have our gods, don't we?" I was more than a little upset. How could she continue mocking God? Doesn't God care? I am well aware that there are believers who accept evolution, though admittedly, I don't understand how. Still, they do not mock God in the process.

When I see pro-choice marches with signs that mock Christian standards, I become incensed. When scientists try to tell me that a baby is just a blob of tissue, or that a woman has a right to do what she wants with her own body, I'm angered. How long can God allow this slaughter to continue? Why are abortionists driving Mercedes when you and I struggle with the monthly payments on our Ford? Where is the fairness in all this? It's not fair. That's right—life is not fair, but it is just, and we will see why in a moment.

Prosperity and the Wicked

Look at them—the wicked! They are always at ease,
and they increase their wealth.

Psalm 73:12

The real problem in Asaph's thinking is finally revealed in this verse. It is not just his confusion about the fairness of life, but his misunderstanding of prosperity. In his depressed state, he defines prosperity as wealth. That is blatantly wrong, and it is the root of the problem. We think people are prospering because they have great wealth. We find ourselves secretly admiring the rich and famous. If the truth were known, we wouldn't mind a little slice from their pie. So when we get stale meatloaf, we sense life has dealt us an unfair blow. After all, at least we attend church on Sunday.

Prosperity is not normally defined in Scripture as wealth. It is defined rather as a victorious life. Psalm 1 tells us that if we meditate day and night upon the Word of God, then all we do will prosper. I don't rule out material prosperity, but that is never the primary understanding of biblical prosperity. Therefore, laboring under a misconception of what prosperity is can bring a Christian to a depressed state. This led Asaph to question the fairness of God. Life will always be seen as unfair if we think wicked people prosper because they have great wealth. This is a temporal prosperity that can never fill the eternal void that is within all of us. Life is not fair; no, but it is just, and we will see why in just a moment.

Half Time

For I am afflicted all day long, and
punished every morning.

Psalm 73:14

When I tried to understand all this, it seemed hopeless.

Psalm 73:16

Just what was it that was so painful for Asaph? He began to summarize how rough life was for him and how easy it was for the unrighteous. His feet had almost slipped out from under him as he sulked about how unfair life is. However, God rescued him from such mental anguish and gave him a mountaintop experience. His new vantage point gave him a bird's-eye view of the past, present, and future. None of this could take place "until I entered God's sanctuary" (Ps. 73:17).

The word *until* is the key word in this entire text. Everything hinges on these two syllables. It is the pivot upon which the psalm revolves. It acts as the transitional element that takes us out of the darkness and into the light.

Have you ever been to a high school football game and looked up at the scoreboard? The home team of Franklin High has its name printed in lights while their opponent is usually labeled VISITORS. For the purpose of analogy, the home team is the world, and we are the visitors. At this point in the psalm, we are losing fifty to nothing. The world has taken charge, they are prospering, and we are being trampled under foot. Nothing seems fair at half time *until* we go into the locker room for a pep talk and learn the difference between fairness and justice.

Fairness versus Justice

If you have felt a bit teased by the phrase "life isn't fair, but it is just," the time for explanation has arrived. In the first half of the psalm, Asaph has been living under self-imposed pressure. He feels that life should be fair. This is how most of us feel, particularly in a western society where our rights are highlighted and material possessions are idolized.

You see, fairness deals with the physical. It has to do with material gain and its close relatives *health* and *wealth*. Fairness is seeing the good and bad in life placed on balance scales with no resulting bias. Everything is on an even keel. It is looking around to see how we measure up to others.

Justice, on the other hand, deals with God's retirement plan for the ages. It has to do with eternal prosperity and contentment. Justice says that all will be measured out in the hand of God. Justice tells me that everything works together for good to those who love God. Justice says there are no loose ends—God will eventually tie it all together. "These all died in faith without having received the promises [fairness], but they saw them from a distance [justice]" (Heb. 11:13).

When you and I view life with fairness in mind, our discernment goes down the tubes. We get angry with the prosperity of the wicked as we start to desire what they have. Some have gone so far as to chuck the whole thing and seek the pleasure of the world. "Demas has deserted me, because he loved this present world" (2 Tim. 4:10).

This is often done out of the rationale that life should be fair, and since God isn't doing his part, I'll just take control and seek what is best for me. When we look at the great saints of Scripture, we don't see this. Paul never demanded a good life from God, nor was he angered when he lacked what the world exalts. "I have learned to be content in whatever circumstances I am" (Phil. 4:11).

As a parent, I never developed the art of breaking a candy bar perfectly in half. Nor did I have the gift of dishing out equal amounts of ice cream to my children. If there is one cookie and two kids, the only *fair* way to handle the situation is to break the cookie in half. However, no mortal parent has ever broken a cookie exactly in half. Any attempt to do so will be met with a challenging remark from the child who received the smaller piece. They are pros at eye-balling each other's portion and assessing who got the greater amount. Do you know what they say if their piece is one crumb shy of their brother's—"It's not fair!" But now you have a biblical response: "You're right, Johnny, life is not fair, but it is just."

Their Just Dessert

*Indeed You put them in slippery places; You make them
fall into ruin. How suddenly they become a desolation!
They come to an end, swept away by terrors.*

Psalm 73:18–19

God is a God of justice. Nothing escapes his eye. There will be a last
chapter written in the lives of all those who live in ungodly ways. There is
the law of the harvest. The crop does eventually come in. I can't help but
consider Proverbs 7 in relation to this whole matter. If you haven't read it
lately, it deals with the strange woman, a prostitute. It tells the story of the
foolish young man who is taken in by her dress, eyes, and flattering lips.

It reads like a twenty-first century novel. Why does God record such
sensuous activity in Scripture? How is this different from the drugstore
paperbacks? It is different in two essential elements. First, it leaves out all
the sordid details, and second, it doesn't leave out the consequences.

It is said of this foolish young man that he is led away to the
slaughterhouse, that her steps will lead him to the grave. Every rock star,
movie star, or athletic star who has achieved success through pride and
wicked means will some day pay the price. "They will eat the fruit of
their way and be glutted with their own schemes" (Prov. 1:31).

Why does God reveal this to us? Are we supposed to be pleased when
they get their reward? Are we to cheer them on in their folly? No! God
simply wants us first to see that this is nothing that we should desire, and
second, to show us we are not to envy their lifestyle. We are not to consider
what they do and the benefits from it as prosperity.

None of us really knows what's going on behind the scenes. I have no
idea what mental anguish they experience. I can't sense what the guilt factor must be; I can only go by what the Lord has declared about their lives.
Someone once said, "This is the only heaven the world will ever know, and
it's the only hell the Christian will ever know."

A few years back *U.S. News and World Report* did an article on a man by the name of Ivan Boesky. Boesky was one of Wall Street's wheeler-dealers. He made countless millions in the grand art of "takeovers." He boasted a twenty-hour work day. Clocks lined the walls of his office in order to keep him posted on all the time zones throughout the world. He lived out his life in time slots. He kept in constant communication with other high-rafter bats in the financial community with a complex phone system. The article went on to say that "Boesky attributed his success to . . ." I did a double take as my eyes went back over the word *success*. If that is success, then count me out. Never home for a meal with the family, no time for church or developing friendships, no time to "stop and smell the roses." If we are not careful, we find ourselves describing people like Boesky as successful when, in fact, he is a pathetic figure best described as having failed at life. By the way, he was later found guilty of insider trading and served a lengthy jail sentence.

In Psalm 73, having gone into the sanctuary of the Lord, which represents fellowship with God, the psalmist acknowledges the horrible state of the wicked. His entire perspective changes, and he now understands their end. He sees them in slippery places. God really is in charge, and all things will be made right. This brings to mind another truth regarding the law of the harvest, which says, "For whatever a man sows he will also reap" (Gal. 6:7). The psalmist has come to see that no one gets away with anything. However, if we fall for worldly logic and human reason, we will be fooled by what we observe and miss what God has revealed. Asaph felt he had been cheated and secretly wished he could enjoy what the wicked were indulging in. Once he came to his senses, he saw this divine law of the harvest at work. There are three parts to this law. We reap what we sow, we reap more than we sow (Hosea 8:7), and we reap after we sow.

It is this last part of the law—we reap after we sow—that few ever seem to observe. A young freshman in high school has been told all his life how bad people get punished. He sees his classmates experimenting with drugs, alcohol, and sex. He secretly watches and waits for them to reap what they have sown, but nothing happens. "They'll get theirs," he says to himself as he enters his sophomore year. Still nothing happens and the perversion has increased. He waits for the shoe to drop, but they seem happy in their sin. Surely the consequences of depravity will arrive on their doorstep over these next couple of years in high school, but somehow they have all dodged the bullet. He begins to believe that he has been lied to and is missing the pleasures of sin. He soon joins the ranks of those who walk in the flesh and parties his way through college, abandoning all spiritual loyalties. God is removed and all that counts is a good time. But then something begins to happen. His friends who were having so much fun for so long are now in slippery places and in a "moment are consumed." Marriages fall apart, alcoholism sets in, and a host of other ills beset them, including mental anguish. He soon realizes he has been duped by the ways of this world. "Don't be deceived: God is not mocked" (Gal. 6:7), Paul warns.

Asaph goes on to say that he was foolish and ignorant for so long to not know those things about God's ways. He rejoices in the fact that it is never too late and says, "You guide me with Your counsel, and afterwards You will take me up in glory" (v. 24). He has made the necessary mid-course corrections, which is an encouragement to all of us who lose sight of our pilgrimage. The psalm ends with the clear declaration: "Those far from You will certainly perish" (v. 27).

Lord, Are You Asleep?

Like one waking from a dream, Lord, when arising,
You will despise their image.

Psalm 73:20

The psalmist has been sensing that the Lord has been asleep when, in fact, the psalmist has just been awakened to the fact that God has always been at the helm. He is completely in charge. The psalmist has come to see that God will bring out the balance scales. Only this time cookies will not be weighed, nor will gold and silver or real estate. Hearts will be hung in the balance. Faithfulness will be weighed. A wise use of time will be measured out, and those who made it big in the world's eyes will be found wanting: "For what is highly admired by people is revolting in God's sight" (Luke 16:15). They will have sacrificed their souls for a little pleasure. Christ will have been rejected for a majority share of the stock.

Asaph goes on in verses 21 and 22 to describe how foolish he feels having allowed this surface view of the wicked to drag him down. He then finds peace as he shifts from a fair view to a just view: "You guide me with Your counsel, and afterwards You will take me up in glory" (Ps. 73:24).

When glory is in view, worldly prosperity makes a quick exit. Eternal values enter, and the pilgrimage is again underway. We tend to forget our temporary journey here. Sometimes we stop for a rest and drink from an empty cistern. This is exactly what Asaph did. He lost his way and started to flirt with the world. But he is soon back in the saddle and sees God in control. Things are beginning to fall into place as he recognizes that all who are far from the Lord shall perish. "But as for me, God's presence is my good. I have made the Lord GOD my refuge, so I can tell about all You do" (Ps. 73:28).

Notice he says he will tell about all God's works. The Lord is at work and in charge. I saw all of this acted out in the drama of life several years ago at our church. A good friend of mine called me from the hospital to inform me that his twenty-one-year-old daughter was in a coma from smoke inhalation. I rushed down to the burn center in Washington, D.C., and was met with the sad news that this young lady was not likely to pull through. I sat with the family in the waiting room for what seemed to be an eternity.

Finally the head doctor came in and asked to meet with the parents privately. They requested that I come with them, to which the doctor promptly agreed. Seated around a large conference table were three burn specialists, three nurses, the parents of this young lady, and myself. The look on the doctors' faces had already spelled out what we had anticipated. She was brain dead. The father immediately thanked the medical staff and then shared his faith that he knew where his daughter's eternal destiny was. She was with the Savior.

As we left the conference room and entered the large, empty corridor, my good friend, who had just lost his daughter, said to me, "Mike, it's been a good day—it's been a tough day, but a good day, because it is the day that the Lord has made, and I will rejoice and be glad in it." He was not in shock or just mumbling Christian phrases. It was very real to him. He grieved his loss, but he looked to the heavenly city where they would be reunited.

Never will I forget those words. I realize most of us can't quite relate to something that dramatic, but it simply shows how one man and his wife saw life from an eternal perspective. Justice was the issue—not fairness.

Life is tough—no doubt about that either—but it is just and we won't see that in a moment but in eternity. It is just because God will see to it that on an eternal scale, everyone will receive his just reward. All of the good and bad will be placed on balance scales, not to determine our eternal destiny, but to bring all things into proper balance.

Failure to distinguish between fairness and justice affects our moral discernment because it questions God's authority over his creation. We begin to wonder if he really cares or if he is even aware of society's problems. We soon adopt the philosophy that wickedness and evil are where the action is. Why suffer for the sake of the gospel if there is no benefit? Why not eat, drink, and be merry if there is no eternal justice in which prosperity is meted out?

If, on the other hand, I am able to see, as Asaph eventually did, that eternity is at stake, I become a different person.

A western jesus has taught us to see life differently. Our thinking has been shaped by a philosophy that says we deserve a good, long, and happy life. The western materialistic philosophy has rubbed off on the church. We don't see Christ as central. If we did, then worldly prosperity would not matter. We would find our contentment in him. To envy those who have more than we have—whether they are wicked or godly believers— reveals a heart of covetousness, which according to Scripture is idolatry. Think this through and recognize it as a real battle. Find your satisfaction in the One who owns it all, because if you find it somewhere else, you will forever cry out that life is not fair.

CHAPTER 11

A Western Jesus and Contentment

*I increased my achievements. I built houses and planted vineyards
for myself. I made gardens and parks for myself and planted every
kind of fruit tree in them. I constructed reservoirs of water for
myself from which to irrigate a grove of flourishing trees.
I acquired male and female servants and had slaves who
were born in my house. I also owned many herds of cattle and
flocks, more than all who were before me in Jerusalem. I also
amassed silver and gold for myself, and the treasure of kings and
provinces. I gathered male and female singers for myself, and
many concubines, the delights of men. Thus, I became great and
surpassed all who were before me in Jerusalem; my wisdom also
remained with me. All that my eyes desired, I did not deny them.
I did not refuse myself any pleasure, for I took pleasure in all my
struggles. This was my reward for all my struggles. When
I considered all that I had accomplished and what I had labored
to achieve, I found everything to be futile and a pursuit of the
wind. There was nothing to be gained under the sun.*

Ecclesiastes 2:4–11

The Whens of Life

Ecclesiastes seems more relevant today than when originally written. This is because the philosophy it was designed to challenge is more pronounced today than it was three thousand years ago. Though it has always been alive and well, the belief that "man can improve his lot in life" is in its heyday. Spawned by the technology of the twenty-first century, many have bowed their knee to the baals of materialism and technology. I often refer to this as the "whens" of life. Life will be better when _____ (you fill in the blank). The whens of life are those fantasies you play out in your mind that once fulfilled, will finally make you content.

We all have our secret list of "whens." At the risk of sounding negative, too many have been led astray only to find disillusionment a high price to pay for such empty dreams. The simple fact is that life will not be better "when." That is a western dream. You want it so badly you can see it and taste it. But like a mirage, it disappears and you awake from your dream only to find another "when" staring you in the face. The writer of Ecclesiastes declares plainly that the pursuit of happiness is vanity of vanities apart from God.

In no way do I wish to imply that life never gets better. Experience rebukes such a notion. I enjoy my present standard of living more than that of ten years ago. Though material possessions and circumstances may improve my standard of living, they do not determine the quality of my life. There is a distinct difference between quality of life, which relates to the inner man, and a standard of living, which relates to the outer man.

The blunt fact is, materialism and technological "whens" of life are totally unrelated to "the peace of God, which surpasses every thought" (Phil. 4:7). This has always been a hard pill to swallow, and it is for this reason that I ask the following questions. Since technology is designed to simplify life and make the world a better place in which to live, how many people are getting home earlier from the office now that computers are doing all the work? How many businessmen travel less now that communication is so advanced? How many people have less stress in their lives as a result of man's increased wisdom? The whens have been experienced, but when will inner peace come?

Living in the Future

To illustrate the deception of this temptation, let's take inventory of our past whens. Believe it or not, most of us are presently living in what was only a pipe dream ten years ago. That's right! We have forgotten that our present standard of living is what we longed for in the past. Ten years ago most of us were saying, "Life will be better when I get a new job." You now have that new job, but in all likelihood, things probably haven't changed much. And wasn't there a time when you felt all your problems would be solved with a salary increase? Barring inflation, most of us are making more today than we ever dreamed possible, but are we really better off? I suspect things are just as tight, maybe more so. We are presently experiencing the whens of yesterday. Fulfillment is always within our reach but never within our grasp. The lesson never seems to be learned as we cling tenaciously to the whens of tomorrow.

Some are now living beyond their past expectations, but the promised satisfaction has yet to show its face. It's an elusive butterfly. Your health is great, but your children are rebelling. You love your job, but the long hours are putting a strain on your marriage. Your income is substantial, but the bills are even more so. The cycle is seemingly endless, and the search for the perfect life slips through our hands like a greased eel.

Satan's Ploy

Sometimes it is hard to believe we have been duped. Pride turns a deaf ear to truth, even when truth reveals we have labored under a false concept of life. No one ever lived happily ever after because of TiVo. Mary and John will not ride off into the sunset because of new carpeting in the den. No, the roots of happiness tend to go deep in search of eternal refreshment.

How happy is the man who does not follow the advice of
the wicked . . . his delight is in the LORD's instruction, and he
meditates on it day and night. He is like a tree planted beside
streams of water that bears its fruit in season and whose leaf
does not wither. Whatever he does prospers. (Ps. 1:1–3)

As a deer longs for streams of water, so I long for You, God.
(Ps. 42:1)

It should be obvious to the most casual observer that this philosophy
of materialism bringing happiness has not only failed to stand the test of
time but has been left threadbare in the life of every individual who has
engaged its counsel.

Since we are not ignorant of his (Satan's) devices, or at least not supposed to be (see 2 Cor. 2:11), it will forever be to our advantage to discern
the *real* purpose behind any temptation, philosophy, or logical argument
that promises a better future without God.

What I am saying here is not new. Even the unbelieving world often
confesses that things never really satisfy; but as often as we preach this
truth to ourselves, there is something within our fallen nature that denies
this, and we continue in the pursuit of stuff. I think I know why we don't
accept the gospel of money-won't-make-you-happy. Experience is hard to
challenge. There are those who have made millions, yet they remain desperate and admit that such wealth has not brought them happiness. On the
other hand, there are those who had it, lost it, and would admit they were
happier living in a beautiful home with a pool out back than they are now
in a one-bedroom apartment without air conditioning. So what are we to
make of this?

We must distinguish between cosmetic physical comfort and spiritual
rest. I have often said that though money can't make you happy, it can
certainly keep you from being sad. Here is what I mean. Though I would
much rather live in an air-conditioned house than a mud hut, I have come
to realize that physical comfort may relieve me of discomfort, but I am not
prepared to say that a person sipping champagne on a yacht is happier than
a godly believer imprisoned for his faith. We wind up comparing apples

and oranges. The apples represent our physical comfort while the oranges represent our spiritual rest. The apples are the outward man who perishes, while the oranges are the inner man who is being renewed day by day (see 2 Cor. 4:16).

Since the world knows nothing of its spiritual need, it will forever try to quench that thirst by drinking from the cup of materialism. They are not aware that their longings have a spiritual heritage damaged by "the fall." There is a spiritual longing that is interpreted as a physical need. This is why we sound foolish when we tell the world that money doesn't satisfy or you can't buy happiness. They know full well that it does. But we are back to our apples and oranges again. I have often been physically refreshed and satisfied by the "apples" that money can buy but even more so I have been spiritually refreshed by the "oranges" money can't buy. From the looks of the western church, few understand this. The statistics show that giving goes down as a society increases in its wealth. I often tell our people to turn to the one verse in their Bibles that no one really believes. They know by now that I'm referring to Luke 12:15, where Jesus is confronted by a man who has been cheated out of his inheritance. Jesus tells the man that "one's life is not in the abundance of his possessions." I am quite convinced that few if any in our culture really believe that. We want the apples more than the oranges. Give me the physical pleasures and I'll pursue spiritual wealth later. Life will be better when the apples come in.

This is exactly what the Scriptures mean when they tell us that the eyes of a man are never satisfied (see Prov. 27:20). Herein lies the truth of man's nature. Once he has in his grasp what he has always wanted, he wants more because the dream never quenched his thirst. This is why Jesus said when you have him, you will never hunger and never thirst. He is talking about oranges not apples. However, in the spiritual realm we also desire more, but for a very different reason. Once the apple has been tasted and found wanting, we look for bigger apples. However, once the orange has been tasted, we want more because it did quench our thirst, and God gives us a greater capacity to taste and see that he is good. The desire for more oranges is very different from the desire for more apples. The person who has all the stuff says to himself, "That just didn't do it for me. I need something more." The person who finds Christ says, "That really did it for me, and he has so expanded my capacity to know him that I want more."

I'm afraid the western jesus has presented the church with apples and no oranges. Preaching is often along the lines of felt needs. We herald forth ways to have a better life and toss apples to our congregation when what they need are oranges that will quench their thirst. We tell them God wants them to have a great life now, but how transcendent is that message to those meeting in an underground church in China? This type of message is western to the core—the apple core, that is. "I have come that they may have life and have it in abundance" (John 10:10) has been butchered. People already had physical life when he came, so he is not addressing the physical. The life he is talking about is his life. The abundance is not measured by apples but oranges. Paul spoke of life in Christ, and he pursued nothing in this world, yet he lived an abundant life.

Back to the Basics

I wonder what Satan's strategy is in keeping this philosophy alive. Could it be to paralyze, neutralize, and immobilize the church? Has our salt lost its savor (see Matt. 5:13)? Do we find ourselves seeking what is temporal and not what is eternal (see 2 Cor. 4:18)? Are we laboring for the meat that perishes and not the meat that endures (see John 6:27)? Do we seek those things that are below and not those things above (see Col. 3:2)? Have we learned to walk by sight and not by faith (see 2 Cor. 5:7)? Are we laying up treasures on Earth and not in heaven (see Matt. 6:20)? Have we sown to the flesh and not the Spirit (see Gal. 6:8)? If honesty is still part of our character, we will admit the enemy has the upper hand.

Let's see how the whens of life have replaced the simplicity that is in Christ. Be painfully honest with this question: How many of the following whens have sidetracked you from time with your family or the Lord? How many have complicated, rather than simplified, your life? The list is not designed to condemn. Although some of the items are clearly evil, most are neutral, and some are even positive and worthwhile.

Sports	Travel
Martial arts classes	Drugs
Heavy metal music	Complex toys
Computers	Mind-bending games
Television	Ten-speeds
TiVo	Self-improvement classes
MP3 players	Intellectual societies
Shopping malls	Gossip columns
Video arcades	Subliminal advertising
Movies	Fantasy football
Pornography	Fast food chains
Fitness centers	Credit cards
Lavish vacations	Amusement parks
No-fault divorce	Three wheelers
Jacuzzis	Scuba diving
Hot tubs	Snowmobiles
Yachts	Lotteries
Living together	Alcoholics Anonymous
Skateboards	Monday Night Football (ouch!)
Pyramiding schemes	Weight Watchers
Two-income families	High society magazines
Trial marriages	Cell phones
Marathons	Aerobics
Tanning rooms	My Space

Is it any wonder that so many within our society are frazzled, frayed, singed, charred, burned-out, drained, or on their way down it? Consider this: how many of the above items would be totally unfamiliar to your grandparents? Would you believe this list was comprised of those things that have been introduced to our society within the last thirty to fifty years?

Although most present-day pastors have addressed the subject of "life in the fast lane," I'm hard-pressed to find one printed sermon from yesteryear dealing with the subjects of boredom, eating disorders, divorce, stress, depression, suicide, burnout, or the midlife crisis. These existed in the past but not in epedemic propositions. Much of this is western misery. Like AIDS, our spiritual immune system has shut down. We have become defenseless against every spiritual disease known to man. Our high-tech society has produced a low-tech joy. We have, in fact, been taken in by our own craftiness (see 1 Cor. 3:19).

The Riddle of Riddles

The fact is, we are "always learning and never able to come to a knowledge of the truth" (2 Tim. 3:7). How ludicrous for this to be dubbed the "Age of Communication" when we interface more with computers than we do with people. How strange to be inundated with books, tapes, and seminars on marriage as we stand idly by watching the divorce rate skyrocket. How does one explain the increase in crime when behavioral psychology is so scientific? And dare we stop without mentioning that the drug culture has sunk its roots deep into the elementary school system, while mental institutions are glutted with inmates, and pollution is choking our cities? It is truly an enigma.

Does this paradox have an explanation, and better yet, does it have a solution? For the non-Christian, there really is an easy explanation: his blindness prevents him from seeing his condition. He has amassed great volumes of knowledge but lacks the biblical wisdom for its application. He is not aware that he needs the orange more than the apple. This is spiritual blindness from which the natural man cannot escape without the saving knowledge of the gospel. He continues to slap Band-Aids on polio. Life's problems stem from man's spiritual estrangement from God, and all his social ills and conflicts are born out of an evil heart. The church should lead the way back to God, but it has bitten into the forbidden fruit, which in this case happens to be the apple, while the orange waits to be picked. Perhaps it is true that "one rotten apple spoils the whole barrel."

Life on a Treadmill

General Electric had a slogan many years ago: "Progress is our most important product." There can be little doubt that progress has been a priority in the western world. This, after all, is what we are told makes for a better life. Our standard of living rests upon the pillar of progress. So why is man struggling? The paradox again begs to be explained.

There seems to be an inexorable law that goes into effect with every pioneer advancement to improve life. Much like a seesaw, when one side is up, the other is invariably down. We build cars and planes to satisfy our transportation needs, while at the same time polluting the atmosphere. We build bigger TVs and watch in amazement as the SAT scores drop to an all-time low. We improve the shelf life of a product but soon discover the preservatives are a cause of cancer. We develop faster computers and spend more time at the office, which is the very problem they were designed to solve. All is vanity.

Technology is not evil, but when technology replaces God, then we have committed the greatest of sins—*idolatry*. This is when God gives man over to his own devices. God has a way of keeping us humble when we trust in our own wisdom. The apostle Paul put a burr in the humanist's saddle when he said, "Hasn't God made the world's wisdom foolish?" (1 Cor. 1:20), and "For the wisdom of this world is foolishness with God. . . . He catches the wise in their craftiness" (1 Cor. 3:19). Guess what? We've been taken. I say "we" because many Christians have fallen for the humanist philosophy that states, "Life will be better *when* . . . ," but *when* never comes.

Shortly after the discovery of penicillin, man predicted he was on the cutting edge of wiping disease from the face of the globe. Today such prophecies are not too highly esteemed by those in medical research. Complex viruses continue to lobby for control and at present have the upper hand. "Stop the world, I want to get off" is the battle cry of humanity, as many view life as a purposeless treadmill.

Something keeps man from moving toward his ultimate goal of happiness. There seems to be a monkey wrench in every gear, and the circumstances of life don't mesh. The oasis is a mirage and the pot of gold is filled with ashes. His ship never does come in, although he sees it lingering so plainly on the horizon. This is the plight of the lost and those who follow a western jesus.

Instead of the Christian community changing the world, we find that our salt has lost its savor as we submit to the secular belief that "we only go around once in life, so we better grab for all the gusto we can." We begin to feel cheated if we don't have a new car, computer, or microwave. Our lifestyle becomes cramped as experience pronounces judgment on our philosophy. It's checkmate! The apple is rotten to the core. This is one reason I so detest the gospel of health and wealth. It is man-centered. It's all about me and my present happiness. It's all about the whens of life. The focus is temporal, and that which is temporal is terminal.

Excuses for trusting in the whens of life have run aground. We pause to regroup and find ourselves eyeball to eyeball with the sobering fact that most of our materialistic and technological whens are in the attic, in the basement, lost, broken, rusted, out-dated, or scheduled for the auction block at the next garage sale. Christians, too, find themselves knee-deep in warranties, guarantees, titles, contracts, deeds, lawsuits, bankruptcies, and the like. Is there a way out?

The Solution

In an effort to guard against the peril of the pendulum, a few mid-course corrections are in order. You may by now feel that you have been wandering in the apple orchards more than the orange groves and want a way out.

Keep in mind that no biblical solution at this point has been offered. The reason? Because the problem first had to be defined and all of man's attempts at solving the problem exposed for what they are—folly. Christians might then realize they too have been seduced by the whens of life. Humanistic efforts at solving the paradox had to be examined in order to highlight the biblical solution, and for the sake of credibility, the temptation to believe that "life will be better *when*" needed to be identified.

One of the most fascinating truths of Scripture states that the world is on a collision course with its own wisdom. Every generation predicts great things for the future. Somehow man, through technology and human effort, will extricate himself from the jungle of problems inherited from his less intelligent ancestors. It seems only logical to think this way, as human wisdom increases. Yet history proves exactly what Scripture promised—that God would make foolish the wisdom of the world. It doesn't require prophetic insight to see that the world is close to its breaking point.

Life Will Be Better When

High school and college graduation speeches never cease to amaze me. The theme is always the same: "You are the generation that will lead us into a better future." The speaker then plagiarizes the same speech given at the tower of Babel: "Come, let us build ourselves a city and a tower with its top in the sky. Let us make a name for ourselves" (Gen. 11:4). It always has the elements of "you can do it." It's a Nike speech: "Just do it." It's the world's version of "name it and claim it." They just use different wording, such as "Whatever the mind can conceive it can achieve" or "If you can just believe in yourself, you can do anything." Do you know how many of these speeches have been given? As many as there have been graduation ceremonies.

Try to imagine this being said at Harvard's graduation ceremony.

What a privilege it is to stand here today and address this highly gifted and intellectually elite group of graduating seniors. You have distinguished yourselves as the brightest and best our nation has to offer. I would love to tell you that the future is in your hands. I would love to tell you that you may be the ones to usher in Utopia. I would love to tell you that you will make the world a better place in which to live. But if I told you that, I would give you false hope and would be lying to you. The truth is that a curse has been put on this world due to the sin of Adam, and there is nothing that has or can escape its consequences. All of your human wisdom isn't worth a hill of beans when it comes to reversing the curse. Only God can do that, and he will when he ushers in the new heavens and the new earth. In the meantime, you should use all the abilities and wisdom that you have to help rid this planet of poverty and disease, with the full understanding that all of this will not be eliminated until Christ returns. The big question for all of you graduates is, "Have you come to the Savior?"

Needless to say, the speaker would be ushered off the platform the minute God is mentioned.

Solutions, much like problems, need to be defined in terms of a context. Everything happens within a context of time and/or circumstances. The solution will have little impact without a historical framework, so let's go back to the beginning and find out where this paradox originated.

In Genesis 3:14–19, we are given revelation on what we often refer to as the *curse*. In other words, had not God revealed the curse to us, we would be left with no understanding as to why the world resists our attempts to improve it. Not only do the peoples of the world struggle amongst themselves, but the physical earth refuses to cooperate: "The ground is cursed because of you. You will eat from it by means of painful labor all the days of your life. It will produce thorns and thistles for you, and you will eat the plants of the field. You will eat bread by the sweat of your brow" (Gen. 3:17–19).

The earth has been divinely programmed to resist man's attempts to bring it under control. If it isn't the wind, it's the water; if it's not the desert, it's the dust; if it's not a fire, it's a flood. It's the age-old story of three steps forward and four back. As stated earlier, the apostle Paul in Romans 8:18–23 comments on Genesis 3. We are told that the creation is in bondage to corruption and decay. It groans to be released. It has been made subject to vanity (see Rom. 8:20). Will man and his humanistic wisdom overthrow God's sovereign plan? Because of the fall, God has put this world under the curse of frustration. He uses this to draw people to himself.

This explains why there is such frustration in life. All human effort apart from the revealed wisdom of God is doomed to fail. This is the beauty of biblical revelation. As believers, we don't see this as a riddle or a paradox but the result of sinful pride and declaring independence from God. Just think how it would change our way of life if all people believed the Scriptures. NASA could save billions of dollars. No longer would it be in search of how the universe came into existence. Genesis 1:1 would solve the mystery: "In the beginning God created the heavens and the earth." But don't hold your breath; I doubt NASA will take this chapter too seriously.

Anthropologists would not have to spend their lives in African dust bowls in search of the missing link because God says that everything gives birth after its own kind. How sad to spend millions of dollars and as many man hours in search of something that doesn't exist. Jesus was quite clear when he said, "'Haven't you read,' He replied, 'that He who created them in the beginning made them male and female'" (Matt. 19:4).

And what about those poor souls whose bodies have been frozen in hopes that man will someday find the solution to death. Again, biblical revelation relieves the frustration: "And just as it is appointed for people to die once—and after this, judgment—" (Heb. 9:27). "Therefore, just as sin entered the world through one man, and death through sin, in this way death spread to all men, because all sinned" (Rom. 5:12).

Disillusionment mounts as humans continue to fight against the divine current. Since many are ignorant regarding biblical revelation, they are unaware that bondage and frustration will meet them at every turn. The Christian, however, cannot claim ignorance as an excuse for his wilderness wanderings. His confusion stems from the fact that he has allowed the world to creep into his thinking. When we borrow from the world's philosophy, we can only expect the world's results—futility.

In preparing to present the solution, I feel somewhat compelled to share that I am not offering some nifty panacea verse from Scripture that will free us from the temptation to believe that "life will be better *when . . .*" Like all biblical solutions to any problem, there is a growth process that takes time. I am not presenting a spiritual get-rich-quick scheme.

With that said, we must first realize that a fulfilled life is not based on what is material or circumstantial. Although all Christians have been told this and claim to believe it, few actually live by it, myself included. Second, we must come to grips with a very significant truth: namely, you can only be disillusioned when you have expectations in anything other than God. "God must be true, but everyone is a liar" (Rom. 3:4).

The Lord impressed on me several years ago that to the degree I don't know *him,* I will trust in other things, such as the whens of life. If I don't know God as Jehovah-Jireh ("my God shall supply"), then I am forced to place my confidence in money, employment, stock options, and other things. This must have been what Paul meant when he said, "More than that, I also consider everything to be a loss in view of the surpassing value of knowing Christ Jesus my Lord . . . My goal is to know Him and the power of His resurrection" (Phil. 3:8, 10).

All of our whens are simply areas in which we don't know God. Hence the solution: knowing God. What!? Knowing God? "But that's so general," you say. I know. You were looking for six easy steps to avoid that plaguing temptation, but knowing God? Before you decide to string me up by my thumbs, hear me out. Knowing God is not a vague solution. God makes it quite clear that he wishes to be known. Our problem is that we are not responding to the invitation.

The whens of life are satanic decoys designed to keep us in a state of constant frustration. Jeremiah exhorts us to guard against the philosophy that life will be better when I'm wiser, stronger, or richer: "The wise must not boast in his wisdom; the mighty must not boast in his might; the rich must not boast in his riches. But the one who boasts should boast in this, that he understands and knows Me" (Jer. 9:23–24).

We must be careful not to look to things, people, or circumstances to fulfill our expectations. The more we know God, the more he delights to work supernaturally in our lives, and the more he expands our capacity to know him.

Paul's security was not based on the secular philosophy that life would get better when he could franchise his tent business. "But everything that was a gain to me, I have considered to be a loss because of Christ" (Phil. 3:7). Daniel did not think life would be better if he could get out of Babylon. He purposed in his heart that he would not defile himself (see Dan. 1:8). Moses did not think life would be better if he stayed in Egypt: "For he considered reproach for the sake of the Messiah to be greater wealth than the treasures of Egypt, since his attention was on the reward" (Heb. 11:26).

Here is the bottom line of the solution: God may wish to bless our lives through material possessions or circumstances. Yes, life will be better as a result, but not because of *what* he provided. Life will be better because *he* was the provider. God becomes the prime mover in making life better. He breaks through the cloud of frustration and fills our hearts with the joy of seeing him provide. Our security is transferred from the whens of life to the provider of the whens, which allows us to testify of his goodness: "The Lord's blessing enriches, and struggle adds nothing to it" (Prov. 10:22). "For the eyes of the Lord range throughout the earth to show Himself strong for those whose hearts are completely His" (2 Chron. 16:9).

When there is a supernatural testimony behind our job, home, marriage, and family, then God is glorified and we are satisfied. And here's why. We are spiritual beings. We can only be fulfilled when God is at work in our lives. The whens of life frustrate the flesh. The provider of the whens satisfies the spirit. Our spiritual capacity is greater than our physical capacity. Thus our spiritual makeup is really who we are. The world and the enemy have blinded us to the truth, thus we seek fulfillment in everything but God. The western church has filled its basket with apples as we skip merrily through the orchard.

We started this chapter with a quote from Ecclesiastes. It seems only fitting to end with the same. Solomon, having experienced all the whens of life, closes his observations about vanity with these words: "When all has been heard, the conclusion of the matter is: fear God and keep His commands, because this is for all humanity" (Eccles. 12:13). We'll add to that the words of the psalmist: "Those who seek the LORD will not lack any good thing" (Ps. 34:10). All the whens of life are eliminated for those who seek the Lord. Yes, life will be better when . . . we know God.

[CHAPTER 12]

A Western Jesus and Discernment

A HUMANISTIC WORLDVIEW HAS become so pervasive in the West that the church is rapidly losing its ability to discern truth in the moral, doctrinal, and ethical arena. I hope to shed some light on this subject in this chapter.

Moral Discernment

Perhaps the biggest influence the western jesus has had on his followers is to convince them that holiness is legalism. This chapter may ruin your day, but more importantly, it may save your life.

In the summer of 1985, my family and I were invited to a friend's house to see a new Hollywood release. Since I had not been to a movie in several years, perhaps due more to busyness than a disdain for movies, my level of discernment had not been dulled by the entertainment industry. (Please understand, I am not denouncing all entertainment but only those forms of entertainment that are immoral. Not all entertainment is evil. Not all movies are evil.)

Though I was somewhat shocked at how far Hollywood had come, I was far more alarmed at what believers considered "family entertainment." As a pastor and shepherd, one of my responsibilities is to warn, through careful teaching, those whom God has entrusted to my care. I'm convinced my sensitivity in this matter was heightened by the fact that I was not a frequent moviegoer and was thus better able to assess the changes than those who attended the theater more frequently.

Driving home that night with my family in tow, I was confused, bewildered, and hurt. Many within the body had recommended this movie. Solid believers had seen it and apparently saw nothing wrong. The next weekend I stood before the body and told them that in three weeks I was going to give a special message, and I wanted everyone there even if they had to shift their own funeral arrangements. Boy did they show up to find out what was on my heart. I believe the Lord gave me a calm, loving, but firm exhortation to my people. Not one person responded negatively. Most everyone admitted that they had let down their guard in this area.

As I began to search the Scriptures regarding moral issues, I became painfully aware of two things. The first is that this issue is not vague or debatable. It is clearly revealed from Genesis to Revelation what God thinks about morality. Second, and of equal importance, is the fact that the church will fight to the death on issues that are either nonessential or vague at best. We split over issues we can't control (e.g., when Christ will return) and demand total agreement on matters that are seen through a glass dimly. However, on biblical morality—which is necessary to maintain fellowship with God—we feign ignorance, and with a western jesus by our side, we fog up the lens of clarity with excuses that will never pass the test of Scripture.

It is the express purpose of this chapter to expose the morality of a western jesus. "Dear friends, I urge you as aliens and temporary residents to abstain from fleshly desires that war against you" (1 Pet. 2:11). I have no intention of making anyone feel guilty or ashamed. I simply wish to reveal how far we have come in what we are allowing into our world of entertainment.

I realize that by today's standards what I saw twenty-one years ago is mild in comparison to what is viewed today. I'm fully aware it is considered family entertainment. Have we not been taken captive by the standards of a western jesus when judging what is right and wrong? Is there not a higher standard? Have we reversed the standard? "Woe to those who call evil good and good evil" (Isa. 5:20). Thirty years ago if an unbeliever had wanted to see films like those believers watch today, he would have waited until out of town on a business trip, worn dark glasses, flipped up his collar, and slipped into the back of the theater for a cheap thrill, all the while experiencing the chill of conviction. Today Christians queue outside the theater with their entire family, rehearsing all the way home the movie's dramatic scenes, and then call their Christian friends to tell them what great family entertainment it was. Movie guides are now standard fare in Christian magazines. Anyone who wishes to know the contents of a movie need do nothing more than consult the entertainment page of their local paper. It will say "rated PG-13 for sexual scenes, crude humor, and brief nudity."

A Tolerance for Evil

We are no longer asking the right questions. Our intellect, not our spirit, has taken over. We can find all kinds of excuses for wallowing in the mire. In 1939, *Gone With the Wind* was released and along with it the first curse word in Hollywood's film history. Clark Gable said, "Frankly, my dear, I don't give a d___." Consider how far the industry has come. Now consider how far the Christian has come. Somehow we have adopted the belief that as long as we lag a few steps behind the world, we are morally upright. This arm's length from the world is the new standard for a western jesus, and we feel safe in our relative morality. However, what we have failed to discern is that a PG rating today would have been PG-13 fifteen years ago, and PG-13 would have been rated R. Hollywood's present condition was never intended to be a relative standard for the church. While the lost world was shocked sixty-five years ago by "I don't give a _____," believers now talk about Hollywood hotties. We need to remember that the Word of

God is our standard. "To the law and to the testimony! If they do not speak according to this word, there will be no dawn for them" (Isa. 8:20).

I suspect the major contributing factor in our moral decline is our ability to tolerate evil. A steady diet of TV and movies keeps our spiritual system in tune with iniquity. As the entertainment industry increases its dosage of sex, violence, and verbal abuse, our ability to discern that which is morally corrupt becomes dulled.

It wasn't until the mid-1950s—when I was ten years old—that my family purchased a television. How well I recall watching such innocuous shows as *Ozzie and Harriet* and *Father Knows Best*. This is where my generation tuned in. We had a low tolerance for evil. As the years have passed, however, our level of tolerance has increased. We are now exposed to clothing commercials that would have been banned in Sodom. My real concern, however, is not how far we have come. We need to be sensitive to the fact that the present generation has entered at a much higher tolerance level than we could have ever imagined. Since we can see how far we have come, can we not project what our children will be viewing in ten years? Just imagine what this generation will tolerate in the future, knowing their present entry level. This chapter was taken from a little booklet I wrote about eight years ago. Guess what? That day has arrived earlier than I thought. Now we have mp3 players that download movies right out of the sky. Kids have cell phones that can do the same. MySpace.com is wide open for any perversion we can think of. Proverbs 27:20 says, "People's eyes are never satisfied." This is exactly why the world comes out with new levels of perversion every year. They understand biblical concepts better than the children of light do. They operate with the full knowledge that man will never be satisfied with his present pleasures. There must be greater and greater stimulation in order to keep the world—and the church—coming back for more.

Excuses from a Western Jesus

What is it about human nature that makes us work so hard to defend activities we know are wrong? Why do we make every attempt to justify and rationalize what our conscience condemns? Could this be what the Lord refers to when he speaks of a seared conscience in 1 Timothy 4:2 or a deceitful heart in Jeremiah 17:9? Someone once said, "An excuse is the skin of a reason stuffed with a lie." While I was visiting Russia a few years back, a Russian pastor spoke forcefully to those of us visiting from the West. He said that our morals and movies were slowly making their way into the Soviet Union and destroying the nation. Our western jesus offers many excuses. Have you ever justified your viewing habits with all or any of the following?

1. *I never watch anything worse than PG-13.* The movie rating system, as we have seen, is based on humanistic reasoning. The inexorable decline in our country's morals dilutes the rating system's credibility. God's standard never changes, but as evil increases in society, the standard by which evil is judged becomes relative to what society will tolerate. By definition, a standard is something that does not change. There is a standard for weights and measurements by which all weights and measurements are compared. When the standard is lowered, that which is compared to the standard is lowered. The standard by which movies are rated is lowered each year. It requires more violence and immorality to qualify for a PG-13 or R rating than it did the previous year. When we fall for this arbitrary rating system, we soon lose our moral discernment. What the world once called adult entertainment, the church now calls family entertainment. The movie industry's present condition was never intended as a relative standard for the church.

2. *Going to the movies helps me stay in touch with the culture.* With this reasoning, why don't we test the quality of the latest crop of marijuana? Do we really need to know what is going on in the world of evil? There was a great statement made in the 1700s about the relevance of Scripture: "Give me a candle and my Bible, lock me in a dungeon, and I will tell you what the world is doing." Is my witness less effective if I avoid Hollywood's latest releases? Listen to the words of the apostle Paul: "But I want you to be wise about what is good, yet innocent about what is evil" (Rom. 16:19). I have never known the gospel to be in jeopardy because the messenger hadn't been to the latest James Bond flick. This is humanistic thinking at

its best (or should I say at its worst). For more on this line of reasoning, I strongly recommend Josh Harris's book *Not Even A Hint* (Multnomah, 2003).

3. *But the movies I see are tame in comparison with the rest of the films.* Yes, and so is strychnine in comparison with arsenic. This is typical western-jesus thinking. We tend to think if something else exists that is far worse, it automatically dilutes the inherent evil of what we consume. I'm fully aware that much of what believers watch is mild in comparison with what the world watches. Let us not forget that what the world watched sixty-five years ago was mild in comparison to what believers watch today. If greater evil becomes the standard by which we evaluate our morality, then morality becomes relative, and the standard will forever shift in the direction of the world and not the Word.

4. *Everyone else does it.* Why do we as believers always look for another standard? Why are people, movements, and Christian leaders the measuring stick for right and wrong? Why do we consult others when God has clearly spoken regarding such matters? Don't ignore what he has to say in the following Scriptures, but consider their relevance to the subject at hand:

- "But put on the Lord Jesus Christ, and make no plans to satisfy the fleshly desires" (Rom. 13:14). How much of what we view provides opportunity for the flesh? How much would have to be removed from our viewing habits to obey this verse?
- "Therefore dear friends, since we have such promises, we should wash ourselves clean from every impurity of the flesh and spirit, making our sanctification complete in the fear of God" (2 Cor. 7:1). What about senseless violence and gore? Would God have us view this for our pleasure?
- "Nevertheless, God's solid foundation stands firm, having this inscription: The Lord knows those who are His, and everyone who names the name of the Lord must turn away from unrighteousness" (2 Tim. 2:19). "Depart from iniquity" in the Greek actually means *depart from iniquity.*

- "Do not love the world or the things that belong to the world. If anyone loves the world, love for the Father is not in him. Because everything that belongs to the world—the lust of the flesh, the lust of the eyes, and the pride in one's lifestyle—is not from the Father, but is from the world" (1 John 2:15–16). If the lust of the eyes is not of the Father, then where does it originate?
- "Adulteresses! Do you not know that friendship with the world is hostility toward God? So whoever wants to be the world's friend becomes God's enemy" (James 4:4). Is not the movie industry the height of worldliness?
- "But I want you to be wise about what is good, yet innocent about what is evil" (Rom. 16:19). To consider being entertained by sex and violence is a frightening thought.
- "For God has not called us to impurity, but to sanctification" (1 Thess. 4:7). To be holy is to be set apart for God's purposes.
- "Dear friends, I urge you as aliens and temporary residents to abstain from fleshly desires that war against you" (1 Pet. 2:11). What damage is done to the soul? How much wrong thinking is put into the mind? Where will it lead the next generation?
- "Finally brothers, whatever is true, whatever is honorable, whatever is just, whatever is pure, whatever is lovely, whatever is commendable—if there is any moral excellence and if there is any praise—dwell on these things" (Phil. 4:8). How many films or TV shows could be filtered through this verse without leaving a residue of corruption?
- "I will not set anything godless before my eyes. I hate the doing of transgression; it will not cling to me" (Ps. 101:3). It is one thing to stumble across evil; it's another thing to pay for it.

What would we have to remove from our lives if we took these Scriptures at face value? Should we take them at face value? If not, what do they mean? Did Christ really mean it in John 14:15 when he said, "If you love Me, you will keep My commandments"? Would a genuine love for Christ cause us to rearrange our entertainment schedule? I have often heard of believers visiting third-world countries and telling the believers there, "I wish I could take you back to America with me." The response is not what you might think. Many will say, "We don't want to go to the United States because materialism and entertainment will cause us to forget God."

5. *What's wrong with a little entertainment?* Such a question reveals a deeper problem. Why, for example, are many developing nations experiencing revival and spiritual growth? Why does church history reflect this to be one of the weakest ages of all time in western culture? Why are there so many problems in the home? Why is contentment at an all-time low? Why are there so many defeated Christians? The answer is really not that complex. Our need for fulfillment is on a spiritual, not an entertainment, plane. Amusement often robs us of time with the family and fellowship with believers. Sapped of spiritual energy, we soon lose our direction and drift aimlessly in a sea of moral confusion. There is nothing wrong with a little entertainment, provided it honors the Lord. "Whether therefore ye eat, or drink, or whatsoever ye do, do all to the glory of God" (1 Cor. 10:31).

6. *But the movie/book had such a clever plot.* We have come to think that if evil is sugarcoated, it must be all right. It is strange how we would never use such logic when it comes to eating. Would you consider taking poison glazed with honey? Why then is an entertainment format fit for consumption when the meat of the message is corrupted?

7. *I've been viewing movies like this for years, and they have never affected me.* You and I are the least capable of making such an assessment. For example, we can't see ourselves aging, but just bump into an old college friend who we haven't seen in years; he or she will be only too quick to point out that we are getting a little thin on top and plump around the waist. In the same way, we can't detect our own moral decline. It requires the Word of God to reflect our present spiritual condition. Any person who uses this excuse and can honestly say that today's movies do not cause sexual stimulation is lying to himself and fools no one.

8. *I have not been convicted in this area.* A particular thought comes to mind when I hear this. It is true that we should not follow someone else's

convictions in areas that are not explicitly revealed in Scripture. However, we are not dealing with a subject that is fuzzy, vague, unclear, or hazy. In my opinion, God's guidelines for moral purity are among the clearest teachings in his Word. This would be equivalent to saying, "I'm not convicted about shoplifting." It is a matter of obedience, not conviction.

9. *All sin is the same.* Why has Hollywood been the target when there are so many other pressing issues, such as greed, hate, jealousy, and materialism? Why single out the sin of immorality over all the rest? Aren't all sins the same in the eyes of God? While these all sound like fair questions, they are really nothing more than an excuse. Here's what I mean. "Some people speed, others gossip, I go to dirty movies. It's all the same to God." It's the nobody-is-perfect excuse. Here is what's wrong with this rationale. Is it true that all sin is the same in the eyes of God? Yes and no. Yes, all sin is the same for the unbeliever. One sin will keep him out of heaven. Heaven is perfect, and no sin as small as a lie or as great as murder will be allowed in. However, for the believer all sin is not the same. In the Old Testament, some sins had the death penalty attached to them (i.e., adultery), while others were treated in a far less severe manner. All sins are not the same for the believer. To argue that procrastination and adultery are the same in the eyes of God is ludicrous, but it sure comes in handy during those dark moments of temptation. Another interesting observation regarding lust is that every list of sins mentioned in the New Testament, to the best of my knowledge, starts with sins of immorality: Mark 7:21–23; Romans 1:29; 1 Corinthians 6:9–10; Galatians 5:19–21; Ephesians 4:22–26; and Colossians 3:5–6. There is a hidden motive behind the excuse of claiming that all sins are the same. It is a futile attempt to place a decoy before our conscience in hopes of redirecting its powers of conviction away from our moral compromises.

Perhaps the main reason for singling out immorality is that it seems to be universal in nature. Not everyone struggles with lying, stealing, or cheating, but most everyone struggles with the lust of the flesh. This is why the movie industry does so well. It attempts to satisfy a need, which in reality can only be satisfied in a righteous way.

The Ultimate Excuse

A generous amount of space has been afforded this last alibi because of its recent popular and widespread use. The last excuse for indulging in immorality is possibly the most insidious. Perhaps you have armed yourself with this final defense in hopes of dismissing all that has been said thus far with a western jesus by your side. This is the big gun used by many believers to continue with viewing habits that dishonor the Lord. It's the I-have-liberty-in-Christ excuse.

Four key words come into play at this point: *liberty, holiness, legalism,* and *grace.* These terms are often used and defined to excuse sinful habits. They are often employed to lay boundaries where God has not spoken or to remove them where he has. Some definition at this stage may clear the path for truth to run on.

Perhaps one of the greatest discoveries in the believer's life is the truth of "liberty in Christ." The law can no longer condemn me. Christ has set me free from the law of sin and death. There could be no greater joy! However, liberty is not freedom from holiness, but a call to holiness. "For you are called to freedom, brothers; only don't use this freedom as an opportunity for the flesh, but serve one another through love" (Gal. 5:13). *Holiness* means to be set apart. It is the word from which we derive the terms *saint* and *sanctified.* In John 17, Jesus described holiness best when he referred to believers as *in* the world but not *of* the world. Unfortunately there is a strong cry from the pew when issues of holiness arise. *Legalism!*

This issue of legalism versus liberty has been hotly debated through the years, particularly in our materialistic, pleasure-oriented western culture. It might be profitable to define these terms and see where our entertainment habits fit in light of these definitions. Legalism essentially falls into three categories:

1. *Trying to keep the law to be saved.* The law cannot save; only God's grace can save.
2. *Believing that God will love me more, for example, if I pray more, read my Bible, and stop going to the movies.* God unconditionally loves

you and me. No amount of dos and don'ts will increase His love for us.

3. *Adding rules to God's Word where he has not spoken.* "Thou shalt not play cards." "God is angry with anyone who doesn't attend Wednesday night prayer meeting." This type of legalism is nothing more than adding the doctrines of men to the Word of God. Legalism is regulated by the flesh and is an outward response to a set of rules that make us appear righteous. The Pharisees kept their list of rules, but God exposed their hearts: "Woe to you, scribes and Pharisees, hypocrites! You are like whitewashed tombs, which appear beautiful on the outside, but inside are full of dead men's bones and every impurity" (Matt. 23:27).

Does God's Word speak against movies? Categorically not. To say so would be adding to the Word of God. Does God's Word cry out against lust, foul language, and immorality? Categorically yes! Therefore, we are not dealing with a gray area but a black-and-white issue.

Regarding Christian liberty, where do we stand? Liberty is regulated by holiness, which is an inward spiritual response to God and his Word because of who I am in Christ. We have lost our way when we confuse holiness with legalism, which has now taken over the western church. My great concern as a pastor is that those whom I shepherd, as well as myself, can discern the difference. When we start throwing everything into the category of legalism, where will this take the church? Is the day approaching when denouncing premarital sex will be called legalism? Are we far from demanding that drunkenness, homosexuality, and pornography be protected under the banner of Christian liberty?

To call holiness *legalism* is to profane the name of Christ, prostitute his Word, mock his command to be holy, blemish this great doctrine, cause our hearts to become hard, and prepare us to accept greater evil. I would certainly agree that just as we are saved by grace, we are to live by grace. If we try to hide under Romans 6:14 ("you are not under law but under grace"), then we must be honest enough to find out what grace does for the believer. Paul gives us a clear and unmistakable answer. "For the grace of God has appeared, with salvation for all people, instructing us to deny godlessness and worldly lusts and to live in a sensible, righteous, and godly way in the present age" (Titus 2:11–12). Do these verses indicate freedom to do anything I please? Quite the opposite. The indwelling grace of the believer instructs him to flee evil. False teaching on this subject has diluted the power of grace and left the church anemic. We are drowning in senseless entertainment. There is a place to denounce legalism and embrace liberty, but it requires discernment to know where and when.

Again, the question begs to be answered: Do my viewing habits pass through the test gate of Scripture? Do sentinels of truth post a Do Not Enter sign? Do I surrender or try to counter his Word by drawing from my quiver of western excuses? Once excuses have carried out the supreme mission of desensitizing the heart to evil, we soon find ourselves suffocating under a blanket of moral pollution. We have seen the danger of excuses and must be careful students of their nature—lies disguised as good reasoning. They prey on our weakness and turn the compass of our conscience south, escorting us from one entertainment venue to another. Once a weekend pattern of flesh feeding sets in, we discover that excuses have nasty offspring called habits, which are in relentless pursuit to put our soul behind bars. Request for parole—denied. The prophetic side of Scripture that has been so longsuffering begins to lose patience and bares its teeth like an angry canine: "Don't be deceived: God is not mocked. For whatever a man sows he will also reap" (Gal. 6:7). Consequences of sin soon appear like unwanted guests who have come to crash the party. We begin to realize excuses are like tentacles that squeeze holiness out of the believer, who soon discovers the harsh reality that sin is subtle and a callous heart cruel.

I write this out of a heart of compassion. If you could sit in my counseling chair and see the damage a western jesus and his entertainment have done to families, you would grieve. The dermatologist looks daily at premature wrinkled skin. He sees melanoma and other varieties of skin cancer. He says to his patients, "If only you had regulated your exposure to the sun, this would not have happened." But the looks of a great tan far outweigh the possibility of an early death. I think we need more exposure to the Son.

The Way of the Fool

In Proverbs 7, we have the account of a foolish young man who is in the wrong part of town at the wrong time of night. The observer of this young man says he lacked judgment. A woman dressed like a harlot took his eyes captive. Her seductive ways brought him into the realm of death.

We read this and smugly say to ourselves, "I've never done anything like that. I have never visited a prostitute or been taken captive by an immoral woman." Let's not be too hasty to dismiss this text as addressing some wayward youth. This actually addresses the lifestyle of many believers today. For you see, our technology now allows us to visit her home without ever leaving ours. Our local video store invites us to an evening of entertainment hosted by a harlot. A few clicks on the Internet or a late-night cable movie and we have played the part of a fool.

A Moral Contradiction

There is a strange twist in the western church regarding this subject matter. The following scenario is being played out daily across the nation. Pastor Jones, while out of town on a speaking engagement, purchases a men's magazine. A member from his congregation on travel witnesses the purchase but remains quiet until he can privately meet with his pastor. The member lovingly confronts him. The pastor openly admits that several times a year he makes such purchases while on travel. The pastor and member agree to inform the church leaders of the problem. He is asked to step down for six months and get help. Word leaks out to the body, and he eventually moves out of the area to avoid further embarrassment. Meanwhile, a few miles away, Pastor Smith gives a culturally relevant illustration in his sermon from a movie. The congregation and spiritual leaders of the church applaud his abilities to relate entertainment themes to real-life situations, particularly if they have a redemptive theme. His people are proud that he doesn't live a sheltered life but is in touch with the real world.

The strange twist centers on the fact that the illustrations are taken from movies that display nudity or have blatantly immoral themes. What is the reason for this moral contradiction? Cultural acceptance from a western jesus. If the world system accepts it, so does the church. As the world goes, so goes the church. This same logic has wormed its way into most Christian homes. Parents are devastated to find sexually explicit material under their teen's mattress but have no problem dropping them off at the theater to view in public what they have hidden in private.

The world is not embarrassed by sins that are socially acceptable; however, there are some sins the world looks upon with a certain amount of disdain. Getting stone drunk at a company Christmas party might get you a reprimand from the boss the following day. Drunkenness shows a lack of self-control and smacks of an undisciplined life. Reading pornography has a social stigma attached to it. The movies, however, fall into an entertainment category. Somehow there is a double standard that says it is perfectly OK to view pornography on the screen but not in a magazine. There is not the embarrassment associated with being seen walking out of an R-rated film as there is being caught walking out of an adult bookstore. Strange, is it not?

No doubt some will find the movie-magazine comparison contrived, since most believers go to the movies for the value of its storyline, not its sexual content. To this I would agree. After all, reading a pornographic magazine could be for no other purpose than for sexual stimulation, whereas to see a movie might be for a different reason. At this point we may find ourselves at ease, comforted by the fact that this comparison of movies and magazines is forced and lacks substance. However, if honesty were summoned to render a verdict in this matter, I believe it would find us guilty on three counts:

1. Though we went to the theater with the singular purpose to enjoy a night out, our fallen nature secretly hopes an illicit scene is waiting in the wings. When it makes its appearance, we will be armed with the ever-ready defense that we didn't come for that purpose, and therefore, cannot be held accountable for what we saw.

2. From past experience, ratings, talk around town, and newspaper reviews, we probably knew in advance that the movie contained sexually explicit material. To plead ignorance at this stage is a bit weak.

3. Intent never nullifies consequence. Downing a bowl of vanilla fudge ice cream with the singular intent of enjoying the flavor does not erase the caloric content. With flavor often come calories, and with calories comes weight. With sensual entertainment comes immorality and with immorality, lust. Though we may justify our viewing habits and even make distinctions between movies and magazines, God does not accept our rationalizations. Our eyes still behold that which is not pleasing to God. "I will not set anything godless before my eyes" (Ps. 101:3).

A Backslider Speaks Out

As we examine the pilgrim and his morals, I can't help but draw the reader's attention to the following words by the apostle Peter in his second epistle, where he says: "And if He rescued righteous Lot, distressed by the unrestrained behavior of the immoral (for as he lived among them, that righteous man tormented himself day by day with the lawless deeds he saw and heard)" (2 Pet. 2:7–8). Now here is a man not exactly known for being a spiritual giant. He doesn't light up Scripture with the testimony of a Daniel or a Moses, yet he is distressed and tormented in his soul over what he saw in Sodom. Here is what troubles me. The western believer not only is not troubled by what he sees but is engaged in the moral pollution of the culture that grieved a backslidden Lot. We have no boundaries at all regarding what we watch.

If the Truth Were Known

I have a few last thoughts as we draw to a close regarding this study on moral discernment. How is it that such blatant evil has crept into the church unawares? Why have so many believers embraced Hollywood's perverted view of love, sex, and marriage? How could we have been so duped? I have pondered this for quite some time, and I hope these final thoughts might give us an answer.

One reason why movies are so readily accepted is that many believers have come out from under the heavy hand of legalistic churches. With the churches' numerous man-made doctrines and rules, movies were usually on the list. Denouncing movies smacked of legalism because the rest of the list fell into that man-made category. The pendulum often swings back to the extreme—all movies and TV shows are now permissible because they were once denounced by legalists. Therefore, to be free from legalism is to be free to watch anything we want. Paul responds, "Should we continue in sin in order that grace may multiply? Absolutely not! How can we who died to sin still live in it?" (Rom. 6:1–2).

The entertainment format clouds the mind from detecting the evil blatantly or subliminally woven throughout the film. This sinister intruder disguised as humor, action, and romance makes his way past the gate-keeper of our soul, who has long since fallen asleep, and does what evil does best. It sears the conscience (see 1 Tim. 4:2), desensitizes the heart (see Eph. 4:19), and defiles the mind (see Titus 1:15).

Once the entertainment industry has taken root in our souls, it is very hard to renounce—thus, all the excuses and rationalizations. The fact is, we have grown to love entertainment no matter what the content. We feel it is our right. It helps take the edge off, much like a stiff drink at the end of the day. We have our video library and the weekly entertainment guide close at hand. We look to see what the latest must-see film is. We can't wait for Friday night to put our brain in neutral, our flesh in drive, and our spirit in reverse. After all, we deserve it. It's been a long week. Then one day we sense something isn't right. We never seem to be in the Word, and when we are, it's dry as dust. Prayer seems meaningless. Our soul is parched. We lack real joy, and the Christ we claim as Savior seems distant and elusive. Church is dull and our testimony stale. What happened? The entertainment industry took up residence in our heart. There is now a TV in every room, and our video rental card is more tattered than our Bible.

Truth and Consequences

The ultimate damage done to any society that puts no restraints on the entertainment industry cannot be adequately measured. It seems clear, however, that what damages the individual, damages the nation:

- *Entertainment desensitizes us to evil.* The more perversion we allow into our minds, the more callous we become in detecting evil. The more callous we become in detecting evil, the more perversion we allow into our minds. The cycle becomes vicious and leads to an intoxication of lustful thoughts. Our minds soon become their new residence, and serving an eviction notice is of little use. We can no longer think with spiritual clarity, and the mind of Christ is only a doctrine taught in seminary.

- *Entertainment deadens the pain of reality.* Life soon becomes make-believe. Reality becomes distorted. Movies take us back in time and forward into the future, shrink people, enlarge people, exaggerate pleasure, and create fantasies that will never be experienced. Reality soon becomes difficult to accept. We see people we will never look like. We experience romance that is totally unrealistic. We are given imaginary power. All this frustrates the human soul. God has made us to experience that which is real, not that which is illusory or imaginary. Our western jesus has led us far from the transcendent Christ—who is not an illusion, but who is very real.

- *Entertainment directly affects our society.* Why is the current divorce rate among Christians 50 percent when it was drastically less one hundred years ago in the world of unbelievers? Has the flesh changed? No, but the ability to frustrate it has changed. The movie industry encourages fornication and adultery. It demands that we have a better life. It reduces the vow "until death do us part" to a disposable preference. Society is seduced by fantasy planted in its soul but is eventually awakened by a harvest of decay. Hopelessness sets in. Life is dull. Another soap opera or movie will only deaden our conscience a few more hours. An overindulgence of lustful thoughts eventually leads a society to become angry. We demand our rights to have it all. But it appears only on a screen. We have been defrauded. There is no way to righteously satisfy what the world promises. It's a dead-end street. For example, we now have road rage, angry teens, bench brawls at sporting events, and endless lawsuits. Though not all of this can be attributed to the movies and TV, a great deal can. There is a clear biblical connection between immorality and anger. The young men involved in the Columbine High School massacre in April 1999 were steeped in pornography, as are those involved in almost all violent crimes.

What Now?

Some hard things have been said here regarding our viewing habits. There has been no attempt to be judgmental, as I have found this to be a major battle in my own life. I made some corrections a few years ago that I trust might be helpful to the reader:

- Recognize your viewing habits to be perhaps your greatest battle. It is the Achilles' heel for the church today. Renouncing this will not be easy.
- If you are a regular television or movie watcher, take inventory of your program selections. Are these shows honoring to the Lord, or do they create lust in your heart?
- Reread the section on excuses. Ask yourself if you have used these to justify watching that which you know is not pleasing to the Lord.
- Humble yourself before the Lord by confessing your sin and seeking his grace to be set free.
- Tell another believer about your decision and ask him or her to pray that you would have the strength to maintain your new desire to live a holy life before God.
- Remove any temptation from your home, such as videos and cable programming that might cause you to fall in this area.

A holy life brings us into the presence of God. This is where he dwells. It is a safe place for the mind. It cleanses and purifies. This is where we sit at his feet and learn of his ways. Tom Cruise is not his substitute. God is our all in all.

A Final Word

In my years of pastoring, I have learned it is far more important to tell people what they *need* to hear than what they *want* to hear. God is not a killjoy. He knows what brings genuine joy, and he knows what destroys the soul. This is the very reason he has chosen to reveal to us how we should live. I have come to realize that when I can't stop what God commands me to stop, I'm admitting to addiction. When I won't stop, I'm admitting to rebellion. I trust the reader will exercise this compelling truth of moral discernment in all areas of life. Entertainment is just one small segment of the believer's walk affected by this discipline. The world through books, magazines, TV, nightclubs, videos, and a host of other avenues of entertainment invites the believer's eye to wander from its heavenly gaze.

Is this chapter really about movies and TV? Yes and no. Clearly we have touched on the subject of morality, and I trust it will encourage the reader to consider what has been said. However, there is a greater issue at hand. I have used this chapter as a dipstick into the moral condition of the church to show that if this is how far we have fallen as a western church and how much our culture has impacted the church in a negative way, then doesn't it stand to reason that we have also been influenced in other areas covered in this book, namely how we view the church, our pilgrimage, our reasoning, and our faith.

The movie issue is just a measuring rod. When we see how much we have been discipled by a western jesus and how we view the Scriptures through a biased lens, is it any wonder that our morals have hit rock bottom? This has not been easy to write because I never wish to sound judgmental. I know my own heart, and I certainly don't measure up to all that I have written. Much of what has flowed from my pen comes from the realization that I have fallen prey to much western thinking. I began to wake up a few years ago and was sobered by what I was seeing in the church in America. I started reading Tozer voraciously and was convicted by where he saw the church heading over forty years ago. He was so prophetic, and I became very aware of my sinfulness. What he and others warned against is now a reality. I came to this realization a while back that once evil enters society, it goes through five stages of evolution. (This is one evolution I believe in). When Clark Gable swore in *Gone with the Wind*, the world went from 1) being shocked by such language, 2) to tolerating such language, 3) to accepting such language, 4) to embracing such language, 5) to promoting such language. This is the fulfillment of Romans 1.

I simply want to point out what happens to a culture that has lots of time and money on its hands. The western jesus shows up in many more places than just the movies, but this area of moral discernment gives us a good objective read on where we are on the other issues as a western church. Believe God when he says, "The way of the transgressors is hard" (Prov. 13:15 KJV). Obedience is not always easy, but the rewards far outweigh the "pleasures of sin for a season" (Heb. 11:25 KJV).

CHAPTER 13

The Pilgrim and His Counterpart

WE OFTEN SHY AWAY from the word *witness*. It seems to conjure up mental images of a fiery evangelist laughed at by the world. It seems pushy, arrogant, and self-righteous to try and persuade others about our spiritual beliefs. We are often told that we are narrow-minded and should keep our thoughts to ourselves. My, how we have obeyed their request. Has it ever occurred to the western church that when we are told such things, that those giving us such advice are evangelizing. They are telling us that there is more than just one way. Isn't that itself a narrow message? We have been intimidated into keeping our mouths shut in spite of the clear command to open them.

Many are presently risking their very lives to preach in areas where Christianity is forbidden, yet here we are with great freedom but enslaved by a fear of looking foolish or believing that we have no business proclaiming the truth. I want to be an encouragement to you in this arena. In order to do so, I need to tell my story, but I have no way of sharing the details without bringing myself into the picture. I'm just a vessel and certainly no paragon of virtue in this Great Commission. The Lord has been pleased to advance the gospel through my preaching and witness, and I enter into this personal testimony with fear and trembling. We must always remember that the gospel is the power of God unto salvation and not our personalities or clever answers to the lost. So with that as a disclaimer, I invite you to enter my world starting in the summer of 1970.

In the opening of this book I shared how I came to know Christ in Copenhagen, Denmark. When I returned to the United States, I had no money, no job, and no place to go. I decided to move to Miami, Florida, and got into the life insurance business. Armed with my newfound faith, God providentially had my path cross with another believer who was moving out of the apartment that I was moving into. He immediately saw that I was a new convert in need of discipling. He took me under his wing and my journey began with regard to telling others about Christ.

Since I was in the business world and he was finishing up his senior year of Bible college, we decided to start an adult Bible study where he would be the teacher and I would be the provider of lost souls. It wasn't long before we began to see conversions as well as new believers strengthened in their faith. My friend graduated a few months later and moved across the state, leaving me with the study. I was as wet behind the ears as they come, but I was excited about the process. The very first time I spoke at the study I knew this was what I wanted to do for the rest of my life. Many were converted and demonstrated fruit in their lives, which remains to this day. I left the business world and spent two years in Bible college, which gave me the basics of theology, for which I am most grateful.

Through a series of events, I felt called to plant a church in Reston, Virginia, where my wife Kay and I moved in May 1974. My pilgrimage was baptized by all the trials and tribulations of getting a church started in a community where I knew absolutely no one. How could I possibly pull this off without divine assistance? As the apostle Paul said, "Who is equal to such a task?" (2 Cor. 2:16).

A generous couple whom we had never met before knew of our desire to plant a church in Reston and allowed us to stay with them until I could secure work and find an apartment. I applied for a job at the local country club and was hired as a glorified locker room attendant. I was sure the

Lord had made some kind of mistake. What was I doing working at a country club, cleaning toilets, vacuuming the floors, cleaning the pool, and shining shoes? I had spent four years at Annapolis, had a political science degree from a reputable university, and a degree from Bible college. Why wasn't this being put to good use? Why wasn't I an assistant pastor of some large church using my skills? Where was God in all this?

The pressure was on. I had to have converts or there would be no church. I began to strategize as to how I would engage people in a discussion of the gospel. In June 1974 we planned our first Bible study to be held at the home of the couple who had invited us to stay with them. But whom would I invite? I had come to know a number of people at the club, so I had my list of potential attendees. I started with the manager, who quickly informed me that at best he was agnostic, but out of courtesy he agreed to come. I then went after the athletic director, the golf pros, a chef, and the lifeguard staff. The study was to begin at 7:00 p.m. on a hot Tuesday night in June. As the time approached, I became very nervous. The driveway was not exactly filling up with cars. As a matter of fact, there were no cars. I walked out on the golf course behind the house and began to pray, "Lord, please bring someone out tonight." A few moments later a car pulled up, and I immediately recognized it as belonging to the manager of the club. I ran up to greet him and asked if he knew whether or not the athletic director would show up. He said he seriously doubted it. The owner of the home called the athletic director and said, "By the way, the study tonight is informal attire, see you in a few minutes" and hung up. Out of a sense of obligation, the director and his wife came. So we had the couple who owned the home, two of their friends, my wife and me, the athletic director and his wife, and the manager. None of the golf pros showed up or any of the other invitees. By the way, when you invite people to something like a Bible study and they say they will try to make it, what they actually mean is "I will not, under any circumstances, be there." More on this later.

The very first night I spoke on the authority of the Bible and how you could know it is the Word of God and how you could be assured of entering heaven. I gave a strong gospel message, closed in prayer, and pointed to the snacks in the back of the room. The athletic director's wife approached me with a few questions and said, "I want to hear more about this."

Each week I continued to invite people from the club only to get the typical response: "We'll try to make it." I soon began to realize that such an invite carries a certain amount of potential intimidation with it. Those being invited naturally worried about being called on to pray or read from the King James Bible. They feared not knowing where various books of the Bible are located. They feared being called on to answer a question. To ask someone to attend a study strikes fear into the hearts of those who have never been schooled in the Scriptures. My approach changed. One morning while hanging around the pro shop, I asked Harry, one of the pros, about coming to the study. He had been invited numerous times but had never shown up. I said, "Harry, I would love to have you come to the study tonight. The format is very simple. I teach from the Bible for about thirty-five minutes. I won't call on you or anyone else to read, pray, or answer any questions. If you don't like the study, I will never ask you again. Just give it a try." Harry showed up.

The athletic director and his wife both became believers, and he went off to seminary and now has a doctorate. The manager and his wife both trusted Christ and have served in numerous churches, including the great Denton Bible Church. Harry, the golf pro, became one of our elders and now lives in Atlanta. Each one of these people has gone on to lead others to Christ. Third generation believers have come out of that study.

This, however, was just the beginning. Another golf pro, Bill, showed up with his fiancée, Cheryl. They came out of curiosity more than spiritual desire. After each study they would get in the car and head to the West Virginia border to play the slots, laughing all the way about the silly Bible study. They eventually got married and fell on tough times. My dear friend John, whom I had gone to Bible college with, came up to help me with the new church plant. He also worked at the club and led Bill and Cheryl to Christ. Bill and Cheryl are both now on staff at our church where Bill has headed up our missions outreach for the last eighteen years. Under his leadership our church has given more than $20 million to world missions. God is good! But it doesn't end here. A young high school sophomore named Bob was also impacted when he came out to our youth group that had just started. He soon called upon Christ to save him and has been my youth pastor for the last twenty years. His ministry to the lives of our youth cannot be calculated.

While I was still working at the club, which lasted from June 1974 to September 1975, I had a shoeshine concession in order to make a few extra dollars. My actual club salary was $6,000 a year, so the shoe deal was a big help. My partner was a young man named Pat who had come out of a religious background and was very disillusioned with anything that had God at the helm. I couldn't help but think what an easy target this guy would be. As we shined shoes together, I started pouring the gospel into his life, expecting him to come to the Savior within a few days. Months went by and his questions were daunting. He had really thought through the issues and was no pushover. I tried everything from apologetics to logic to reason, but nothing would penetrate. He eventually started to attend our church service and after some period of time, the Holy Spirit convicted him of his need, and he called upon the Lord for salvation. He left the club and went to Washington Bible College and was one of our first missionaries. Having served in Thailand for a couple of years, he returned to the D.C. area with a passion to reach the Laotian and Thai population in our area. The fruit of his labors are more than abundant. One morning I picked up the *Washington Post* and there was Pat on the front page with a story about him helping a Thai family that had been in a train wreck. I said to myself, "Wait a minute here, Pat's on the front page and I've never even made the classifieds." God is good.

The early days at the club produced three converts in the golf pro shop, the manager, the athletic director, three lifeguards, a locker room attendant, a bookkeeper, and one chef. All have gone on to serve the Lord in various capacities.

Not too long after the church got underway, I received a phone call from a carpenter who wanted to come in and see me. He had apparently been doing work for a couple who attended our church. The wife worked in our junior church department and could not attend the services, so each week she was given a copy of the sermon on tape. While Theron, the carpenter, was working in her house, he overheard the message being played. He was at that time attending a very liberal church and could tell from the tape that this was what he believed. He came to my office and told me his story about how he and several other couples were very uncomfortable with the teaching they were getting and asked if it would be OK if they tried out our church. I was thrilled to get him out from under such teaching; and out of that incident of overhearing a tape, the following resulted. One couple that came heard the gospel and was converted. The husband later became one of our elders. Theron came on staff as our youth pastor and later went into missions. One of the men who came was separated at the time, and this was no small marriage problem. They had been apart for about two years with two small children. I said, "Wallace, do you think Linda would come in and talk with me?" He said that all he could do was ask her. She agreed to see me. We met three times, and on the third meeting I told her that she needed to let her husband back into the house and start working on the marriage. She left my office in tears; and with much resentment and anger, she allowed Wallace back into the home. She eventually was converted and some twenty years later we sent Wallace and Linda out to plant a church about fifteen miles west of Reston. They just broke ground for their first building. This couple has led many to Christ and has been used by God to reconcile many damaged marriages. God is good.

Also out of the group that left the liberal church was another very troubled couple. Tim and Sandy had major marriage problems. Tim was a believer, but Sandy was not. She called upon the Lord one Sunday morning after the gospel had been given and life has not been the same from that day on. Now listen to this. Their son, Scott, from Tim's previous marriage came to live with them. He smoked pot and had a rebellious nature, but after many hardships, Scott eventually became a believer and entered New Tribes Mission. He and his wife were sent to Thailand to reach a tribe in the northern part of this great country. After many years of being baptized into the culture and learning the language, the tribe was reached with many conversions. Those in the tribe started to reach out to other local tribes and are now having their own missions conference.

Scott just returned home to work with his dad, who is the missions pastor at a large Bible church in Winchester, Virginia.

This is all the result of linking one faithful situation to another. This is not the Mike Minter show, but the obedience of countless people throughout the years to whom God has shown himself faithful. There was the young man who in those early days ran off the sermon tapes before there were duplicators. There was the faithful lady in junior church who listened to them. There was the obedient carpenter who knew he needed to get out of the liberal church he was in. There were those who followed him. This all led to reaching a tribal people who are now reaching their next-door neighbors with the gospel. However, the real key to all of this is a sovereign God who providentially arranged for these events because he cares for a lost world.

Also in those early days were the long intellectual battles with my older brother, who at the time was working at the Pentagon. Fresh from getting his master's degree in oceanography, he simply could not reconcile evolution with the biblical view of creation. The gospel, however, can break through human reason, and not long after, he and his wife became believers. They eventually went with New Tribes Missions to Papua, New Guinea, to reach a tribal people who had never heard the gospel. Though they went to language school, it was not like learning French from someone who knew French. No one knew this language. They built their home and an airstrip among the INRU (pronounced Inadoo) people so supplies could be flown in. They gradually learned the language by walking around and pointing to objects and writing down the words phonetically. Eventually the day arrived when they gathered all the people together to see and hear a reenactment of the passion of our Lord. The gospel was acted out and clearly explained. Many came to Christ and are holding church services to this day.

I tell this story because I have watched the western jesus make his way into the church. The pilgrim's mission of being gospel centered and a desire to reach those around us has fallen on hard times. We seem to feel this is the job of someone else when Paul clearly tells us that we have been entrusted with the gospel: "Instead, just as we have been approved by God to be entrusted with the gospel, so we speak, not to please men, but rather God, who examines our hearts" (1 Thess. 2:4). His passionate plea is "How can they hear without a preacher?" (Rom. 10:14). The West is now the mission field. How sad to see what materialism has done to the church. We don't wish to release funds for the cause of the gospel, but we build bigger churches for the purpose of ministering to ourselves. There is literally a ministry for every need but almost nothing for those who have yet to hear.

The West has the vast majority of funds needed to spread the gospel. Randy Alcorn has many statistics on the weakness of the western church in releasing its money because we tend to love this world. We live to make more money so we can improve our standard of living, without one passing thought of using the extra income to raise the standard of living for the poverty stricken throughout the world. Note carefully that I say "we." I am guilty as charged and have made some corrections, but I am far from what I think the Scriptures call us to.

When I was being trained in the life insurance business, we learned quickly the importance of prospecting. We were taught to keep our eyes and ears open for potential clients. Were they young, healthy, and moving up the corporate ladder? If so, then they would be a good prospect. As believers, I don't think we should look at the unbeliever as a prospect, so to speak, but we should look at them as Jesus did: "When He saw the crowds, He felt compassion for them, because they were weary and worn out, like sheep without a shepherd" (Matt. 9:36). We need to be constantly aware of the fact that God has placed an unbelieving world at our feet.

This is not meant to put anyone on a guilt trip. It is just a reminder that we, as believers, are called to tell those around us about salvation. As you well know, many are losing their lives in hostile foreign lands sharing their faith while we are embarrassed to open our mouths in a free country. Give it a try. You just might be surprised how the Spirit will move forward and bless your witness by taking what you say and multiplying it even to northern tribes in Thailand and the southern regions of New Guinea.

CHAPTER 14

The Pilgrim and Those Who Walk with Him

WE CANNOT POSSIBLY GO through life without recognizing the varied personalities that are all around us. God is so unique in his creative powers that the number of different personalities are as many as there are people. One of our favorite expressions when describing someone is to say, "I really like them, but . . . ," followed by some negative aspect of their personality. Here is another one: "They are always under the control of the Spirit. You can tell by how calm they remain in any situation." Assessing personalities can be fun but can also lead us to make false judgments about people's lives.

I don't quite know what it is about me, but I always take everything to its logical conclusion, which can ruin your day. For example, you may conclude that a person is walking in the Spirit because they are so kind, peaceful, and joyful. You rest assured that your assessment is on the money. Now let me tell you how I think about such matters. If being joyful or peaceful is a sign of walking in the Spirit, then what am I to do with

Christ-denying people who are every bit as calm and joyful as a believer? Or worse yet, what do I do with an unbeliever who is considerably more at rest than most believers. A typical western view of lost people is that they are always in inner turmoil and only in Christ can we have true joy and peace. Life seems to tell a different story. I have seen many happy lost people and many sad believers.

Spirituality versus Personality

Have you ever wondered why some people who are not believers display the fruit of the Spirit in a greater and more consistent way than you do? Yet we know that such fruit can only be the product of a true believer. Makes you kind of wonder, doesn't it? I like to refer to this enigma as spirituality versus personality. The fruit of the spirit is found in Galatians 5 and is listed as follows: love, joy, peace, patience, kindness, goodness, faith, gentleness, and self-control. Does it not gall you to lose your temper with your children when the couple next door—who have never once entertained a spiritual thought—remain calm in the midst of spilled milk and sibling rivalry? What are we to make of this?

We must keep several things in mind. The unbeliever is perfectly capable of doing good things and behaving in a kind way. Also keep in mind that the believer is quite capable of displaying sinful behavior. In other words the flesh of the unsaved can perform good works, while the flesh of the believer can do what is wrong, but the source is still from the flesh. For the unbeliever that just may be his temperament or personality.

The real key to understanding this seeming contradiction has to do with at least two things. The first is the source of our behavior. I used to have a very volatile personality, which usually was evident during athletic contests. I have broken golf clubs, pool cues, ping pong paddles, tennis rackets, and have even been known to throw fishing rods into the water if the fish weren't biting. When I became a believer, such behavior seemed to evaporate. I have other issues that have not been uprooted as easily. One thing I know is that the change was not personality but the work of the Spirit in my life.

The second issue is motive. Why does the couple next door never raise their voice at their children? Is it motivated by a love for Christ? Is it a desire to be a good testimony or witness? The real motive might be that they want children who will turn out well and not embarrass them. They may want children who will learn self-control and thus do well in school or athletics, resulting in scholarships that will save the parents lots of money. We may never know the motive, but we do know that it is not empowered by the Spirit of God.

We see this in Christians who we know do not take their faith seriously yet seem to manifest the fruit of the Spirit. They may even wonder why you can't act more like them. You may wonder the same thing. Remember, it may not be spirituality but personality.

Camping with Paul and David

But an hour is coming, and is now here, when the true worshipers will worship the Father in spirit and truth. Yes, the Father wants such people to worship Him.

John 4:23

Could there be two people any more different than Paul and David? I love to study the lives of people in Scripture, and I love to study the spiritual nature of those alive today who comprise what we call the body of Christ. God has made us unique by employing his creative powers. Our personalities are as distinct as our fingerprints. David was a lover of God. He was the supreme worshipper, who danced before the Lord and loved the sound of music. He turned the heavens into a mural painted across the sky: "When I observe Your heavens, the work of Your fingers, the moon and the stars, which You set in place, what is man that You remember him, the son of man that You look after him?" (Ps. 8:3–4).

Paul was a passionate evangelist who had little time for romantic notions of life and nature. He used nature as an apologetic to prove the existence of God: "From the creation of the world His invisible attributes, that is, His eternal power and divine nature, have been clearly seen, being understood through what He has made. As a result, people are without excuse" (Rom. 1:20). Paul appeals more to the intellect, while David touches our emotions. Paul gave evidence for God's existence, while David gave reasons to worship. Paul gave us polemic (argument) while David gave us poetry.

Paul built arguments and forced man to see his condition before a holy God. David weaved poetic expression and appealed to the emotions perhaps more than he did the intellect. Certainly there were overlapping truths that both shared. David said, "The fool says in his heart, 'God does not exist'" (Ps. 14:1).

However their basic natures would have clashed had they been forced to work together. I can just see Paul and David after a hard day of church planting, lying down under the stars only to have David romantically describe the moon and the mighty hosts of heaven. Paul might respond with, "Will you be quiet? I'm trying to sleep, and we have a big day ahead of us."

Don't you see yourself in these characters? We often have conflict in life over the very beauty of our differences. What should be used to supplement what we lack is often seen as a frustration or threat. Maybe we need to go camping with someone who looks at life differently than we do.

There are other instances where personality and spirituality play a major role. Paul and Barnabas clashed over John Mark. Was this simply a theological issue or a clash in personalities? Many western believers think it is ungodly to take a secular personality test like the Myers-Briggs. We fear the world entering in where only Scripture should be used. Scripture certainly is the final authority, but the world being "more astute than the sons of light" (Luke 16:8) often does a far better job analyzing our "fallenness" than we do. The Myers-Briggs has numerous categories that describe the basic personality traits in people, and then it tells you which types clash with other types. No matter what the test registers—and it is usually very accurate—it is nothing more than a distillation of our fallen nature. They can make all the evaluations they want, but only Scripture has the solution. My point in all this is that we, as pilgrims, often make false assessments of people. Some people by nature are jovial and happy. Some by nature are more sullen. Some are extroverts and others introverts. This may have nothing to do with being led of the Spirit.

One of my good friends on staff has traveled with me a great deal. He is by nature an introvert, but you would never know it if you heard him speak. He is one of the funniest men I know, yet he tells me he would be perfectly happy if he lived on a mountaintop and never saw another person other than his family. Here is what is so great about traveling with him. Paul never gets ruffled, and I always look like I just got out of the rinse cycle of a washing machine. I have a fairly wound-up personality. If there are three ants crawling up my leg, I will refer to them in the billions. Paul and I were recently in Germany where I was preaching and he was leading worship. He took one of the preaching sessions and happened to mention that people often compliment him on how calm he remains in difficult situations. In his typical self-effacing manner, he told the audience it had nothing to do with spirituality but that was just the way he was wired. Though I do think Paul walks in the Spirit, I appreciated the fact that he pointed out the DNA of his personality.

In our sojourn as Christians, we will come across many to whom we attribute godliness when in fact that may not be the case. I have had many praise me for my passion in the pulpit, but I know full well that by nature I am a passionate person. No doubt the Spirit has moved me at times, but I think it is far more a reflection of my personality than my spirituality.

Now with this in mind, let's put some traction to the practicality of this truth. In my years of pastoring, I have seen every type of personality on the planet. I love to study people and see what makes them tick. Though most of the people I have ministered to through the years have been a great blessing, I have come to see that American Christians are more easily offended than perhaps any other group of believers in the world. Our culture breeds a whining mentality. We get offended so easily. Yes, we can blame much of this on how we were raised, but if we really believe the gospel, I think we will begin to see that this is really an issue of shared glory. Here is what I mean. Our western lips give God the glory, but our hearts want to share it, and we are thus offended if someone else gets praised for what we did, or we are hurt because our name didn't appear in the credits.

My first awareness of this in my own life came right after I had started a singles ministry in our church. Each week I would gather all the singles together and have a different person give their testimony. After several weeks, it was Tom's turn (not his real name). Tom had been raised at our church and had sat under my preaching his entire life. He had just finished college and joined our group. Now before I tell you his testimony, there is something you need to know. I always give the gospel at the end of each service. I make it very clear that salvation has nothing to do with man's human goodness or being religious or keeping the law. I carefully explain that the very righteousness of Christ is imputed (placed to our account) to all who put their faith in him and him alone. The gospel and its clarity are very important to me. Naturally knowing that Tom had heard me preach a billion times (there I go again), I expected him to praise me for being faithful with the gospel. Here is what Tom shared with the group: "Ever since I can remember, I have been here at Reston Baptist Church. However, it wasn't until I went off to college and attended a Campus Crusade meeting that I heard a clear presentation of the gospel." He was as serious as he could be and had no intention of making me look bad. I smiled through his testimony and said, "Praise God." My insides were going nuts. How could he sit under my preaching and not get saved? Is he telling everyone that I don't give a clear gospel? My lips praised God, but my heart was far from him.

When I left that night, I knew my response was ungodly. What was being exposed was my desire for shared glory. If I really believed the full essence of the gospel, why would I care how Tom got saved? But you see, there is a western jesus that still has his way in my life. Our culture exalts self, and it has infected our hearts and the church. We exalt people above God. The ugliness of pride is all throughout the church. Being easily offended is a form of pride. I see it often. I have many times told our people that we need to give up our right to being offended. "Abundant peace belongs to those who love Your instruction; nothing makes them stumble"

(Ps. 119:165). I have tried to live with this truth the best I know how. Many years ago I gave up my right to being offended, and it has served me well, though there will always be the Tom situations that I need to deal with. Wanting the praise and the glory will forever be a battle.

I love to watch the TV show *Jeopardy*. Many years ago when my son David was just a little boy, he would sit in my lap and watch it with me. One evening he said, "Dad, you should go on *Jeopardy*." What a great opportunity to fish for a compliment and get a little praise from my son, who obviously thought his dad was pretty smart. "David," I said, "why do you think I should go on *Jeopardy?*" Without hesitation, he responded, "Because they give Nintendo games to the losers." So now I'm a loser who can't give a clear gospel.

Offense will come. Some will be major and some minor, but pilgrims have no time to lick their wounds. This western pride must be put on the cross. When you are offended, let me suggest three possible solutions. These have served me well through the years. First, ask yourself, "Did the person try to offend me?" Most people do not get up in the morning with the intent of being offensive. If we can accept the fact that the person who hurt us had no intention of doing so, this will help alleviate the pain. Second, let's say they did. If that is the case, then we need to have compassion on that person. They have a serious need and we must help them through it. Third, ask yourself if you were too sensitive. No matter what the offense, one of these solutions should be an escape route. This is not a formula but a biblical solution. The Scripture tells us to overlook offenses: "A person's insight gives him patience, and his virtue is to overlook an offense" (Prov. 19:11).

Why We Need to Encourage and to Be Encouraged

But encourage each other daily, while it is still called today, so that none of you is hardened by sin's deception.

Hebrews 3:13

We are called to encourage one another daily and to pray for one another. Here are a few helpful hints on walking with those who are on the same journey.

1. *Because through much tribulation we must enter into the kingdom of God.* We all need to be stroked by the warm hand of encouragement. Whom can you think of who just might need some right now?

2. *Because we receive far more criticism than praise.* Our emotional ledger sheet tells the truth. It sure would be nice to get it to balance before the final account. You can help make the difference.

3. *Because it develops friendships.* We naturally seek out those who refresh us with words of comfort rather than those who destroy with words of criticism.

4. *Because it gives health to the recipient.* "Pleasant words are a honeycomb: sweet to the taste and health to the body" (Prov. 16:24).

5. *Because we hurt far more deeply than we will admit.* Most people carry burdens, the weight of which cannot be estimated by an outsider. Learn to encourage when you sense a need.

How to Encourage

And let us be concerned about one another in order to promote love and good works.

Hebrews 10:24

1. *Learn to encourage daily.* Remember—a person's worth in Christ hangs on the thin thread of encouragement, and some are at the end of their rope. Don't wait to give words of comfort.

2. *Learn to relate to those who have similar needs.* Be sensitive to those who are going through a trial similar to what you have already experienced. How did you weather the storm? Let them know how God used that difficulty in your life.

3. *Learn to be a good listener.* We all need to learn to read between the lines. People rarely unload their problems in bulk. They usually deliver

them in small packages just to see if you're concerned enough to open it. If you do, they will likely make another delivery. No one will expose their deep feelings to people who show little or no interest. Be a person who cares!

It will never be the nature of a man to encourage, but it will forever be his need.

Giving and Receiving Criticism

No one will escape critical words. It is part of life, so we might as well accept the fact and learn from Scripture how to handle it best when it comes. The following is foreign to western thinking.

We should consider several things before looking into the subject. We must first ask ourselves if we are by nature critical, and second, we must consider how well we respond to criticism. Pride and insecurity make us bristle at the thought of being corrected. No one enjoys being told that they are lazy or are not doing a good job. This goes right to the heart of our very being. So let's take a look at how to give and receive criticism. This should help us within our families, our jobs, and our church.

HOW TO GIVE CRITICISM

1. *Earn the right to correct.* This means that you should have poured words of encouragement into the person over a period of time. They will then be far more receptive to correction when it is needed (see Prov. 8:33).

2. *Be gentle but not evasive.* The Scriptures tell us that the servant of the Lord must not strive but be gentle (see 2 Tim. 2:24). If we combine this with Ephesians 4:15, which tells us to speak the truth in love, then we should have an excellent balance in our approach.

3. *Always show the recipient of your correction that you care* (see Prov. 27:5–6). People are far more receptive if they know you have come to them with a pure heart and a desire to help.

4. *Always follow up.* Thank them for any improvement that you see as a result of the correction. This builds confidence and will help you bond with them.

Remember, we all have blind spots that only others can see. Only a fool despises correction (see Prov. 9:8-9).

HOW TO RECEIVE CORRECTION

The flip side of the coin is how to receive criticism. Proverbs has much to say about how a wise man becomes even wiser after correction and how a fool despises any type of rebuke. None of us wants to be labeled by Scripture as a fool, but I must say that few people receive good correction well. So what does God tell us?

1. *Avoid being defensive.* Realize that the one who comes to us may very well have some good advice that will help us in our careers, home life, and other relationships.

2. *Always view correction as protection.* Even if the person who performs the surgery fails to do it skillfully, it may benefit you in the long run. Don't focus on how it was said, but on the truthfulness of what was said.

3. *Recognize that you don't see yourself the way others do.* We generally have a higher view of how we come across, which is why we relate to others the way we do. We feel it is right. Those who are around us most feel the radiation of our personality that we don't experience. The source of the radiation doesn't feel it. This is why we need honest feedback from those who love us.

4. *Don't expect people to correct you in a godly manner.* Most people don't know how to do this, including many believers. Consider the following:

- *What was said?* Ponder any truth that comes with the correction.
- *Who said it?* The amount of truth is directly proportional to the credibility of the one doing the correcting.
- *Let them say it.* You can dig through and remove the bones later.

The Law of Defilement

I recently taught through the book of Haggai and was stopped in my tracks by a verse that I had never heard mentioned, much less preached on.

In the second chapter of this two-chapter book is a life-changing truth that I call, "The Law of Defilement." A simple question is put before the priests regarding defilement. It goes like this: If consecrated (holy) food touches food that has not been consecrated, will it make the nonconsecrated food or drink holy? Answer: No. If an individual who has touched a dead body then touches food or drink, will that food or drink become defiled? Answer: Yes!

We see this law of defilement in every area of life. You would never take spoiled food and touch it to fresh food in hopes that the fresh food will make that which is spoiled fresh. The reverse, however, is true. Why is that? Don't you wish it worked the other way? I'm afraid it goes way beyond food. It spills over into relationships. Build into a person's life for twenty years, and on a bad day speak harshly (defile) and all the good that you have done is now spoiled. Lifelong relationships have been destroyed by an errant word. The Scripture says, "An offended brother is harder to reach than a fortified city" (Prov. 18:19). Will it work in reverse? You have been an offense for twenty years to your spouse and then one day you speak kind, encouraging words. Will those consecrated words make all the past offenses consecrated? Will the good turn the bad into good? "Bad company corrupts good morals" (1 Cor. 15:33). So why don't good morals consecrate bad company?

This is the law of defilement, and if it is not reversed, it can make life seem quite bleak. Asking forgiveness can certainly reverse things, but what if you're the one who has been defiled and the defiler never asks forgiveness? If a baseball player hits five homeruns in a row and then strikes out, the team does not feel defiled. You average how many times he gets a hit. The average is what counts. However, if a friend tells you the truth 999 times in a row and lies on the 1,000 time, you don't commend him on his average of telling the truth. You lose confidence in him totally! Can I ever trust him again? is the big question in your mind, even though you know you have lied at times also. "God must be true, but everyone is a liar" (Rom. 3:4).

The law of defilement went into effect the day Adam and Eve fell. This law has run roughshod over all creation, humanity, and especially the church of the West. Just take a moment and consider the number of potential ways we taint the lives of others and how they do equal damage to us. You also may want to consider that our very biased nature plays down what we have done to others and exaggerates the hurt inflicted upon us.

Here is just a short list to consider. You offend others if you are habitually late, but you see it as no big deal. Sarcasm takes a bite out of close friends, but they never tell you. Procrastination hurts a business partner and delays progress. A raised voice damages your spouse or children. Making fun of someone is more hurtful than you might expect. Borrowing tools from your neighbor that are eventually returned upon his request builds friction. Quick decision makers intimidate those who are slower, and those who are slower frustrate those who are quick. People who see life as black-and-white are upset by those who live in the gray.

The list could be multiplied a thousandfold. Is it any wonder that God tells us, "Love covers a multitude of sins" (1 Pet. 4:8), and it is wise to overlook an offense (see Prov. 19:11)? Are we to just accept this as part of life and live with contamination? Here again, what offends the western jesus would never offend the transcendent Christ. We are too easily offended.

As a pastor, I have received my fair share of defiling letters, e-mails, and verbal assaults—some deserved, some not. If I give way to the law of defilement, then all I have to look forward to is a life that will simply fade away.

Nullifying the Law of Defilement

There would be far less conflict in the church if we could overlook the petty issues that have no relevance at all to the gospel. This law of defilement is reversed in only once place—the cross. That which is clean (Christ) touches that which is defiled (us) and *makes us clean.* Perhaps this is why Paul said to boast only in the cross (see Gal. 6:14).

We are called to appropriate the cross in all areas of defilement. If we have bitterness, anger, and hatred toward those who have defiled us, it will only hasten our own demise. This is certainly no way to live. We must view people as fallen, flawed, and capable of defiling. The middle verse of the Bible says, "It is better to take refuge in the LORD than to trust in man" (Ps. 118:8). Why? Because people are defiled by nature and thus will defile those with whom they come in contact. Every spouse defiles his or her mate. Every parent defiles his or her children. Friends defile each other without even knowing it. So where do we go to wash and get clean? We bathe in the law of the Spirit of life in Christ Jesus (see Rom. 8:2). You forgive without waiting for the offender to ask for it. This is the Christ of the New Testament church. This is the only place where the law is reversed.

You can now see believers as forgiven defilers, clothed in the righteousness of Christ. You will see unbelievers who defile you as your mission field, with a compassion to see them freed from the law of sin and death. Forever keep this truth in mind.

Lessons to Live By

At my age, I have started to gather lessons from life as seen through a biblical lens. Here are six lessons to live by:

1. The Christian life is war (see 2 Tim. 2:4).
2. There is a real enemy, and he will capitalize on your weaknesses (see Eph. 6:11).
3. Christians have weaknesses (see Rom. 7:14).
4. God is sovereign and will combine the evil of Satan and the flaws of believers to ordain difficulty in our lives for our good and His glory (see Gen. 45:1–8).
5. If we harbor bitterness toward someone who hurt us by not seeing others as flawed and God as sovereign, we will do the same to someone else (see Gen. 31:7).
6. Rejoice in the providence of God that he has called you for such a time as this (see Esther 4:14).

When I entered the evangelical world, I was naïve about Christian relationships. I had spent four years at Annapolis living with the same group of men in the same company. I don't recall ever having a falling-out with any of them. As I look back over my pilgrimage as a Christian,

I'm afraid I can't say this. Probably many of you reading this have left one church and gone to another over some type of hurt inflicted by another believer. The psalmist says, "Even my friend in whom I trusted . . . has lifted up his heel against me" (Ps. 41:9). As you draw security from this psalm, just remember that someone else is drawing from it, only they see you as the familiar friend.

Proverbs 18 is not far behind with "An offended brother is harder to reach than a fortified city" (Prov. 18:19). Paul tells us in 1 Corinthians 11:19 that "there must, indeed, be factions among you," and Paul certainly experienced this in his own life. He had a major falling out with Barnabas over John Mark, and we later read Paul's painful assessment when he says, "Demas has deserted me, because he loved this present world" (2 Tim. 4:10). Even Scripture paints a realistic picture of fractured relationships within the body of Christ.

This should be a sobering reality that the potential for conflict is much greater within the church than it is in the secular world. Would you like to know why that is? The answer is really quite simple. Our piece of real estate is infinitely greater than that of the business world, military, or government. Here's why. We have all the issues that the world deals with regarding personality, conflict, money issues, rights, hurt feelings, and the list goes on. But we also have the added dimension of the spiritual world, which is no small matter. Throw the Bible into the mix and you now have endless doctrinal issues, moral issues, and judgment issues that complicate life beyond measure. Here again I can't help but raise the western jesus banner in all its glory. You see, in the West we have lots of time to be offended and grumble over issues that no one is discussing in the underground church in China, and because we hate the word *compromise*, especially as it relates to Scripture, we become unyielding on every subject raised in Scripture, from music to the issue of women passing the communion plate.

There are many subcultures in our western churches. We tend to hover around certain doctrinal matters that attract our attention, such as the baptism of the Holy Spirit. This is huge in some circles. There are other subcultures that believe we are to eat only certain foods as are mentioned in Genesis. Years ago a couple came to me very concerned about the snacks we were giving the children during their Sunday school break. They asked me if I believed the verse that says, "Do you not know that your body is a sanctuary of the Holy Spirit . . . therefore glorify God in your body" (1 Cor. 6:19–20). I agreed to allow them to handle the snacks. Did you ever see a four-year-old who liked dried apricots? Yet that couple was back in my office within weeks because those who had volunteered to bring in healthy snacks were bringing in apples and raisins that were not organically grown.

There are others who feel the ultimate compromise is to believe that the world is older than six thousand years, thus giving an open door to evolutionary theory. I am not here to take sides on any of these issues. What I am here to tell you is that there are reasons there are so many battles within the body of Christ, yet we are called to live at peace with one another and to walk in harmony. All this seems impossible with the number of issues before us.

If you have been a believer for any length of time, no doubt you have heard the very heartwarming statement, "In major things unity, in minor things liberty, in all things love." I have no doubt that the person who came up with this little adage desired to see the church walk in unity. There is one minor problem with this major proposal. Who decides what is major and what is minor? You may laugh at my illustration about the snacks for the children, but the couple who came into my office put this issue on the same level as the gospel. We all have our pet doctrines. Look at the homeschool movement within our country. When our children were being raised, we tried Christian school, homeschool, and public school. I even thought about reform school. (Just kidding!) I have four great children who are grown and love the Lord. But again I raise the issue about the passion with which we enter many arenas.

Are you waiting for me to give you the definitive answer on predestination versus free will, public school versus homeschool, premillennial versus amillennial, divorce and remarriage, hymns versus praise songs, the NIV versus the King James, and ten thousand other issues? Don't hold your breath. I will, however, tell you why this is more of a western issue. When the church lacks a wartime mentality, we tend to engage in doctrinal battles that we would otherwise allow people to arrive at their own conclusion. Though not all doctrinal issues can fall into the category of "each one must be fully convinced in his own mind" (Rom. 14:5), many can.

As westerners, we tend to become evangelists in every arena. We find something that works for us, and soon we are trying to persuade all our friends that this is the narrow road to success in the pursuit of the victorious Christian life. Do you mind if I put my pastor's hat back on for a minute? One of the great joys of pastoring the same church for more than three decades is that I have been able to follow most of the trends on philosophy of ministry, child rearing, and doctrinal issues. Here is what I have found. I have seen the good, the bad, and the ugly in all these arenas. I have watched children who were homeschooled rebel, and I have seen homeschoolers go off to Yale as a great witness. I have seen the same from those who sent their children to Christian school and those who sent them to public school. A western jesus loves formulas. I have known godly, victorious Christ-honoring saints who are fully reformed in their theology, and I have known godly, victorious Christ-honoring saints who are nonreformed. I have known victorious believers who practice the sign gifts and victorious believers who don't. I have met godly amillennialists and godly premillennialists. I have rubbed shoulders with victorious apologists and those who are equally victorious despite not knowing what an apologist is. I have walked with victorious believers who emphasize prayer over Bible study and victorious believers who emphasize Bible study over prayer. I have seen vibrant God-honoring scholars as well as vibrant God-honoring saints who have no formal training at all. I have also met many who hold tenaciously to these various views and disciplines who are defeated believers. However, I have never met any victorious believer who did not see Christ as central. I am not talking about a nebulous let's-all-love-Jesus mentality. I am talking about the Son of God who became the Son of man so the sons of men can become the sons of God. I am talking about the One who is fully God and fully man. I am talking about the One who becomes sin so that I might be declared righteous.

Perhaps in God's infinite wisdom he has allowed our differences to spread us throughout the world and plant new churches. I dearly love the many people who have left Reston Bible Church through the years. We may not always agree, but they are still wonderful saints whom God will use to spread the glory of his gospel. Every church has experienced the same thing.

According to a radio program I heard, George Whitfield and John Wesley had very different views regarding the doctrine of predestination, yet Whitfield admitted that when the rewards are to be dished out in heaven, Wesley will be in the front of the line. I recently went online to hear from a great reformed scholar on the subject of the Holy Spirit. In the process of his talk, he mentioned being filled with the Spirit. He said that in his lifetime he knew of only a very few people who he felt were under the constant influence of the Spirit. He went on to say that the one person who came closest to living a consistent life of being led by the Spirit was none other than Bill Bright, the founder of Campus Crusade. I was not at all surprised to hear such a testimony about Dr. Bright. What surprised me is that someone in the reformed camp picked the poster child of "free will" as his living hero of walking in the Spirit. So you see, all of us from time to time let down our doctrinal guard and admit that others can still be victorious and not believe all that we believe.

People on the front lines never have time to engage in such arguments. Their pursuit of lost souls is plenty to keep them busy. But give us the good life with excessive time on our hands, and we will blog away our day arguing over every known issue. I personally have settled with the issue of the gospel as my main battleground. I also keep a close watch on issues that are tangentially related to the gospel. Then there are those issues that I feel strongly about but certainly don't break fellowship over. There are no easy answers. John Piper faithfully reminds his people to be Bible saturated and Christ honoring. God will sort out all the rest as we enter into his glorious eternal kingdom. But as for now we will "see indistinctly, as in a mirror" (1 Cor. 13:12) and the ways of God will be past finding out (see Rom. 11:33).

CHAPTER 15

The Transcendent Christ and the Word of His Grace

And now I commit you to God and to the message of His grace, which is able to build you up and to give you an inheritance among all who are sanctified.

Acts 20:32

WE HAVE COVERED A great deal of western real estate. As I have tried to expose some of the cultural, traditional, generational, and western biases that keep us from seeing the Word as clearly as we should. In this chapter I hope to take you on a journey through the Scriptures regarding what the Bible says about itself and how to get the most out of it. Getting rid of our western lens, we will be able to see more clearly what his divine revelation intended us to see.

For purposes of bragging rights, many Christians often toss out the fact that the Bible is the best-selling book of all time. As uplifting as this might sound, the wind is taken out of our sails when we discover that very few read it regularly and even fewer have read it in its entirety. The Bible is given as a gift at graduations, weddings, and other special occasions. It finds its place on the family bookshelf wedged between *Moby Dick* and *Huckleberry Finn*. The spine of its black leather binding says *Holy Bible*. It is viewed by many as a good luck charm to keep the demons away. So why do so few read it? Could it be that we don't know the Author and are therefore fearful about taking advice from a stranger?

The study before us is about the Word of God. Paul commends the Scriptures to us so that we might be built up. Believers have an invitation to drink deeply from God's eternal truth and to feast at his banquet to their hearts' content. I selected this as the last chapter because grace is our instructor, mentor, and friend, "instructing us to deny godlessness and worldly lusts and to live in a sensible, righteous, and godly way in the present age" (Titus 2:12), and understanding the Word will help us through all we have discussed up to this point. We don't read the Bible so we can master it; we read it so it will master us. To discover its truth is to discover who I am and why I exist. We will never know all about the Word, but the Word will forever know all about us.

The following thoughts about the Word of God have been collected through years of study and meditation. Though personal, I trust the truths will go beyond the bounds of my own life and benefit others. I believe that these expressions about his divine revelation are from his Spirit, who promises to guide us into truth. My intentions for writing this chapter are fourfold:

1. To encourage the believer to fall in love with God's Word.
2. To help the believer prepare to hear from his Lord and experience a deeper intimacy with Christ.
3. To show the believer how to grasp more deeply what is revealed in Scripture.
4. To free the believer from the western jesus.

Approaching the Mountain

The standard cry from many who know Christ is that the Bible is just too hard to understand. "I don't get anything out of it when I read" is the common refrain. The assumption is that we will go to church and have someone else explain the Bible to us. Though sympathy may run deep for those who make such statements, I can't help but wonder why Scripture would command us to study what can't be understood. First, let me note that the Bible is a profoundly deep book with many baffling statements and difficulties. As we begin studying, we find ourselves at the base of a mountain. This is where Moses was before he was given the Law. I believe there is a lesson to be learned here. We, too, must begin the upward climb. The higher we ascend, the greater the vantage point to understand what lies below. The view becomes breathtaking, and the ability to climb to greater heights is supported by the strength we have gained through the exercise—precept upon precept. We are challenged intellectually, spiritually, and emotionally with every step. The journey is not easy. All who take this lifelong climb will experience the rugged terrain of "things hard to be understood," the dense forest of "things seen darkly," the cutting edge of a "two-edged sword," and the guiding light of a "lamp for my feet." Certain skills are necessary to learn and to apply to our lives as we ascend to new elevations. Whether you are a new believer or a seasoned saint, I believe there is much here to feed on because it is based on God's Word. Different skill sets are needed at each level, as every new elevation broadens the view of what lies below and draws us closer to what lies above. The general purpose of this chapter is to help equip each hiker with the necessary skill set for the climb.

Preparing for the Climb

From a distance, we look at the mountain in all its grandeur and assess its character and nature. The base is broad, secure, and nonthreatening as it is accessible to the most inexperienced climber. Vegetation at this lowest level is nourished by water descending along its gentle slopes. The foliage is green and thick, inviting the eye to study its varied forms. As the prospective climber scans the higher elevations, he notices a progression of thinning trees, small shrubs clinging tenaciously to rocks, and formidable ridgelines that lead to the summit. He's unsure of this challenge. The base of the mountain seems safe, but if he does not proceed, the climber will never see beyond the forest. The static view will become monotonous and boring. This example of the climber's first step also illustrates a believer's approach to the Word. Some may never wish to move beyond the elementary principles of Scripture. They understand basic doctrine but remain buried in the shadows of the fundamentals and never see light from higher elevations.

How to Approach the Word

When the believer turns to Scripture, he must be aware that he is standing on holy ground. A teachable heart will enable the reader to learn and remove the sting of boredom:

- Approach the Word with all the reverence of approaching God himself: "My hand made all these things, and so they all came into being. This is the LORD's declaration. I will look favorably on this kind of person: one who is humble, submissive in spirit, and who trembles at My word" (Isa. 66:2).
- Approach the Word prayerfully: "Help me understand the meaning of Your precepts so that I can meditate on Your wonders" (Ps. 119:27).
- Approach the Word with a pure heart: "If I had been aware of malice in my heart, the Lord would not have listened" (Ps. 66:18).
- Approach the Word with the expectation of hearing from God: "I am a stranger on earth; do not hide Your commands from me" (Ps. 119:19).
- Approach the Word with the full understanding that you will obey what it says: "Teach me, LORD, the meaning of Your statutes, and I will always keep them. Help me understand Your instruction, and I will obey it and follow it with all my heart" (Ps. 119:33–34).

This attitude of the heart will prepare the soul to receive the Word as the Lord speaks to those desiring truth.

Four Methods of Learning God's Word

As I spend time in Scripture, there seem to be four basic learning approaches, with each supplementing our understanding of God's revelation. The first approach is to *read*. "Until I come, give your attention to public reading, exhortation, and teaching" (1 Tim. 4:13). Reading is like walking through the woods. As we walk, we gain information about our surroundings. We notice beautiful trees, ferns, moss, and streams meandering through the forest. When we read Scripture, we learn various truths. For example, we read the account of Joseph being sold into slavery in Egypt, his attempts to flee from an immoral woman, his subsequent jail sentence, and his final release. We can rehearse the highlights with others and tell about Joseph's encounter with Pharaoh and learn about Pharaoh's promotion of Joseph to second-in-command of all of Egypt. This is a good start to understanding Joseph's life, but does it end here?

The second method of learning God's Word, taking us to yet a higher elevation, is *study*. "Be diligent to present yourself approved to God, a worker who doesn't need to be ashamed, correctly teaching the word of truth" (2 Tim. 2:15). At this new level, we gain insight that is a step beyond information. Now the hiker begins to identify the trees and ferns. He takes note of the fact that streams have a destination and merge with other streams, giving birth to rivers. Details become important. Joseph's life is not just an account of a young man who rose to power through difficulty. That's information. Through study and careful insight, we discover that his obedience is woven into the providential working of God. "You planned evil against me; God planned it for good to bring about the present result—the survival of many people" (Gen. 50:20). At this elevation, we have a greater understanding because we begin to have God's perspective. But does it end here?

The third method is to *memorize* Scripture. "I have treasured Your word in my heart so that I may not sin against You" (Ps. 119:11). Strengthened by the two former exercises, we are ready to move to an even higher elevation. The hiker now memorizes the identifying marks of an oak or maple tree. Memorization protects us in time of need and gives us direction, like guideposts that keep us on the trail. We recall from Joseph's life that he told his brothers, "Now don't be worried or angry with yourselves for selling me here, because God sent me ahead of you to preserve life" (Gen. 45:5). As we find ourselves in difficult situations, Scripture can provide us a lifeline to heaven. We see ourselves as pilgrims who have learned the lay of the land through memorization. As we tuck away the Word of God in our hearts, our souls will be comforted by the fact that God uses even the bad things in life for redemptive purposes. But how much further do we have to go?

We are now above the timberline. The summit is just ahead, but it cannot be reached without this final biblical discipline—*meditation*. Reading gives information, study gives insight, memorization comforts and guides, but meditation gives life. As we meditate, Joseph's life becomes very real. It is no longer just biblical information sacrificed on the altar of exposition for another message disconnected from real life. Meditation doesn't give life to the Word, it gives life to the one who meditates on the Word. The message of life and fruitful living will never be fully experienced at the base of the mountain. The Scripture promises that those who meditate will be "like a tree planted beside streams of water that bears its fruit in season and whose leaf does not wither. Whatever he does prospers" (Ps. 1:3). As mentioned earlier, I learned through meditation of Joseph's simple question as to the well-being of his two cell mates. That changed the course of history.

As the hiker moves gradually through the forest, he gains information, insight, and guidance from careful observations along the way. However, the best part of any hike is taking the time to reflect on what cannot be experienced when we move too rapidly through the forest. Remember the illustration from chapter 2 where my dad would take us hiking and make us sit quietly? Things began to appear—things we would have otherwise missed because of a quickened pace. The same is true of Scripture. Learn to read a few verses and meditate on them.

The Nature of His Word

We have seen that the Word has much to offer as we ascend to its heights. It would be unfair, however, to make the climb seem easy. The Word is stubborn in yielding its secrets. "It is the glory of God to conceal a matter and the glory of kings to investigate a matter" (Prov. 25:2). God wants us to dig, labor, and toil in the areas of reading, studying, memorizing, and meditating. I believe that as we exercise these related disciplines, much fruit will be harvested. We must not be discouraged as we encounter difficult passages. Revelation comes by degree, and the process may cause frustration until we understand what the Lord says about his Word. From my own study of the Scriptures, I have come across six categories of revelation that the reader must keep in mind.

We must understand the mind of God regarding his Word. When we hear people say, "The Bible has the answer to all questions," we will become disillusioned when we find that there are issues on which the Scriptures are silent. I have labeled these issues with categories of revelation, so as difficulties arise, I can assign the appropriate category of revelation ranging from 1 to 6—1 representing no revelation and 6 representing personal revelation. For example, "Why did God create Adam and Eve if he knew from eternity past that they would fail the test?" Answer? The Scriptures don't tell us. This falls into category 1, which is classified as *secret*. "The hidden things belong to the LORD our God, but the revealed things belong to us and our children forever, so that we may follow all the words of this law" (Deut. 29:29). Scripture reveals that there are some issues the Lord keeps to himself for his own reasons. We must learn to trust him.

The second category is defined as *hard to understand*. "He speaks about these things in all his letters, in which there are some matters that are hard to understand. The untaught and unstable twist them to their own destruction, as they also do with the rest of the Scriptures" (2 Pet. 3:16). The Bible tells us that some revelation is hard to comprehend. Each person has his own area that may fall under this heading. It is not a secret; these passages are clearly revealed but difficult to accept. Perhaps you know that Scripture teaches that Christ is the only way to heaven. This is a very clear teaching, but you might feel it's unfair. After all, there are many who have never heard of Christ. Although the first chapter of Romans may help us better understand God's plan, for many it does not erase feelings of unfairness. Thus it is hard to understand.

The third area deals with revelation that is *partial* as we read in 1 Corinthians 13:12: "For now we see indistinctly, as in a mirror, but then face to face. Now I know in part, but then I will know fully, as I am fully known." Here we have biblical revelation that leaves out some details. We know that heaven is a perfect place with no more pain or sickness, and my assumption is that human language can't describe it, so we are given partial revelation on this subject, though there is more revealed about heaven than we think. I highly recommend Randy Alcorn's book, *Heaven* (Tyndale House, Wheaton, Ill., 2004).

Fourth, we have revelation based on *maturity and need*. Jesus told his disciples, "I still have many things to tell you, but you can't bear them now" (John 16:12). Revelation is often based on obedience and maturity. As we grow in our knowledge of the Lord, the Holy Spirit as our interpreter and illuminator will expand our capacity to understand the deeper truths of his revelation. "The secret counsel of the LORD is for those who fear Him, and He reveals His covenant to them" (Ps. 25:14).

Our fifth point can be labeled as *obvious*. Clear revelation is just that. These are the fundamental doctrines of the faith that have stood the test of time. It is clear from Genesis to Revelation that salvation is by grace and not human effort. This is manifested in typology such as the men on board the ship with Jonah where it is recorded: "Nevertheless, the men rowed hard to bring it to land; but they could not . . ." (Jonah 1:13 KJV). Here we have Jonah telling them that he must give his life in order for them to live (grace) yet the men resisted this message and tried to row to safety (works). We have the message clearly revealed to Abraham where it is said, "And he believed in the LORD; and he counted it to him for righteousness" (Gen. 15:6 KJV).

I believe the sixth and final degree of revelation is perhaps the most important—*personal revelation*. Though this has been previously expanded on, I just want to remind the reader that God personally reveals himself to us in the Word. In Psalm 119:105 we read that his Word is "a lamp unto my feet and a light unto my path." Stepping into revealed light is what guides us down the path. There is no path for those who refuse to obey the light that is presently given.

The Authority of the Word

The Word of God is always the final authority. Any personal message from the Holy Spirit through the Word must never contradict the Word. "In my quiet time the Lord told me to leave my wife because He wants me to be happy." Such foolish interpretation counters the clear teaching of God's Word and can be dismissed immediately as a false conclusion. There will always be the temptation to fall for some satanic lure that suggests the Word is not the final authority. There are four factors to consider as you read Scripture:

1. *The Word is more authoritative than a sign.* "He answered them, 'An evil and adulterous generation demands a sign, but no sign will be given to it except the sign of the prophet Jonah'" (Matt. 12:39). Here the Lord Jesus rebukes any who would put a sign above the written Word. Jesus then uses Scripture to support his point.

2. *The Word is more authoritative than a miracle.* "He told him, 'If they don't listen to Moses and the prophets, they will not be persuaded if someone rises from the dead?" (Luke 16:31). We have the clear testimony of Christ explaining that even the miracle of a resurrection will not bring about conversion if the observer denies what was written by Moses and the prophets.

3. *The Word is more authoritative than human reason.* "We also speak these things, not in words taught by human wisdom, but in those taught by the Spirit, explaining spiritual things to spiritual people" (1 Cor. 2:13). The apostle Paul addressed the issue of human reason resisting divine revelation. This is a major temptation, which is all around us. We must be on guard and compare all human wisdom and reason with Scripture.

4. *The Word of God is more authoritative than any experience.* "So we have the prophetic word strongly confirmed. You will do well to pay

attention to it, as to a lamp shining in a dismal place, until the day dawns and the morning star arises in your hearts" (2 Pet. 1:19). Peter speaks of his experience at the Mount of Transfiguration and then goes on to tell us that Scripture (the more sure word of prophecy) is more reliable than any experience.

Always keep the Word as the final authority.

The Place of Scholarship

Many believers are intimidated by the Word because they are not graduates of seminary or Bible college. They feel inept and secretly ask, "What right have I to interpret God's Word when I lack the tools for such an endeavor?" Certainly this is an honest question and one I asked years ago. Since I have no original language study, can I really draw as deeply from the well?

This is where we must call for balance. There are those who feel scholarship is cold and lacks the work of the Spirit. Scholarship is quick to defend its position by denouncing the loose handling of the Word and the more subjective reliance upon the Spirit to tell the reader what the Scriptures say. Do we need scholarship? Absolutely! Do we need the Spirit for illumination? Absolutely!

I believe the balance is found in the truth that both scholarship and a reliance upon the Spirit are needed. I never preach on a text of Scripture without first consulting the scholarship of a commentary. I want to know what the words mean. I don't want to be sloppy with the text. However, I don't allow this to detract from what I draw out of the text for personal application.

For example, in studying the life of Abraham, scholarship helps me understand the various meanings of God's names, such as Adonai, Jehovah, and El Shaddai. Meditation reveals to me that Abraham's life typifies the Christian life. We see the ups and downs. We see hope and doubt. We see victory and failure. In Genesis chapter 12, we find Abraham lying about his wife, claiming she is his sister. Many years later in chapter 22, he willfully offers up Isaac, his son. Meditation reveals the following:

- In Genesis chapter 12, Abraham went down to Egypt. In Genesis 22, he went up a mountain.
- In chapter 12, Abraham went down to sin. In chapter 22, he went up to sacrifice his son.
- In chapter 12, Abraham feared man. In chapter 22, he feared God.
- In chapter 12, Abraham was rebuked by the heathen. In chapter 22, he was rewarded by God.

All the scholarship in the world would not have revealed this to me, but meditation and the Holy Spirit did. All the meditation in the world will not tell me what Jehovah means, but scholarship does. I trust we can see that both are essential. Scholarship keeps me honest with God, while meditation keeps me in touch with him. Certainly this is not an exhaustive study of either discipline, but hopefully it will help the reader see the need for cooperation.

Biblical Patterns

When reading through Scripture, look for consistent themes, cause-and-effect relationships, and common denominators. These are very helpful in understanding the mind of God. One biblical pattern that I noticed a few years ago is what I call *the saturation principle*. In Genesis 15:16 we read, "For the iniquity of the Amorites has not yet reached its full measure." I began to inquire if there were hints in other portions of Scripture that would indicate when the Lord would say, "Enough is enough." In Genesis 6:13, the Lord tells us, "Then God said to Noah, 'I have decided to put an end to all flesh, for the earth is filled with violence because of them; therefore I am going to destroy them along with the earth.'" The fullness of man's evil brought a deluge upon the world. We then read of the wickedness of Sodom. Immorality encompassed "the whole population" of the city (Gen. 19:4). There again we see fullness. Destruction was soon to follow. Daniel tells us in Daniel 8:23, "The rebels have reached the full measure of their sin." Nineveh had reached a level of wickedness when God sent Jonah to warn them of impending doom.

God had a point of saturation for the city Sodom, the nation Israel, and the world. What might this say to us who live in present-day America?

Obedience and Revelation

In Psalm 119:105 we read, "Your word is a lamp for my feet and a light on my path." When this text was written, there were no flashlights or lasers. People used simple lanterns to find their way in the dark. The analogy that Scripture uses here is quite significant. If I hold my lantern, it will cast a certain amount of light to allow me to see my way, but not *all* the way. As I step onto the safe ground revealed by the light, it advances the light and reveals the next step to me. New revelation only comes as I obey previous revelation. Many believers continue to stare at the same piece of property all their lives and never take that next step of faith. God reveals nothing new to some believers because they have failed to obey what has been revealed.

The Lord's teaching on this is brought to light in many Scripture passages. In Acts 10, we have the vision of the sheet descending from heaven. Peter had no idea what this represented (see Acts 10:17). In verse 20 he was instructed by the Holy Spirit to carry out a task without doubting. He obeyed. The next thing we find out is "but God has shown me" (Acts 10:28). The Lord revealed the meaning of the vision. This is consistent throughout the sacred Scriptures. Joseph, Daniel, Paul, and others obeyed, feared the Lord, and were given understanding. Not only were they given more revelation for their lives, they were given a greater capacity to understand the revelation.

I am not talking here about receiving new revelation. The Scriptures are complete. Understanding them, however, is another matter. Obedience to what we do know yields greater understanding of what we need to know next.

Theological Bias

Most theological systems contain some truth and some error. Many of these systems have been the brainchild of brilliant Bible scholars who have wanted to systematize the ways of God. It is dangerous to subscribe to a framework that defines God. He simply defies all efforts to be systematized or categorized. The Lord has a way of placing speed bumps throughout his Word that thwart all attempts to put him into a box. The problem arises when we have a preexisting reference point from which to operate, which forces interpretations of a text in an effort to fit the theological mold, often distorting the truth.

There is a certain danger inherent within theological systems because they leave no room for mystery. They are rigid and must give answers to all difficulties. There is a subtle arrogance that surfaces, and we become excellent debaters who sling scriptural grenades back and forth as though we were at war with anyone who would dare to question our thinking. I don't wish to be misinterpreted at this point by implying we can never drive a stake in the ground and say, "Thus saith the Lord." I have very strong convictions about doctrine, but I leave room to listen to others whom God might use to sharpen my position or help me see a different perspective. Believe it or not, God blesses people who don't agree with you or me, and he doesn't bless us because of our knowledge but in spite of it. That's what makes God gracious.

Prospecting for Wisdom (Proverbs 25:2)

This section needs a special introduction. Wisdom is such an important quality of life, and Scripture puts a great premium on it. It is particularly special to me because I had a difficult time in the academic environment in which I was raised. School did not come easily to me, and I floundered from the day I entered the classroom until the day I graduated. Recently, a young man from our congregation politely asked me if I ever had a complex about being stupid. He phrased it differently than that, but I had no trouble reading between the lines. I told him I don't ever recall having had a complex, but if I did, it was quickly resolved when I understood the difference between being intelligent and being wise. *Intelligence* speaks of the inherent capability to grasp information and process it. *Wisdom* is a skill for living; it is seeing life from God's perspective. I have known many intelligent fools in God's eyes. The Scripture refers to those who profess themselves to be wise to be fools. These are intelligent people who reject the revelation of God. Not everyone has the mental capability of being intellectual; their IQ may be limited. However, all believers have the capacity to become wise because the Holy Spirit illuminates our minds.

The Scriptures exhort us to search for wisdom as we would a hidden treasure. First, this implies that the Lord considers wisdom as greater than gold or silver: "Happy is a man who finds wisdom and who acquires understanding, for she is more profitable than silver, and her revenue is better than gold" (Prov. 3:13–14). Second, the Word shows that wisdom is not easily found. We must "prospect" for it. Third, it demonstrates that what is valuable does not lie conspicuously on the surface but must be unearthed. Value is usually based on the availability of an item. The less available, the greater the value. This is why wisdom is so valuable and why so few people possess it, for we live in a day when intelligence and human wisdom are highly desired. Parents drive their children to excel in academics, which is not wrong, but may very well be out of balance if wisdom is not sought with equal fervor.

How do we search for wisdom? Diamonds and gold must be mined, and they are usually found in places that are not as accessible as jewels of lesser value. This is where careful study and meditation pay great dividends to uncover the precious nuggets in the Scriptures. Prospecting for wisdom means spending time in the Word.

Doctrinal Discernment

Time magazine once had a featured story titled, "Does God Want You Rich?" The article told of the battle among believers over this issue. It listed on one side of the page all the Bible verses that those in the prosperity camp use to support their view that God wants us rich. There were an equal number of verses on the other side of the page supporting those who see this as a serious breech of sound doctrine. I have often thought that many theological issues can better be resolved without using a verse here and a verse there to prove one's point. Yes, Scripture must be applied, but when it is obvious that neither side is going to cry uncle, we just might have to rely on discernment.

One of the reasons I use the word *transcendent* is for this very reason. If doctrine is truth, then it will transcend all culture and all time. Can the prosperity gospel of God-wants-me-healthy-and-wealthy pass the test of transcendence? Suppose you are a missionary called to the jungles of Brazil to reach a wandering nomadic tribe. How will you prosper materially since there is no material in which to prosper in the middle of the jungle? Suppose you are called to work as a doctor in a leprosarium in Africa. Where will you park your Rolls? Better yet, where will it get repaired? Add to the list Calcutta, Bangladesh, and countless small towns in third-world countries. How can this gospel survive in such places? It can't, because it is not transcendent. It won't survive in the hot dusty sands of the Sahara or the bitter cold winds of Siberia. Maybe we should just forget the poverty stricken places on planet Earth because our SUV might get dirty with the fingerprints of little children who have never had a prosperity manicure. No, the prosperity gospel only plays on the stage of the West. It can't survive a hundred yards from the mall. This is a man-centered, self-centered gospel limited to those within reach of a Hyatt Regency. No Hyatt, no gospel. This is a gospel that is temporal and not eternal. It is, in fact, no gospel at all. It suppresses truth because of an unrighteous love of money and what it can buy.

Endless one-upmanship using a verse here and a verse there to win the argument rarely wins anyone over to either side. What about divine healing? This is another huge doctrinal issue hotly debated. Certainly there are many verses that speak to the subject of divine healing. It's not enough to say that all miracles went out when the canon of Scripture was closed or the last apostle died. That is a very weak and rather convenient way to dismiss the subject. As stated earlier, I'm not sure you can prove this from Scripture.

So are there miracle workers today? Perhaps that's not the right question to ask. To say that there are no healers today is a rather sweeping statement since there may very well be one in the outskirts of Siberia whom you and I will never know of. I think the questions should be, are the ones we see here in the West, on TV and in the stadiums, the real McCoy? If they are, then they should measure up to what we see in Scripture.

Perhaps the most celebrated healing, at least regarding all the details is concerned, is of the palsied man who is healed by Peter and John in Acts 3. We are given many facts about the man. He was a beggar, crippled from birth. He was carried daily to the temple gates. His healing was not just that his anklebones were given strength but that he knew how to jump and walk. Coordination takes time. Another very interesting fact was the testimony of those who witnessed this miracle. They were amazed. But perhaps the most noticeable detail is that he was more than forty years of age, and the Scriptures tell us that all Jerusalem knew of this man and were all praising God for the miracle. Keep in mind this is just one man, not great numbers of healings as we see today on TV. Also, the enemies of Christ said: "And since they saw the man who had been healed standing with them, they had nothing to say in response. After they had ordered them to leave the Sanhedrin, they conferred among themselves, saying, 'What should we do with these men? For an obvious sign, evident to all who live in Jerusalem, has been done through them, and we cannot deny it!'" (Acts 4:14–16). They readily admitted that no one questioned what had happened, and they themselves were forced to look at the evidence and say, "Truly a miracle has been done and we cannot deny it."

Is this what we see today? On TV or at healing meetings many supposedly get healed but Christ deniers who go to scout out the meetings *never* leave saying, "We cannot deny it." They leave laughing all the way back to the press room, where they write their mocking columns or show the hoax of it all on national television for the rest of the unbelieving world to laugh at. Do you want to know why? Because the healing on TV cannot be observed. The healing is always internal, *never* external. "In the name of Jesus, heart valve be replaced, tumor be gone, backache be healed." Notice how none of these can be proven. Why not "leprosy be gone" or "cerebral palsy be gone"? Can you imagine what the press would say if a man was carried onto the stage with his bones twisted and gnarled from his mother's womb and they were straightened out before the eyes of the critics? Could they claim trickery if the man's therapist was right there to verify all this? Hardly! To the best of my knowledge, the recorded healings of Jesus were always observable. Leprosy, withered hands, palsy, and the replacement of an ear were seen by the masses. People may not have believed in him, but they didn't leave denying what happened. Again, I say the question is not can someone heal today, but are those claiming such a gift the real deal? You don't need to know all the arguments about canonicity and apostolic authority. You just need some basic biblical discernment.

Ethical Discernment

I am appalled at Christian marketing. I'm not talking about genuine advertising of a concert, DVD series, or a sermon series. I'm talking about the promotion of a product we know is false from the get-go. Much of this is found on Christian radio. Are we that desperate for the advertising dollar to keep the station on the air? Have you heard the ad where the man comes on and tells you that with the purchase of his material you can take a rebellious, angry, whining child and within a minute have him under control? No more back talk or rebellion. Now just pause for a moment. Does anyone in their right mind really believe that such a program could live up to such claims? Many apparently do. Such a claim short-circuits all biblical teaching on how to raise children. Essentially the promoters are saying the Bible is wrong about foolishness being bound up in the heart of a child. It is wrong to teach them when you rise up and walk by the way. With this new program you can have peace and sanity back in your home in less than one minute. Does the station manager really believe this?

Then there are the vitamin ads that make similar claims. Your health is no longer in jeopardy. I have heard of shampoos that eliminate male-pattern baldness. If just one man grew hair, don't you think that all of his friends would inquire how? They would then try it and have the same success. Each of them would have friends who would then try it. In six months there would be no baldness in the United States. But integrity and ethics give way to the almighty dollar. How does this look to the world that is watching the western jesus in action? They think this is the Jesus of the Bible. They mock him, laugh at believers, and question our sanity.

The western church must come back to Scripture and develop a spirit of discernment. Believe me, I don't like airing all this dirty laundry. I don't wish to lift myself up as the one who has all the wisdom. I know I have much to learn in my own life, but in the name of biblical discernment, these areas we've been discussing are not ones that require a seminary degree. Basic biblical truth is all we need.

God's Word about His Word

It has been said, and rightly so, that the greatest commentary on the Word of God is the Word itself. Perhaps the most succinct statement about the Scriptures within the domain of Scripture is Hebrews 4:12: "For the word of God is living and effective and sharper than any two-edged sword, penetrating as far as to divide soul, spirit, joints, and marrow; it is a judge of the ideas and thoughts of the heart." This wonderful revelation tells us what the Word is and what it does. It is alive and it does pierce. It is powerful and it does divide. It is sharp and it does discern. This verse must be squeezed in order to extract every bit of its spiritual nourishment.

Let's address what the Word is:

- *It is alive.* Unlike Shakespeare or great poetry that stirs the heart and warms the soul, the Word of God imparts life: "Since you have been born again—not of perishable seed but of imperishable—through the living and enduring word of God" (1 Pet. 1:23). The Word takes us into the spiritual arena by giving us new birth as we understand and accept the gospel. We are made right with God. The Lord can now communicate with his people through the Scriptures by his Spirit, who illuminates our minds.

- *It is powerful.* It gives spiritual energy to the believer who needs to feed daily upon it because our pilgrimage is difficult. We need the exhortation to keep on persevering through the trials of life.
- *It is sharp.* Here we have the illustration of being able to cut and divide. This is necessary because life is filled with hazy issues that leave us perplexed and confused. How often do we hear the question, "Where do you draw the line?" Though Scripture may not give us an exact answer to every issue, it serves as a guide to help us navigate the narrow channels of decision making.

Now let's consider what the Word does:

- *It pierces.* This is the penetrating character of the Word. It penetrates into hidden areas of the mind. It searches out the secret places without a warrant. It plays no games as it brings the soul under conviction.
- *It divides.* Its razorlike quality is like the precise scalpel of the surgeon, whereas human reason is like a machete being wielded by a wild man. The Word can actually tell us what thoughts or actions emanate from the inner man, which is that part of us that relates to God, and the outer man, which is that part of us that relates to the world. "I do believe [inner man]! Help my unbelief [outer man]" (Mark 9:24).
- *It discerns.* Because of its living quality, the Word can discern between the thoughts and intents of the heart. This is why Hebrews 5:14 tells us that a mature believer in the Word can discern between good and evil. Many believers today are handicapped in this area of discernment. Once the Word sinks deeply into our spirit, we become sensitive to evil and are able to avoid it.

The Profitability of the Word

"All Scripture is inspired by God and is profitable for teaching, for rebuking, for correcting, for training in righteousness" (2 Tim. 3:16). We are told in this verse that Scripture is profitable for:

- Doctrine—sound teaching.
- Reproof—conviction.
- Correction—brought to an upright state.
- Instruction—nurture and discipline.

The end result is "that the man of God may be complete, equipped for every good work" (2 Tim. 3:17). When I consider the great promises attendant with reading the Word, what is it that keeps us from it? Peter Lord, a well-known pastor in Florida, often inquires of large audiences: "How many of you believe everything you read in the newspaper?" He waits to see if anyone will raise their hand. He then follows up with this question: "How many of you believe everything you read in the Bible?" The response, of course, is that usually everyone or nearly everyone raises their hand. He then asks, "How many of you spend more time reading the newspaper than the Scriptures?" He knows what the agonizing response will be. His final word of conviction is, "You mean to tell me that you spend more time reading what you don't believe than reading what you do believe?" Though convicting, it is certainly an excellent question. One of my desires in writing this is to remove the excuses we often give about not spending time in God's Word.

Because the Word is profitable, it is imperative that we learn to benefit from its . . .

- *Reproof.* Doctrine brings about conviction (reproof). This is vital to our spiritual growth; for if we are not convicted, we will not see a need for change. The psalmist speaks to the importance of this issue when he writes, "I gain understanding from Your precepts; therefore I hate every false way" (Ps. 119:104). I love this verse because it tells me that without the guidance of God's Word, not only will I not hate every false way, I won't even be able to identify the false way. This is a sobering thought because Proverbs 14:12

warns me of the consequences of going in the wrong way: "There is a way that seems right to a man, but its end is the way to death." This is why so many believers today seem oblivious to the immorality that not only surrounds them but has overtaken their lives.

- *Correction.* This word carries with it the idea of returning to an upright state.

- *Instruction.* This brings us to the point of being nurtured and disciplined. We are now strong and mature to carry out the good words to which God has called us.

Defining What We Learn

Through the years it has become very helpful to me to take a biblical truth and put it into my own words. This forces me to think through an issue in a precise and relevant fashion. The Scriptures reveal to us the purpose of the law. If I take the time to examine several verses regarding the law—"The law, then, was our guardian until Christ, so that we could be justified by faith" (Gal. 3:24) or "For no flesh will be justified in His sight by the works of law" (Rom. 3:28)—I can put some definition to the overall truth regarding the law. I have distilled the subject of the law to this singular definition: *The law states where I should be but condemns my every attempt to get there.* This succinct definition will help me explain the purpose of the law to others, particularly the lost.

Another example of putting truths into my own words is in Paul's writings on contentment. Paul, in several Scriptures, addresses the issue of contentment. In Philippians he tells us, "I don't say this out of need, for I have learned to be content in whatever circumstances I am. I know both how to have a little, and I know how to have a lot. In any and all circumstances I have learned the secret of being content—whether well-fed or hungry, whether in abundance or in need" (Phil. 4:11–12). In 1 Timothy 6:5–6, he is even more definitive in his exhortation: "Constant disagreement among men whose minds are depraved and deprived of the truth, who imagine that godliness is a way to material gain. But godliness with contentment is a great gain." My own definition of *contentment* is "coming to a place in my life where I desire nothing, as opposed to coming to a place where I have everything." We can do this with most any subject of Scripture. From Deuteronomy 8, I have learned that material possessions are not wrong, but if they cause me to forget God, they become wrong. Therefore, *materialism* is "enjoying the pleasures of this life independent of glorifying God." Having looked at the life of Jesus, I conclude that *leadership* is "that quality of life which by its very example encourages others to follow." While teaching through Romans, I tried to distill for my people what our relationship is to grace and the law, since we are no longer under the law but under grace (see Rom. 6:14). Here is how I related it to them. *I now have a right relationship to the law and to grace because I have a right relationship to Christ who kept the law for me and by his grace gave me the righteousness that the law demands.*

Our definitions need not be profound, but they should be basic expressions of major truths that help us see the big picture in a simple way.

Asking the Hard Questions

Scripture is of little value if we are not personalizing it. Information about the Bible is collected in the brain. Application of biblical truth penetrates the soul. This comes from asking yourself hard questions. Let's analyze a very simple statement from the Lord Jesus found in the twelfth chapter of Luke's Gospel. As Jesus was addressing a large gathering, a man from the crowd came up to Jesus and asked him if he would be willing to settle a dispute about an inheritance between this man and his brother. Read carefully Jesus' reply: "He said to him, 'Who appointed Me a judge or arbitrator over you?' He then told them, 'Watch out and be on guard against all greed because one's life is not in the abundance of his possessions'" (vv. 14–15).

How much simpler could a statement be about what life does not consist of? Having meditated on this verse for quite some time, I started asking myself some hard questions. I wrote them in the margin of my Bible. If my life does not consist in the abundance of things, then why do

I continue pursuing the abundance of things? How does my life reflect the fact that I don't love the things of this world? If my life does not consist of what I have, then what does it consist of? Asking ourselves these types of questions is a good discipline to cultivate, as it forces us to grapple with the practical nature of the Word. It keeps us honest and plants seeds of truth for a future harvest.

The Summit

The summit obviously refers to the top of the mountain. Clearly no one ever reaches the peak knowing all there is about Scripture. While truth is gained through the climb, the summit offers perspective. We can now see the lay of the land. We can see the world scrambling around trying to figure out life. Scientists study diligently for clues about how life began, but we already know that answer if we have read God's Word. Philosophers ponder the meaning of life, but we already know the meaning because we have studied his precepts. Religion seeks to explain how man can reach God, but we already know the way because we have memorized his statutes. The high-tech crowd seeks to make life better, but we already know how because we have meditated day and night on principles that have made us wiser than our teachers. This is not a prideful attitude, but one in which the truth has set us free. This is not arrogance, because we will be humbled by the climb. So put on your boots, shake off the dust of a western jesus, and follow the transcendent Christ.

A Final Word

We have taken a long walk together, and before I say good-bye, I have just a few parting words. I trust that most who read this book are truly pilgrims, but I am also aware that some of the readers may not have joined the ranks of those who are just passing through. You may want to ask yourself some questions. Have I passed from death unto life? Have I been taken out of the kingdom of darkness and been placed into the kingdom of

God's dear Son? Have I truly been forgiven for all my sin—past, present, and future? Do I have the assurance of spending eternity with God?

These are questions of no small import. Our human tendency is to rely on our own ability to perform well enough in life that God will be pleased to welcome us into his kingdom. However, such thinking is not in keeping with what is revealed to us in Scripture. Only perfect people are allowed into a perfect heaven. Since none of us is perfect, then none qualify for entrance. Christ came into this world to save sinners. He kept the law perfectly, earning the righteousness that the law demands. When we put our faith in Christ as our only hope for salvation, then he places into our account his righteousness. His death and resurrection purchased salvation for all who are no longer trusting in their religion, good works, or human effort to achieve eternal life. If you have never called upon the Lord to save your soul, then call on him now. Once you do, your pilgrimage will begin and your final destination will be heaven. Have a blessed adventure.